Leaving No Stone Unturned

Unique cancer recovery stories

Dorit Rishoni-Mandil

Copyright © 2017 Dorit Rishoni-Mandil

All rights reserved.

ISBN:
ISBN-13:

It is prohibited to copy, Xerox, photograph, record, translate, store in a database, broadcast or transmit in any form or by any electronic, optical or mechanical means any part of the material featured in this book. Any commercial use of said material is strictly prohibited, unless given explicit permission from the author in writing.

For my grandmother, the first vegan,

and my father who taught me what true determination is

CONTENTS

Foreword by Dr. Shai Pasternak 1
INTRODUCTION 5
My Personal Story 9
    August 2010 - New Spinal Metastasis 17
    June 2014 - More Metastases 23
Chapter 1 29
    Sorry, but chemotherapy is not for us 29
    Zvika - Metastatic prostate cancer - my wife took responsibility – 4 years after diagnosis 31
    Sara Hamo Lymphoma - Kingston Clinic method – 35 years after diagnosis 33
    Rachel Moran Breast cancer – Kingston Clinic method – 5 years after diagnosis 36
    Ruth Bloch Metastatic melanoma - Gerson Therapy – 3 years after diagnosis 39
    Halima Ben Neria Non-Hodgkin's Lymphoma - Budwig Diet and treatment by aliens – 8 years after diagnosis 43
    Tova Be'eri works with aliens 49
Chapter 2 51
    Arguing with the Doctors 51
    Estelle Baranes Estelle - Sarcoma - insisting and searching for information –5 years after diagnosis 66
    Shuka Eliezer Prostate cancer - independent research – 9 years after diagnosis 70
    Nurit Tzadok Esophageal cancer – changing the conventional treatment – 4 years after diagnosis 74
    Ahuva (alias) Breast cancer - Kabbalistic meditation and nutrition by Nissan Morgenstern - 5 years after diagnosis 78
Chapter 3 81
    Living a full life with cancer 81
    Susie Dvoskin Thyroid cancer spreading to the bones - sports training - 6 years after diagnosis 83
    Nir Malhi Brain tumor - martial arts weapons 12 years after diagnosis 86
    Zalman Pancreatic cancer – doesn't give cancer a chance– 6 years after diagnosis 91
Chapter 4 97
    Faith, prayer, mushrooms, and strengthening the immune system 97
    Shelly Cohen – Mushroom and plant farmer 97
    Dr. Amit Henin Brain tumor - mushrooms – 6 years after diagnosis 99
    Maria (alias) Sarcoma – prayer, faith, and mushrooms - 1 year after diagnosis 103
    Avner Shilo Thyroid carcinoma, metastatic - Guided imagery and emotional work –31 years after initial diagnosis 109
Chapter 5 118
    Deciding to Start Living 118
    Rachel Burstein Metastatic melanoma - mental strength and conviction – 40 years after diagnosis 123
    Or 131

- Metastatic breast cancer spread to the bones - Internal decision to heal – 1 year after diagnosis 131
- Chapter 6 133
  - Dramatic Change in Lifestyle 133
  - Shaike Klein Prostate cancer – nutrition, sports, and supplements – 4 years after diagnosis 133
  - Haya Meron Thyroid cancer - Kingston Clinic method and energy therapy – 12 years after diagnosis 136
  - Michal Metastatic Breast Cancer - self-healing – 7 years after diagnosis 143
  - Vered Gliksman 147
- Chapter 7 150
  - Full Self-Confidence in Recovery 150
  - Avichai Kimhi Metastatic lung cancer spreading to the brain – conventional treatment with faith and guided imagery – 6 years after diagnosis 151
  - Rona Breast Cancer - guided imagery, healing, nutrition, faith – 3 years after diagnosis 160
  - Bracha Steinberg Stage 3 lymphoma - conversations with the lymphatic system - 3 years after diagnosis 163
  - Noa Sehayek Brain tumor - relationship with tumor 4 years after diagnosis 165
  - My Emotions, My Body, and Me 173
  - Suzanna Marcus Breast cancer - changing diet, lifestyle, and emotional work - 16 years after diagnosis 173
  - Shir Metastatic Breast Cancer - nutrition, sports and psychological treatment– 2 years after diagnosis 182
  - Michel Bubta Bile Duct (Cholangiocarcinoma) Cancer - conventional treatment with change in outlook on life, change in diet, meditation – 8 years after diagnosis 188
- Epilogue 196
- Appendix 1 197
  - What I'm doing today following my private research 197
  - Thanks 199
- Appendix 2 201
  - Recommended therapists and complementary treatments 201
- Appendix 3 210
  - Lists to prepare for yourself while and after reading the book 210

Foreword by Dr. Shai Pasternak

Cancer is a very common and severe disease, afflicting mankind from its inception. Even dinosaurs had cancer sometimes, as we know from examining their bones. Cancer becomes consistently more common with the rise of life expectancy and increased exposure to carcinogens. Advances in diagnostic techniques enable wider detection of cancers as well. In Israel today, one out of every two men and one in three women will suffer from cancer during their lifetime.

Until a few decades ago, any cancer diagnosis was almost tantamount to a death sentence, since it was considered an incurable disease. Thanks to recent advances in conventional medicine, nowadays nearly two out of three cancer patients will recover. But there's a catch - the death sentence was only commuted to ongoing, harsh medical treatment that inflicts suffering on patients and their families. Some treatments leave patients disabled, and sometimes those same treatments (not the disease) even kill them. Some patients go to the doctor and get an honest answer - "we're not able to save you!": the tumor is too widespread, or located in a place where it can't be operated or treated with radiotherapy; there is no chemotherapy or "biological" therapy for this kind of tumor; or it is clear in advance that the patient will not withstand the side effects. All doctors can do in such cases is provide palliative care using painkillers and the like.

At a conference held by the Israeli Society for Complementary Medicine five years ago, Dr. Ofer Caspi claimed that "contrary to the false impression given by various publications, there isn't a single alternative therapy administered alone that has been proven effective with controlled scientific tools, such as a cancer clinic". I'll add that no such method will ever be found, if only because such research requires dividing the patients randomly into three groups - one that gets conventional treatment only, another that gets alternative therapy only, and a third groups that gets a placebo only. No ethics committee on this planet would ever approve such a study.

However, many studies have shown that alternative therapy given simultaneously with conventional treatment (that is, as a complementary or integrative treatment), increases the chances of recovery, reduces side effects, improves the quality of life, boosts morale, shortens the duration of treatment, and prevents the recurrence of the disease.

Some alternative practitioners oppose conventional treatment, arguing that it impairs their ability to cure the disease. Indeed, some medicinal herbs are dangerous to combine with certain drugs, and chemotherapy harms digestion, impeding optimal nutrition even in the immune system, which is so vital in terms of the body's ability to cure itself of cancer.

Whatever the reason - faith in alternative medicine, discontent with conventional medicine, or fear of harming their quality of life - some patients consciously choose alternative treatment as the primary or even exclusive method for recovery, not as a supplement.

As an Ayurveda therapist (traditional Indian medicine), I respect my patients' choice to avoid conventional treatment, or alternatively - to receive such treatment concurrently with mine. Most patients choose the second option. In any case - it is their choice.

I believe there are thousands of people in Israel who were cured of cancer, or managed to reduce the tumor or at least stop the growth (and thus transform the cancer from a terminal illness to a chronic disease) while relying only partially on conventional treatment, avoiding the full treatment protocol prescribed by the oncologists, or avoiding conventional treatment altogether. Dorit Rishoni-Mandil calls these people the 'strangely cured'. I know some of the subjects interviewed for this book, and can testify that they are indeed impressive people. Some of them became alternative therapists themselves, following the journey they underwent, or were involved in alternative therapy before getting cancer. Their methods of coping are different, but always include a combination of diet, medicinal herbs, exercise, spiritual activity, and relaxation techniques. Many of them are healthier and happier today than they were before their disease was diagnosed. The types of cancers they had and the stages at which they were discovered are as diverse as in any oncology department. The common denominator among these "strangely cured" is that they all took responsibility for their own care, and did not act passively, despite the pressure they faced from the medical establishment and sometimes from family members and friends.

It wasn't easy for Dorit, who herself became ill with cancer, to reach those people. Painstakingly, she managed to find a few dozen who agreed to speak, and held in-depth interviews with them. Of these, she decided to present twenty-eight cured patients in this book.

This is not a scientific study or academic text, nor is it a full catalog of alternative medicine or a medical advice book. The sample featured in this book does not represent the population of cured patients. Nor does it argue that this method is generally more likely to cure cancer than conventional treatment will. Nevertheless, in light of what I wrote above about the difficulty to conduct research on the subject, anecdotal case studies of this kind are extremely important.

The descriptions in this book are fascinating by any measure, interwoven with the touching story of the author. The work on the book and the research that led to it were an integral part of her personal journey to recovery. The main value of this book is that it instills inspiration, hope, positive thinking, and ideas for possible ways of coping. The book also contains a lot of practical information - full names of therapists and patients, description of various diets, names of medicinal herbs, quotes from leading figures, and more. This is a treasure, which to my knowledge is the first of its kind in Hebrew literature: generally speaking, books on this topic are written by cured patients describing their journey, or by practitioners who treated several patients with their methods. But here we have descriptions from various patients who were cured through a wide range of methods.

The author left no stone unturned in her quest for the 'strangely cured', who themselves turned every stone to get healthy. The result: a master guide to the journey of recovery from cancer. This book kicks off the process, and the rest (including reading additional books) comes naturally. If I had to send just one book to a patient with cancer (or any illness) stranded on an island – it would be this one.

A person who discovers that he has cancer faces a long, steep, dangerous, and sometimes discouraging learning curve. He has no choice but to climb alone up this steep slope. No one can do it for him. He alone bears the burden of dealing spiritually, mentally, and physically with the disease, with its implications, and with the attempt to recover. In any case, he'd be better off doing it his own way, even if advised otherwise by his doctors or loved ones. This book is like a ladder that can lift the sick patient up the curve, and then let him continue on his own. If he falls for a moment - this book will serve as a safety net to support him until he can climb back up. If he drowns in the sea of information or ocean of feelings, this book will serve as a lifeline. If he loses his way, this book will serve as a map, which guides him to different paths and show him where they lead to. Ultimately the patient will choose the right path for himself.

The book "No Stone Left Unturned" is an original and important addition to the existing books on the subject, including "Cancer - Natural Prevention and Treatment", "Living with Cancer" and "Journey to Recovery" - also published by Focus.

Dr. Shai Pasternak,

(December 2014)

Dr. Pasternak is a Western doctor and alternative therapist. He is the medical director of the Northern District at "Maccabi Natural", and treats patients with Indian medicine and Bach flower remedies at "Clalit Alternative Medicine" and private clinics.

drshai@netvision.net.il

www.ayur-veda.co.il

INTRODUCTION

I wrote this book because I wanted to propagate the fact that it's possible to live with cancer in full health. Odd as that may sound, during the past year I personally found proof of this: I met dozens of healthy patients in Israel who taught me that it's possible to cure cancer. They, and thousands of others around the world, were able to eliminate the tumors in their bodies, to their doctors' astonishment, and still live in good health today. Some of them have written books about it and many others continue living their lives uneventfully.

A year ago I made a decision: to find a way to live with the metastatic cancer diagnosed in my body. As a result, I started looking for other people who tried to save themselves with unorthodox methods. I met people who faced cancer up to six or eight times, learned how to curb it, suppress it, and still live a full life. In my encounters with them I learned of more ways to overcome cancer, and was also introduced to wonderful therapists. I learned from all of them how to do what's right and appropriate for me.

Many therapists noted that people usually come to them in a situation of despair, seeking some kind of magic pill. Had they started changing their lifestyle and diet when they just discovered the disease, their chances of healing would be greater. Moreover, it is recommended to make these changes as a preventive measure before even getting sick. But this recommendation is difficult to apply.

I may have grown accustomed to my new condition, and certainly most of the time I am not startled by the fact that my body has cancer. Fear is clearly a major factor in the weakening of the immune system.

Today I live happily. Loving, creating, working in the garden, running, swimming, writing, and spending most of my time nurturing my health and learning from the stories of these special cancer patients. My optimism has grown stronger, and I'm currently starting another journey: naturopathy studies. Through these studies, much like my work on this book, I seek to learn what else can be done to promote health and pass on the knowledge I acquire; there's no reason that my life and the lives of so many others should not continue in good quality, integrity, health, joy, and faith. Now, more than ever, I know that it's possible to dance through life, even with cancer.

Our body can cure itself - even of cancer.

Initiative, perseverance, and tenacity are key qualities in such treatment; with them one can strengthen their immune system and enable it to cope with the disease.

Each of the cured patients presented in this book was unsatisfied with the conclusions and remedies offered by conventional medicine, and took on a great responsibility by embarking on a quest for a different cure. The people I interviewed achieved significant results in stopping their cancer, for the sake of saving their lives. Some of them told their wonderful story to dozens of other cancer patients, but only a few follow their footsteps and take responsibility for self-healing - even though it has been proven possible.

I compiled what I learned from the cured patients into seven major categories that should be emphasized:

- Taking responsibility for my health - no one will make inquiries for me. I can ask for help, but ultimately the responsibility to find a way lies with me.
- Changing my diet – eating only natural, unprocessed foods and removing sugar from the menu. Using herbs and dietary supplements - plants have tremendous healing power. Many studies from around the world explore their effectiveness in cancer treatment. You can browse through article databases on your own, but it's better to go see a therapist who specializes in healing plants and food supplements. Have them find the supplements that are right for you.
- Following my intuition – to be constantly attentive to what's right for me and makes me feel good.
- Letting go of repressed emotions - even if it seems everything is fine now, there are some things from my past that I should process, deconstruct, and let go. It is best to seek the assistance of a skilled therapist for this purpose.
- Elevating positive emotions on a daily basis - constantly searching for what I already have, what's good, what pleases me, and what I'm thankful for. Always acknowledging what's good in my life.

- Getting help - I have learned and still learn every day how important it is to ask people for help and to tell those dearest to me about the path that I chose, in regards to physical aspects and when making decisions about various treatments.

I am not claiming that anyone who takes responsibility for himself, changes his diet, lets out emotions, and does what the cured patients did will indeed get better, just as doctors can't guarantee that everyone who receives conventional treatment only will be cured. Cancer is a complex disease and there's still a lot we don't know about it. In any case, stories of people who cured themselves or manage to keep the cancer dormant ignite my imagination and lust for life. I want to learn from them, and "catch their luck". I think their good fortune is primarily their inner mental ability to do what they did. Again, I believe that undergoing chemotherapy also requires a strong mental capacity. I am not against conventional medicine. I appreciate its practitioners, but regret the fact that many areas related to the healing of the body are excluded from conventional medical studies in our world today.

I call the interviewees in the book my "heroes", because their inner spirit never gave up, because they dared and believed they could choose a different path despite the fear and intimidation from those around them.

During the interviews and the writing process, I asked myself (and attempted to present an answer in the book) how these peoples' stories can benefit me, other patients, and even healthy people who don't want to get sick. Through friends, forums, and Facebook pages, I found these people and interviewed them and their therapists. I even joined some of the cured patients for a few hours to experience their morning routine – the time when most of their healing activities take place. As I got to know one cured patient after another, my inner strength increased, as did my mental capacity to do what's necessary.

The stories in this book are offered as inspiration - they do not constitute a recommendation for treatment. Also, the book does not in any way recommend avoiding conventional treatment.

Dorit Rishoni-Mandil
Ra'anana 2014

MY PERSONAL STORY

Somewhere in the world there is something that can help me, now I need to find it.

When I discovered that the cancer that returned to visit me for the third time was particularly serious, I resumed my search for another way to cure and help myself. It was obvious to me that there must be something in the world that can help me, and all I have to do now is find it. The consistent change in the size of the metastases worried me. I imagined them growing and spreading, and thought I have only a few months left before I'd have to say goodbye to my loved ones. The lawyer who lives down my street raised an eyebrow when I asked him to prepare my will. His wife inquired about my situation, but I politely insisted on keeping it to myself. The situation is dire, I thought. I went back home and organized some paperwork, while imagining myself lying in bed on the second floor of the house, speaking quietly and weakly to my beloved children and to the visitors who came to bid me farewell. I sorted and cataloged all my paintings. I made lists of things to arrange before my departure. I went to the bank to cash out all my funds and savings from back in the days. I must admit that it was a bit fun, too. Getting things in order, sorting, throwing things out, taking care of all the stuff I neglected for years, storing important items in an orderly manner - all this made me feel good and clean inside. I didn't inform my kids on the severity of the situation, but I told their father. We agreed that when we get close to the finish line he would rent an apartment in Ra'anana, the city where I live, and live there with the kids.

Although I made the preparations I deemed necessary before saying goodbye to life, I still wasn't ready to give up. I wanted to set a goal, something for which I'd want to live a few months longer, something that would give me a horizon, a goal to shoot for. What could be better than setting a date for a solo exhibit of my paintings? I thought I'd hold a big and unusual exhibit. So I called the Ra'anana Municipality and asked to use the Lake Gallery as soon as possible because, as I told them, my illness is at an advanced stage and it's unclear how much time I have left. Meaning, the original date for the solo exhibit in 2016 is no longer relevant. The municipality heeded my request and secured two weeks for me in March 2014. I now had a reason to get up every morning and go paint in the basement of my friends, Anat and Shai. Encouraged by Anat, a designer and architect who knows me well since seventh grade, I chose to paint on huge canvases, and once every two weeks I'd go consult with curator Batya Weinshal, owner of the Arsuf gallery on Gordon St in Tel Aviv.

At the same time I did some online research looking for treatments that may reduce the tumor in my liver, and actually found something. Tel Hashomer Hospital accepted my offer to perform pinpoint radiotherapy on my liver. This radiotherapy indeed stopped the growth, but shortly thereafter I started suffering from severe pain in the abdomen, nausea, vomiting, and dramatic weight loss. I didn't understand what was happening to me. I thought the cancer may have spread to the stomach too. A relative of mine who works as a radiologist was asked to look at the imaging results. His diagnosis was very bleak: "The disease is advanced and there's nothing you can do about it", he told me over the phone. "There is a deadly tumor in the spleen and another one in the kidney, and there's nothing you can do about it." The second our conversation ended the pain and nausea worsened. I asked my mother and my sister to come over. We sat around the small kitchen table, three practical and strong women, and talked about a hospice. There's no choice, I said. We'll arrange a home hospice. I could see the sadness and fear in their eyes. I notified my kids' father that it's time to look for an apartment.

I committed myself to the bedroom. The doctor and nurse assigned by my health care provider took responsibility over me. Every day dozens of new pillboxes appeared on the glass shelf in front of me. An infusion was inserted into my thigh and hung on the nail of the picture above me. I was twisting in pain and vomiting incessantly. No one knew how to help me.

The days when I could eat healthy food were gone, perhaps along with my life. I was losing weight rapidly. My collarbones stood out noticeably, with only skin on them.

I always wanted to lose weight, so strangely there was a certain pleasure in this thinness. Beware what you wish for, Vered Glicksman would tell me a few months later.

Another imaging test I took found no tumors in my stomach. The liver tumor had apparently halted too. Did our relative make up the tumors? I never went back to consult with him, but it seemed that the radiotherapy caused a new problem in my stomach or liver. The days went by in pain, vomiting, minor attempts to paint, and a lot of consultations with doctors. My friends accompanied me wherever I asked. I had never been so enveloped in friendship like I was then, which was very pleasant. Despite the suffering, there were some positive points. Besides the exhibit, I now had a new mission that would keep me occupied for many months ahead: to find out what was causing the stomach pain and nausea, and furthermore - how to solve this problem.

Two weeks before the exhibit opened, the paintings were still not ready. I went over to Batya to show them to her. She liked that they were "unfinished", saying it leaves much to the viewer's imagination. I liked the idea of leaving the paintings this way as a statement. I found it visually refreshing. Meanwhile, I chose an ambiguous title for the exhibit: "Not Final", meaning it's neither the end for me nor the last word of the paintings. I had a feeling many people were going to attend the opening. The rumor may have spread in town that I was nearing my demise, because on the opening day over 300 people came, including the mayor and his entourage. My friends from the playback group "Pir Kampir"[1] performed before the large crowd, and my friend Hani Dinur sang with Rami Harel three songs that I wrote. On the side they were screening a film about me by the photographer Haya Gold. My mother was in charge of refreshments. There were never such rich refreshments in the openings of my previous exhibits. The mobilization for my sake reached new peaks. The guest book was filled with words of praise and appreciation. The brother of my spouse Gadi made me a lovely cake shaped like a painting palette. That evening I was happy and my stomach didn't hurt.

But I still couldn't eat. Two weeks later at a routine appointment with the oncologist, he reminded me that it's only a matter of time before the tumors will return.

The exhibit was over and I needed a new goal.

So I thought to myself, I can't eat but maybe I can do other things that can assist my recovery. I need to find solutions. What should I do? I decided to go talk to others who managed to stop the cancer and ask them what they did, what they ate, and what therapists they went to. And thus I

---

[1] The name of the drama group I've been a member of for six years. It means "growing old together", in Bukharian

began a spectacular journey among the cured patients from Israel. They are considered medical miracles but to me they're simply people who persisted, insisted, and succeeded. These people found out they have cancer and began searching through various channels for information on how to aid their body in addition to the doctors' recommendations, or instead of them. Some have lived a full life with cancer for many years, and others experienced a complete remission of the tumors. I visited a woman at a kibbutz near the Sea of Galilee who spoke to her tumor until it stopped growing. I went to the south of Israel to meet a man who is coping with the tumor in his head with martial arts tools. Every week I met another cured patient. The more meetings I had the less anxiety I felt. Sometimes it seemed like it's very easy to eradicate cancer, and at other times feeling the new metastasis in my breast (the one that grew after I was reminded that it's only a matter of time) was terrifying. Towards the completion of the book I had overcome the fear completely. I wonder when exactly it happened. Perhaps after spending a morning of healing with Zalman at his home in the countryside, or a few days later when I spoke with Ahuva, whose change in diet and regular meditation had stopped her breast cancer. Maybe it was when I walked with Shaike in the fields of Hod-Hasharon and learned that he supposedly made few changes in his lifestyle and still stopped his prostate cancer.

My fear didn't evaporate in one specific moment. It happened gradually, from one meeting to another, through a process which intensified as the deadline for submitting my manuscript approached.

I took a deep breath, filled my lungs with the cold air, and smiled.

I remember that morning in August, when I noticed my confidence and tranquility. It was chilly outside and my Swedish cousin gave me her warm jacket so I could walk comfortably in the forest near her house. I sat on a rock overlooking a huge lake. Everywhere I looked there was only nature. I looked at the narrow paths full of peat and gazed at the bright, silvery water. I sat there in silence, optimistic about the future. This was perhaps the first time in this year of struggle that I had even dared to think about the future. I felt alive. It started to drizzle. I took a deep breath, filled my lungs with the cold air, and smiled. I'm alive. I'm in Sweden, in a forest, near the lake. The whole world spans before me and I am free to do as I please.

While meeting with cured patients I scheduled consultations with gastroenterologists in a futile attempt to alleviate the stomach pain and nausea. Again and again I was offered pills that inhibit acidity in the stomach, slow down or speed up bowel movements... but to no avail. By chance I saw a newspaper report on the Ministry of Health warning against taking the Motilium drug (which relieves symptoms of nausea and vomiting) more than three times a day and for over a week. This because, as the paper said, it may be associated with an increased risk of arrhythmia or sudden cardiac arrest. I rushed to check the name of the drug I was given for indigestion relief – and indeed it was Motilium. Of course, that drug was removed from my shelf. I continued to lose weight and to buy pants in increasingly smaller sizes. This trend changed slightly when a doctor advised me to start eating Nutren – a food formula for people who can't chew or swallow. I added Nutren 2 to my diet, which was very good for me. However, the natural therapists I went to were shocked by the ingredients of the formula, so it turned out to be the only thing I can eat which does not induce the reduction of tumors.

Most of the cured patients I spoke to had established an open channel of communication with their doctors during their vigorous quests for information on additional ways to heal their bodies. Each had their own unique story. After hearing all these stories one notices some recurring themes.

In terms of nutrition, the list of strictly forbidden foods includes: sugar, white flour (including pasta made with white flour), fried foods, sweet beverages and sodas, meat, chicken, cows milk and dairy products, preservatives, and all foods which contain ingredients, listed on their packages, whose names you can't recognize. Those who are more cautious will buy organic food and avoid flours of any kind.

Behaviorally speaking, it's widely known and obvious that stress is unhelpful. My many conversations with the cured patients and the information I found online confirmed the strong impact stress has on the body, or inversely, the effect of calmness on our ability to eradicate diseases, not just cancer. The immune system is a key player in one's physical health or illness. Again and again, it turns out that the immune system is dramatically affected by our state of mind. Our ability to influence our mood is complex and requires active involvement in our thought process; in the way we manage our life, our emotions and memories; in the way we realize our dreams, destinies, and goals. I find these activities much harder than choosing good food. It seems that this is the part I have most difficulties with, and I'd like to try it out more. Other factors affecting us are sleep patterns, physical exercise, and controlled exposure to the sun. The methods chosen by the cured patients often vary, and some of the recommendations are conflicting. So how can we tell what's the right way? I believe that each patient must seek their own way, educate themselves on their options, and choose therapists and therapies they feel comfortable with. Intuition plays a huge role in such selections. Reading the stories of the cured patients can give you an idea of the different methods. There isn't one single path to recovery that's better than the others. The stories here serve as a kind of shortcut to the information, but the book is not a substitute for comprehensive research.

Before I got sick I read a lot about what it takes to be healthy, but I didn't take it seriously. It amounted to me nodding to myself and thinking: "yes, exercise is good, and so is drinking water. Yes, sugar is not good". I resumed my stressful routine, unaware that a disease is developing in my body, day after day, year after year.

Today when I see people drinking Coke I'm sure they're drinking poison. But I try to keep my opinions to myself. Sometimes I can't help it.

At the age of 43 I was diagnosed with stage 2 breast cancer. The doctors assured me that the cancer is likely to be suppressed after surgery, 28 sessions of radiotherapy, and six months of four different types chemotherapy. But less than two years after the treatment was completed the cancer returned to a vertebra in my back, and once again I had to undergo radiotherapy and surgery. Three years later the cancer came back and was treated with radiotherapy, only to return again a year later for the fourth time.

In 2013 there were 19,493 women in Israel who were diagnosed with breast cancer, cured, or still coping with the disease. In 2010 alone, 4,036 women were diagnosed with invasive breast cancer. According to the National Cancer Registry at the Ministry of Health, the survival rate after five years reaches 87%. These figures vary dramatically depending on the stage at which the disease is detected. When the disease is in its fourth stage, that is - metastatic, the survival rate after 5 years is only 17%. The average survival period in the case of bone metastases is 2.4 years. One can play with these figures in different ways. When the cancer is detected early on, the years of survival increase. Mine was detected late and the tumor already spread to the glands in my armpit by the time it was noticed. As I write these lines, it's been eight years since the initial diagnosis and four years since the diagnosis of the terminal stage 4. Although I already dodged the statistics, the survival rates are still hanging over my head. So what do I intend to do about it?

Every few months at Tel Hashomer hospital I meet a dedicated oncologist named Dr. Eitan. When we first met he was an intern. I was there with him, observing from the side as he was being examined, and later when he became a full-fledged physician. Eitan didn't rush to send me to chemotherapy. He was concerned about my quality of life. We started with a targeted therapy that worsened my condition, severely damaging my lungs and weakening my immune system. The oncologist at the healthcare clinic said there's no choice but to prepare me for chemotherapy. But when I saw Eitan, he rested on his elbows and leaned toward me: "There is no need to rush", he said, "you can wait". What he failed to say, which I heard from other patients, is that in my case chemotherapy entails a lot of suffering and is unlikely to delay my demise. When I brought up this issue before him, he disagreed with me: "I have patients who undergo chemotherapy and it absolutely increases their longevity", he said. I left the meeting in a good mood, feeling that I'm being listened to and understood. But when I got to my car I realized that I was facing the disease alone and I don't have a plan for conventional treatment. I looked at my kids and noticed how badly I want to live. When my son told me it's not fair that I won't be at his wedding or see his children, I cringed in sorrow. Do I want to live for my children? Yes. That too. Mostly. For the great love I have for them, so I can continue to guide them in this world. To see my eldest son Amit grow up and develop his charm, to see Nadav realize his dreams. Anything besides motherhood? I'd like to figure that out as I look for a way to overcome the disease. The search has become my purpose, perhaps even my life's mission: to prove that cancer can be suppressed.

When I started writing the book I thought I had three tumors in the lymph nodes. I can feel one of them and see how it moves or retreats. I can even feel when it is active. When the spot is warm I know it's active. Six months later, a mammography found at least seven tumors. I didn't know if I still had a chance at stopping them. I wanted to meet people who've been in similar situations and turned their life around by healing their bodies. Is it possible?

"My name is Dorit Rishoni-Mandil. I am an artist and writer with stage 4 metastatic breast cancer. It's been almost eight years since my first diagnosis. I choose to look at the other side all the time. On the other side there are people who managed to stop cancer. If you have such a story you can share your experience here. In doing so, you will encourage others... In other words, you can help save the lives of cancer victims - perhaps a new one every day! If you have a story of a survivor I'd appreciate it if you'd fill out the attached questionnaire and even chat with me later on. Thanks, Dorit".

I posted the above text in various forums of cancer patients in order to find and compile the survivors' stories. Thus I began my search. Then I reached out to therapists and asked them to refer me to their patients who were cured of cancer - it was not an easy task.

I find it hard to understand why people turn to alternative medicine so late. If it's a result of ignorance, then I will now contribute my share to the mass of knowledge. Perhaps it is due to a prejudice that only doctors and drugs can resolve health problems. What else could be the reason? Reluctance to give up sugar and Coke? Maybe it's the suspicion that these sacrifices are ineffective. I saw a film about doctors in Japan who adopted one of the anti-cancer diets and applied it at a hospital. The cancer survival rates at that hospital are among the highest in the world. Hence the notion that it's easier to manage a treatment protocol at the hospital than at home alone. When the nurses squeeze the juices for you and serve you in bed as if they were drugs, the sense of self-conviction and the desire to cooperate increase. I hope one day such a hospital will operate in Israel, one that takes its patients out for exercise, serves juices, requires every patient to undergo psychological therapy and guided imagery and resolve personal conflicts. All of this is monitored by hospital professionals under one roof, so they don't have to run around the country between therapists, physicians, and various 'whisperers'.

All the cured patients I located had set their new path almost singlehandedly. Even if their therapist showed them the right direction, they composed the rest on their own.

I always dreamed of being a researcher. My first choice when I enrolled in university was biology, and though I eventually gave up this track and I decided to study art, I kept hearing in my head my mother's words: "One day you'll find a cure for cancer." She said that sentence to me when I was about six years old, after telling me that her mother, my grandmother, had died of breast cancer that spread to the bones at the age of 43. I am named after her - Dora. The mission I received runs in my blood. And thus, I set out on a quest to find a solution for me and for many others.

August 2010 - New Spinal Metastasis

"There is no full recovery without a change in attitude, full mental relaxation, and inner happiness"

Dr. Edward Bach

We enter a small room in the buildings ground floor. My spouse Gadi takes a seat on the chair on the right. I always choose the left one, which is closer to the doctor's computer.

A young female doctor greets us with a gloomy face. Her eyes rest on the pages in front of her. She dallies... I breathe slowly and examine each feature of her face. What is she doing? I already know the results anyway. I even understand their implication - I read the statistics. I think the doctor is taking the results very hard. I don't look at Gadi, I only feel his presence to my right. I don't lean back. My body is alert, expecting to hear her speak. But the doctor just nods her head, while her mouth releases sounds of sadness. She's chubby, I note to myself, doesn't take care of herself. She's unkempt. What should I do? Reassure her? I'm not going to be another statistic. She doesn't know that I'm a very special patient.

"Do you know anyone who has what I have and survived more than two years?" I ask her. She looks at me, leans forward, and then leans back before speaking. Her eyes search for information on a computer screen and then return to me. "Yes", she says, "of course. That lady who just passed through the hallway had a metastasis a few years ago. We gave her radiotherapy and now cancer is the least of her problems".

So you see - I tell her in my mind - it's not so tragic, so enough with the long face. "I'll be fine", I tell her before we leave, without looking back to see her response. I want to go home. I know exactly what I'm going to do now.

I close my office door and turn on the computer. On the Google search bar I type – "surviving cancer". The quest begins. On notes beside the computer I write the names of unfamiliar plants. I save articles and studies on a special file. For each dietary supplement or herb I find I look up for studies, articles, statistics. Some substances appear repeatedly in the stories of survivors. Survivors mention other survivors and this way I find more and more people. More and more anti-cancer foods. More and more methods. The stories intersect and many of them are supported by research - a plethora of information. At one o'clock I feel it's time for bed. Only at three in the morning do I manage to get up from the chair to get a drink of water. Gadi is asleep for a while now. I go back to the computer, unable to stop because I just found a fascinating and important article…

I have a tumor in the L3 vertebra. This means the cancer has spread. It is in my bloodstream and can appear at any point as it pleases. At present I know of dozens of people who got a tough prognosis and yet beat the statistics by taking action. My information file already has dozens of pages. I go to bed at dawn. By now it is clear to me that there's a lot I can do in addition to the conventional treatment. The information exists and I have to find it, classify it, consult, and then decide what to do with this abundance. The sun rises outside. I fall asleep.

For three months, day and night, I sat at the computer and read stories of American survivors. I crossed-referenced my information and searched for articles that confirm the effectiveness of the substances they take. I learned about the Kingston Clinic method that includes adjusting activity and meals to daytime, transitioning to specific foods, going to bed early and getting up early. I explored the Budwig Diet, which includes adding omega-3 to the menu and eating specific foods such as sauerkraut and organic cottage cheese with flaxseed oil. I read about people who ate only garlic and got cured and others who ate a lot of hot peppers or asparagus puree twice a day. I discovered the Indian Essiac tea that treats cancer. The information is virtually infinite. Of all these options, I formed a scheme based on the "Ann Vigmore" method. It is a diet that favors only unprocessed raw foods. Vegetables, fruits, legumes, grains, almonds, seeds, and wheatgrass juice (see further details in box). I learned that in Israel you can spend a week of healthy eating at Alummot, inspired by Ann Vigmore and featuring lectures, Qigong, and Yoga. I read about Pnina Bar-Sela, who has a PhD in nutrition and vast experience in treating cancer patients. She studied the "Anne Vigmore" method at the Hippocrates Health Institute in the United States.

Before contacting her I read her two books, "Renewal" and "Renewal 2 - The Healing Powers of Food", that describe a lifestyle based on fresh vegetable food (both books were published by Focus).

I went to kiryat Tivon to meet Pnina. She lives in a modest house surrounded by a yard, with wild vegetation, a few fruit trees, and some old steps leading to the front door. I knew that she had treated and cured many patients.

Fresh vegetable diet under the "Ann Wigmore" method

The "Ann Wigmore" method was developed by Dr. Ann Wigmore and her students. She viewed man as a physically, mentally and spiritually whole, and therefore treated human health, not just illness. She holds the patient responsible for the health and lifestyle he chooses, not on his doctors. The method is based on physical and mental cleansing; removal of waste from the body and soul; reconstruction of healthy body tissues; and processes of positive thinking. The main factors known to cause cancer are environmental toxins", says Dr. Pnina Bar Sela, "improper nutrition that burdens the body, lack of physical exercise, personal genetics, and childhood trauma. We try to strengthen the immune system with medicinal herbs and a clean diet. A strong immune system and inner healing powers allow the body to cure infections. Ongoing infections in the body feed the cancer cells, so to help the body deal with infections we eat organic food and avoid processed foods containing chemical preservatives that disrupt the cells' activity. The method excludes eating meat and any other animal product (milk, eggs and fish). The rationale for this is that the structures of our digestive system, stomach, and teeth resemble those of vegetarian animals. By the time the meat reaches our long digestive system it rots away. Under the "Ann Wigmore" method we avoid fried foods and cold-pressed oils added to food. We include in our diet plenty of live juices, mainly wheatgrass juice that has many qualities such as alleviating infections. The exact amount of wheatgrass juice intake is determined by personal recommendation from the therapist. It is recommended to drink four to six cups a day of green juice containing cucumbers, zucchini, lettuce, celery, and cabbage (note that cabbage is not good for people with a sluggish thyroid gland). In addition, drink pickled cabbage juice without salt, anti-infective tea from white oak bark, green tea and lemongrass tea. The "Ann Wigmore" method also includes enemas with water and wheatgrass juice for cleaning the colon and liver. It limits intake of sweets and completely bans sugar, honey, and syrups. The sweets we're allowed to eat are dates, apples, and watermelon.

Those who follow the method eat unprocessed, fresh vegetable food, and avoid any cooked food. Yet many add 20% cooked food to the menu".

Dr. Bar Sela also recommends daily physical activity, not necessarily strenuous, such as yoga, Feldenkrais, or Chi Kung.

Previously, Dr. Pnina Bar Sela championed the method in Israel. Now that she is retired, you can contact Edna Mintz. For more information of the method read Dr. Bar Sela's book "Renewal".

During my visit to Pnina I found myself envious of her great vitality even though it was clear she wasn't so young anymore. I waited as she wrote down the menu for me. "Recovery," she said, "depends on many factors, including mental factors and the type and severity of the cancer".

This wasn't the first time I was told the importance of working on spirituality. Louise Hay's book "You Can Heal Your Life" is placed beside my bed. Louise has a revolutionary message: "I deserve to be healthy." Is that so? It isn't that obvious to me. I often felt guilty about breaking up the family, and perhaps deep down I believed I deserved to be punished for it. "No!" Louise yells at me from the pages of the book, "You deserve to be healthy. You are blessed beyond your wildest dreams". Louise encourages me to write down my happy thoughts, and even add the sentence "I love myself", to the collection of sentences I'm allowed to say to myself. It is recommended to revisit her books at any time. Like a comforting and soothing hand of a big mother, reminding me again and again that I am loved, I am worthy...

In our meeting Pnina also mentioned the Ho'oponopono method, a Hawaiian spiritual healing practice for eliminating bad memories. The word Ho'oponopono means 'to correct the error'.

The main idea behind the method is that we take 100% responsibility over our lives, acquiring the power to release and fix things that are stuck in our lives.

I wrote a reminder in my notebook to reach out. And like many other things I wrote, I'll probably forget the idea for a few years and remember it when writing this book.

Pnina claims that cancer starts in the soul, and that the combination of mental healing and proper nutrition is critical. At our meeting she invited me to get up and grab one of the dietary supplements I brought with me. As I'm holding it with my right hand, Pnina asks me to lift my left hand. She tries to pull it down but has trouble. "This supplement is good for you", she notes and gives me another supplement. This time I can't resist and my left hand comes down easily. "This supplement is not good for you". And thus we went through all the supplements. To vindicate the decision, Pnina took out a pendulum from a small cloth bag and checked each supplement again. The results were the same.

A woman her age believes in the pendulum. So maybe there's some truth to it, I thought. I found that hard to accept, but at the same time I couldn't undo the results. I have the same approach towards healing. I am skeptical by nature, and yet I decided to try it.

When I came across a book by Dr. Eric Pearl, "The Reconnection", I oscillated between skepticism and the desire to try it out. He talks about the sudden disappearance of cancer after energetic frequency treatment. Through reading articles about Dr. Pearl I found that Boaz Ben Uri studied the method. I knew Boaz through Gadi, who studied guided imagery treatment with him back in the day. I knew that Boaz got colon cancer at the age of 48 after diving in the Kishon River during his military service, and that he cured himself in unconventional ways. I went to see Boaz in Karkur for an energetic "reconnection" treatment.

Boaz, a solid man who spent years working in the defense sector and later owned an advertising agency, asked me to lie down on a massage table in the middle of a large room. He told me he does a special meditation on the table every morning, while listening to his favorite music. Due to his illness he left the advertising world and decided to find out what aspect of his life allowed the cancer to flourish and whether there's another way to live the next 48 years of his life. The "New Medicine" theory by Dr. Hamer intrigued him and he studied it. Dr. Hamer describes a mental and emotional approach to the cancer and claims that severe emotional events could remove an organ from the right frequency, hindering its optimal functioning. That's when a disease appears.

"When I got sick, I went 'shopping' in a world which was completely alien to me," said Boaz, "I encountered surreal things before getting to guided imagery and later to healing. I was also interested in nutrition. When you have cancer, the entire game shifts to the immune system. Cancer thrives when the immune system weakens. Guided imagery gives the immune system a chance to balance out and recover. I am convinced that the body can heal itself under the right conditions".

I lay on the treatment table for an hour, feeling Boaz simultaneously in several places around me, as I fell into deep sleep. I woke up in a daze and couldn't speak, ask, or hear anything. I paid him and went out into the path leading to the road. I felt I had a primordial and deep desire to be a therapist. I didn't know what I'm going to do about it. I drove home slowly.

Four years later I would go back and interview him as an extraordinary healer from cancer.

For two years I followed Pnina's instructions: A diet based on fresh vegetable food, wheatgrass in the morning, vegetable juices, strict avoidance of sugar, oak bark tea, astragalus for boosting the immune system, and other dietary supplements. At the same time I went back to work and resumed teaching and painting. Gadi encouraged me to realize my dream and take groups of painters to Italy, which we did together a few times with great pleasure.

It seemed like life had returned to normal. The good and the bad, the love and the hardship all continued to shape our lives. I gradually eased off my dietary restrictions, ate more sugar, and stopped going on walks. One evening we were invited by my brother Shai and his wife Tammy to meet with us at a pub in Ra'anana. Not something we do ordinarily. "We've got news", he said immediately when we sat down. Their faces looked serious. "Cancer?" I asked "No. ALS". Silence. Choked up. What can we do about it? ALS patients jokingly claim it stands for – Ain't a Lethal Sickness. It's an incurable disease, and even worse, no drug company is trying to develop a cure. A year earlier an ALS patient participated in a support group I facilitated, so I understood the situation exactly. I looked at Shai in disbelief. I was speechless. The world turned upside down. I held back my tears until we left the pub. I sought solace with sugar: waffles, chocolate, cakes. Thus the diet was definitively put on hold. The entire emotional protection was gone as though it never existed. There were days when I hoped to die before him to avoid experiencing the sorrow of loss. When I thought about it while eating a tempting chocolate cake, I knew I was inviting back the cancer, but couldn't change those thoughts or my attraction to sweets. In retrospect, maybe I should have tried strengthening myself through one of the spiritual methods.

June 2014 - More Metastases

I can't wait to go to sleep. In the American forum for stage 4 breast cancer patients I read a post by a woman who's been on a ketogenic diet for three years. Initially she was told she had only six months to live. Today her metastases are in remission.

I'm so tired. I want to turn off the computer and go to sleep. But I just found something hugely important... What is a ketogenic diet?

It's after 1:00 AM already. I should have gone to bed at ten in order to rest while the immune system is at its peak. Going to bed late day after day is a nightmare for the immune system. I yank myself from the computer and go to bed. The cancer is clever, its tumor cells secreting substances that disrupt our sleep, further weakening the body's resistance to tumors. In that case, I better find a way to sleep in spite of my insomnia and desire to find more information online.

I wake up at eleven in the morning. Today I'm adhering to the healing morning tasks: cold shower, rubbing the body with a stiff brush to arouse the lymphatic system (slow circular motion from top to bottom), jumping on a trampoline to help the vital lymphatic system and gently massaging the liver and intestines (I once read that Shimon Peres likes to jump on a trampoline every morning). Then I sit in my meditation corner in the garden, under a white mosquito net sheltered from all bothersome insects. I go out for a walk in the sun, absorbing Vitamin D, activating the muscles, and yet again, aiding the lymph nodes. This time I'm strengthening the bones in my legs, back, and hips with through exercise. Then I prepare and drink green juice – a drink full of energy.

Above the kitchen door, the wall clock alerts me that more than half the day has passed. It's already two o'clock and I didn't feel any stomach pain today.

Thanks to these pains I found a new medical method loosely referred to as "patience, it will probably pass". The little sleep I manage to get at night is helpful. Even when it's brief, sleeping separates so well between yesterday and today, so that each morning it seems everything is ok and today I won't feel pain. What causes four days of relief? I recount my new habits: I swallow a huge capsule of omega-3 every morning (albeit with difficulty); I quit the targeted therapy; I write almost every day; and I treat myself with cannabis every night. That's it. Could it be that writing cures the digestive system?

The steep steps lead me to the study: the cocoon that takes me in whenever I find time for it. Quietly waiting for me, just as I left it - full of items, papers, old cell phone chargers, and cables for charging cameras, earphones, and computers.

I look for the charger of the special earphones Gadi ordered for me from abroad for Valentine's Day, but can't find it. So I start consolidating items. The papers go to a pile on the right side of the table and the dishes pile up on their way out of the room. I bring the trashcan closer to me – it's playing a major role now. The mess is cleaned and the long-awaited charger appears on the tabletop, peering under an open envelope.

I sit on my very cozy writing chair, built with springs that let me swing back, comfortable wooden handles, and a soft and comfortable black leather-like seat. Miraculously my feet reach the floor.

On the shelf in front of me there are a few dozen books on health, guided imagery for change, Buddhism, Sanaya's book "Living with Joy", and the excellent book by Dr. Keith Block "Life Over Cancer". A lot of information at hand. I am very familiar with the books and theories, but I have trouble acting persistently to prevent the cells' uncontrolled division.

Something still bothers me... What's a ketogenic diet... I go back to the computer, which I abandoned the night before, and find that it recommends a high intake of fat at the expense of carbohydrates, with the aim of treating epileptic patients by mimicking a state of fasting, which reduces seizures. In his research, Prof. Thomas Seyfried applied this diet to cancer as well. According to him, a metabolic diet of 80% fat, little protein and carbohydrates, and limited calories – would block glucose from the cancer cells, which poorly process fat into energy, and thus starve them to death. I find this diet difficult to implement, and haven't found anyone in Israel who followed it to overcome cancer. During my journey I learn that this diet is also called Paleo and that it's based on the diet of the cavemen, which was rich with animal source food.

The list of therapists who can offer me their services – devise my diet, treat me with acupuncture, cleanse my aura, introduce me to aliens - is almost endless. All the options are available, and even the list of things I can do at home is getting longer. After all, back in 2010 I spent three months gathering information and then made a list of actions and scattered notes around the house to remind myself of the many practices I adopted to preserve my body. I endured for two years: I followed the tasks and my notes, and my cancer cells remained dormant. They were practically snoring. Until one day the tables had turned on our family's fate and all lists and procedures lost their meaning. My stress levels increased, and last spring the cancer woke up.

A year later I seek to force myself back to the same path that proved itself in the past. I ask myself to choose it again. But this time it's more difficult. The damage caused to the digestive system by the radiotherapy is severe. I can no longer eat food normally, but rather must feed myself with special formulas - meaning I can't cure myself through food. Apart from seeing doctors, who at this stage don't know how to help me, I must look for other ways to cure my stomach and the cancer. I start by meetings with Israelis who experienced a halt or remission of the cancer over time due to other actions besides chemotherapy or by avoiding chemotherapy altogether; and I met those who are still alive even years after being diagnosed and after having been told they have a short time to live.

I found 30 stories of cured patients, and I've chosen to broaden on 28 which were particularly surprising.

What do I mean when I talk about a halt or a regression of the disease?

I define a spontaneous regression of cancer as a full or partial disappearance of a tumor with no conventional treatment; or after partial treatment; or treatment administered differently than originally prescribed, because no adequate treatment was found or because the patient defied the doctors' recommendation and yet is still alive many years later. In addition, I included the story of Susie Dvoskin, who underwent every available conventional treatment and continues to live an inspiringly active life despite her advanced cancer. In another story the patient received the standard treatment, but she experienced a complete remission after only two treatments out of six.

In the last century several studies were conducted around the world, compiling data on spontaneous regression of cancer in order to identify a main factor causing it. Dr. Tilden Everson and Dr. Warren Cole of the University of Illinois at Chicago analyzed cases published in the medical literature from 1900 to 1956: they estimated that this occurs once every 80,000 cases. They found more than 600 cases of tumor regressions, and narrowed them down to 47 cases with clear documentation.

I really enjoyed reviewing these cases and constantly reading the sentence: "complete disappearance of the tumors." According to the study, the possible reasons for the cancer's disappearance were: hormonal activity in the body; very low radiation; in one case nitrogen mustard was given and in another Triethylenemelamine - neither known as effective against the tumors they were prescribed for. Even E. coli was given in some cases. In a few incidents, the tumors disappeared after a fever or infection. 11 years later Everson and Cole published the results of their research in a book, which included 176 examples of spontaneous regression.

The subject of spontaneous regression intrigues researchers, and in the medical literature I found hundreds of case studies written by doctors. The potential explanations they offer include: stimulation and strengthening of the immune system; removal of carcinogens (substances that can cause cancer if exposed to them); inhibition of angiogenesis (impeding the creation of a network of blood vessels that feed cancer cells); enhanced apoptosis (the death process of human cells); and epigenetic mechanisms (environmental impact on genes). Also, there are many cases where the regression occurs following an infection in or near the tumor. The infection may have stimulated the immune system to attack the tumors, unlike the situation in which an ongoing infection in the body serves as a platform for cancer cells to develop and grow.

Cole was convinced that the most important factor causing the spontaneous regression is the immune system. The immune system can be weakened by enzymes, infections, hormones, and other traumas. The more stories of cured patients I read, the stronger I felt about the key being in the immune system.

But how do you mobilize the immune system to action – that's a key question. Moreover, how do you get the right cells in the immune system to recognize the cancer cells hiding from it? This may be the subject for another book. However, in each of the stories I present here, steps were taken to strengthen the immune system. As I was finishing the compilation of the material, studies on a new targeted therapy that would strengthen the immune system started being published, showing positive results. This is very encouraging.

Inspired by Cole and Everson, I made a list of the cured patients I met, by type of cancer and possible causes for their healing (according to them). I also added to the list the cured patients I interviewed whose stories don't appear in the book, and others I didn't interview but whose stories appeared in the media.

Possible explanations for recovery based on interviews with cured patients

Type of Cancer (number of cases)	Diet	Emotional Work	Physical Work	Spiritual Work	Incorporation with conventional/unprescribed treatment
Breast (9)	Change in diet, Dietary supplements	Rigorous emotional work: Journey, conversations, guided imagery	Qigong, hiking	Prayer, healing, meditation, prayer	No chemotherapy or radiotherapy
Prostate (3)	Change in diet, Dietary supplements	Guided imagery	Sports, Qigong		Chemotherapy, drugs, and minor doses of radiotherapy or none at all
Brain (3)	Mushrooms, no sugar	Intensive writing about emotions and thoughts	Sports, breathing exercises	Meditation	Different chemotherapy from original prescription. Avoiding surgery despite recommendations
Melanoma (2)	Gerson Therapy		Yoga, working in garden	Meditation	Surgery, partial treatment by medication
Sarcoma (2)	Mushrooms, Dietary supplements	Emotional work		Prayer	Drug prescribed for different type of cancer
Lymphoma (4)	Change in diet, Budwig Diet, "Ann Wigmore"	Emotional work	Sports, Bedtime and wake up schedule	Meditation, Inner conversations addressed at the lymph system	Lower dosage of chemotherapy than normal
Esophagus (1)	Change in diet, Dietary supplements	Guided imagery	Walking, Working in garden		Targeted therapy only, without chemotherapy – despite the recommendations
Lungs - metastatic	Avoiding sugar	Guided imagery, writing		Faith and prayer	Chemotherapy

(1)					
Cholangiocarcinoma (1)	Change in diet	Guided imagery	Sports	Meditation	Surgery
Pancreas (2)	Change in diet, Dietary supplements, Mushrooms	Guided imagery	Sports	Studying Buddhism and observing the "present moment"	Surgery, Experimental drug
Colon (2)	Change in diet	Guided imagery	Bedtime and wake up schedule	Meditation, Energetic treatment	Partial chemotherapy
Thyroid glands (2)	Change in diet Kingston Clinic method	Guided imagery, Emotional work	Intensive sports	Energetic treatment	A combination of iodine treatment, surgery, emotional and spiritual work, as well as changing diet

Description of concepts in table:

Diet – changing diet in order to strengthen the body against the cancer and the side effects of conventional treatment, and to boost the immune system. The various cured patients tried different diets.

Emotional work - processing events from the past, especially those from childhood, which linger as an emotional obstacle in adult life.

Physical work - different kinds of sports and martial arts. Maintaining sleep schedule.

Spiritual work - increasing faith in the ability to heal and faith in the power of life.

Meditation – spiritual work aimed at increasing self-awareness and resolving events from the past.

CHAPTER 1

Sorry, but chemotherapy is not for us

Almost all the cured patients who experienced a miracle had dramatically changed their diet and maintained the new regime over time, without any deviations or exemptions. One of the most important ingredients is organic food. This doesn't merely refer to foods that aren't sprayed, but a cultivation method that allows crops to absorb from the ground more minerals, vitamins, and other substances that are essential to the body. Organic food isn't subjected to genetic engineering. It isn't given hormones or exposed to preservatives. And the soil from which it consumes the materials is richer. Organic fertilizer contains mainly compost made of vegetable food scraps, trimmings, manure of farm animals, and more.

In my garden I grow a variety of vegetables - mostly leafy ones, without spraying them. They're planted in soil that's fertilized with compost we produce in our yard. I buy the young, organic plants at the nurseries of Matan the gardener at Bnei Zion, and from Ori Gani in Ganei Am. Today, on my way home from Shiatsu and Acupuncture, I went to Matan's nursery. Every visit there fills me with joy. I followed his nursery grow, from two trays of seedlings three years ago to several acres of vegetables and trees. To my surprise, I found a seedling of the Moringa tree. I had heard about this magical tree, which we're now becoming aware of, from Noa Sehayek from Kibbutz Ginosar, who planted two trees in her yard this year. She picks their leaves every day to add to the salad.

The Moringa is defined as a superfood. In India it has been used for thousands of years, and it is also known in Africa and South America for its special qualities. This tree, which grows rapidly and needs little water, is rich in vitamins, minerals, amino acids, and antioxidants. You can buy Moringa leaves powder in capsules. The capsule manufacturers cite the following benefits: preserves overall health, improves digestive function, induces weight loss, strengthens the immune system, cleans toxins from the body, enhances liver function, improves vascular function, and reduces joint and inflammatory pain.

I came home from the nursery, with a young Moringa tree in the trunk of my car. I planted it in a pot to make sure it wouldn't grow into a huge tree, and placed it at the entrance to the house – this way I'd remember to tear off leaves for cooking every day. Now that I brought it and found a place for it - I had time to look for more information about the tree. I found that some claim the Moringa cures every type of cancer. I tend to be suspicious of such generalizations. The number of pages of information on Moringa and cancer is huge. I found that the Moringa leaves contain 7 times more Vitamin C than oranges, 4 times more calcium than milk, 4 times more Vitamin A than carrots, two times more protein than yogurt, and 25 times more iron than spinach. In Africa doctors use Moringa to treat patients with diabetes and in India it is used to lower blood pressure. It is estimated that the tree's leaves, flowers, and roots can treat over 300 diseases. A study published in 2006 at Memorial Sloan Kettering Hospital in the United States found that a material distilled from Moringa leaves delayed the spread of ovarian cancer cells in a laboratory, and even killed some cancer cells. Pat-hia, the herbal healer of the African Hebrew Israelite community, whom I met in Mitzpe Ramon, makes a homemade Moringa powder and recommends taking one teaspoon a day mixed with food or juice.

Zvika
Metastatic prostate cancer - my wife took responsibility – 4 years after diagnosis

"We managed ourselves and didn't let others manage us".

Orly

Zvika - age 57, married with three children and five grandchildren, working as an independent consultant - went to bed four years ago awaiting his death, which he was told was very close.

"But my wife Orly had other plans", says Zvika. "She grabbed me by the collar, pulled me out of bed, and started taking me to doctors, therapists, anyone she thought could help me. I didn't have the mental strength to do anything. After the urologist told me he doesn't know any people who survive with my PSA levels and that it seems nothing can be done, rabbi Firer referred us to Dr. Raanan Berger at Tel Hashomer Hospital. Dr. Berger said he doesn't understand why I'm worried. "There are people in your position who live even ten years or more and function normally. New drugs are constantly coming out. There will be bumps along the way, but let's get started", he said reassuringly.

Zvika received an experimental medical treatment, TAK 700, which Dr. Berger ended after eight months when it stopped having an effect. Then he underwent chemotherapy and radiotherapy. By the third round of chemotherapy Zvika was feeling awful and Orly sensed that something isn't working well. She took initiative and asked to check the PSA herself. The results showed an increase in values and they decided to stop the unhelpful treatment. When the doctor recommended another series of radiotherapy, Zvika and Orly noticed that the cancer doesn't return to wherever you radiate, but appears elsewhere. Orly realized that the only place the cancer hadn't reached yet was the skull, and if they'd radiate his back now the cancer would have no choice but to spread to the brain. Dr. Berger was convinced by Orly's point and the radiotherapy was halted.

"Meanwhile, we did everything possible," says Orly. "We managed ourselves and didn't let others manage us. I took it upon myself to help Zvika. Wherever he takes responsibility I take a step back. Every week we went to a naturopath, Dr. Nava Boim. Nava devised a new diet for Zvika and strengthened his immune system through acupuncture. I heard about Professor Zeichek and contacted him. Upon his recommendation, Zvika underwent healing therapy and attended weekly sessions of guided imagery with therapist Billy Shaked.

Meanwhile Zvika was treated with two drugs: Radium23 - included in the health care coverage in January 2014 – which he took for six months; and Extandi, which we buy privately. Following all these measures, the PSA began falling to normal levels".

"I suppress the metastasis through guided imagery", says Zvika, "I have better and worse days, but overall I continue to work, live my life, and try to have fun. The guided imagery and my talks with Billy have turned my world upside down. I am no longer the cranky perfectionist I used to be. Even Dr. Berger told me in our last meeting: 'You are not the same person who came into my office four years ago. "

Carefully considering every treatment proposed to us

Orly: "I think the cancer stopped because we're not fixated. **We are aware of both alternative and conventional medicine.** We manage the disease and the doctors. We ask questions and get involved, carefully considering every treatment proposed to us. Zvika's results are phenomenal. We're no longer part of the statistics described to us four years ago. We are pleased but the job isn't finished yet. We need to keep working all the time, since these changes are for life. Recently we've been taking it easy, but we need to roll up our sleeves again and maintain the diet, exercise, and continue to seek solutions in alternative medicine".

Sara Hamo
Lymphoma - Kingston Clinic method – 35 years after diagnosis

"Of all the methods I discovered, I chose the one that seemed most logical the 'Kingston Clinic' method - a simple, non-extreme method for healthy living with a lot of common sense".

- Sara Hamo

In 1979 Sara Hamo was a 34-year-old mother of two daughters. Following an infection she had that required a tooth extraction, she noticed her lymph node was swollen. Sarah and her dentist attributed the swelling to the infection. When the node continued to grow for two more years despite the extraction and the antibiotics she took, Sara turned to an expert who diagnosed non-Hodgkin's type lymphoma spread to the liver and the abdominal lymph node. She agreed to take the proposed chemotherapy without protest.

"I felt awful during the treatment. I felt it was more of a risk to my life than the disease itself", says Sara. "To the doctor's chagrin, I decided to stop the treatment already after the second session. I shared the decision with my friends, and they all started looking for an alternative treatment for me. "Of all the methods I discovered, I chose the one that seemed most logical - the 'Kingston Clinic' method - a simple, non-extreme method for healthy living".

I went to naturopath Eli Strauss, who taught me how to change my lifestyle based on the principles of the method. I learned what and when to eat. On his recommendation I went to bed early and started taking daily morning walks. Although I had no illusions that I'm going to get better, **six months after I started the Kingston Clinic method I felt I got my life back and I felt healthy and vibrant, to my surprise.** It never occurred to me to go back to the hospital and take dangerous tests to find out if I'm healthy. I gave up on conventional treatment anyway.

Two years after the disease I had my third son in a natural home birth, and my happiness was complete. Then I founded the Natural Home in Ashkelon where I taught people how to maintain a healthy lifestyle. When I had to close down the place, I was free to write my book, "The Golden Path to Natural Healing", which delineates the story of my recovery and the principles of the method. A few decades have passed. I'm not so young anymore. I'm a grandmother of many grandkids - but I still feel wonderful.

In the meantime, I moved to Ein Karem, Jerusalem - a place with cleaner air than in the area adjacent to the power plant in Ashkelon. Here I take people in for counseling and teach courses on the method.

My life's mission is to teach people how to maintain their health and restore it if it's damaged. This is not a magic pill, but a lifestyle that yields quality of life, allowing each person to achieve optimal health based on their condition".

---≪•≫---

Sarah's take on the Kingston Clinic method

"The Kingston Clinic method focuses on matching our lifestyle with our biological clock. The biological clock determines for each system in the body at what time of day it will operate. The muscles, brain, and digestive system are active during the day. The immune and rehabilitation systems are active at night. If we act accordingly, each system will work optimally and contribute to our health. But most of us turn night into day - burdening the digestive system when it needs to rest and not sleeping during the immune system's working hours, when it needs quiet. Most of us also neglect to do morning exercise, which is essential to our health. If we do end up exercising, it's rather during the evening when air pollution is at its peak, the digestive system is loaded with food, and our adrenaline rises and suppresses the sleep hormone melatonin. Sleep schedule and morning activities each account for one-third of the body's healing ability. Proper nutrition in the right hours accounts for the remaining third.

The recommended menu is determined based on the intensity of the digestive system's activity during the day - in the morning it has just woken up and needs highly digestible food such as fruit. In the afternoon it's at its peak - time for raw vegetables that are hard to digest (you can add avocado and goat cheese, which help digestion). In the evening/late afternoon - cooked vegetables, organic egg, and tahini peeled by machine, not chemically. Fine sourdough bread such as rye or spelled, and grains that aren't rich in carbohydrates, just enough to satisfy the appetite. Such a diet - rich in vegetables, easily digestible proteins, and high quality fats, with no sweets or spices, allows all the body's cells to function optimally. In such diets there is also no need for excessive *drinking, which burdens the heart and kidneys and disrupts the digestive system.*

Cleansing processes, such as various infections, influenza, diarrhea, etc., are more common in the first period before the body's tissues are cleansed from harmful substances and we start living a life full of energy and joy. After the primary cleansing, it's recommended to add nuts, almonds, and legumes, which are harder to digest. Those who are healthy and really need it can also eat some organic chicken and fish. Of course, all the aforesaid is just a sample and shouldn't be relied on solely when changing one's lifestyle."

---≪•≫---

Rachel Moran
Breast cancer – Kingston Clinic method –
5 years after diagnosis

"It wanted to make decisions and do things based on what suits me.
It was action that helped me overcome my fear of the cancer"

- Rachel Moran

Rachel Moran - a 64-year-old mother of three and grandmother of eight, resident of Haifa, and a retired Ministry of Education employee - smiles at life, not letting the pain inside her spoil things. Rachel first became ill at the age of 46. A small tumor that didn't infiltrate into the nodes was detected in her breast and she underwent radiotherapy and surgery without chemotherapy. Thirteen years later, at the age of 59, another tumor was detected in the same place. The biopsy showed a link to the primary tumor. Within this tumult of tests and mental stress, her daughter found out she had breast cancer too. The two turned to genetic testing, which revealed that they both carry the BRCA1 gene[2].

"My daughter was treated with chemotherapy and I saw the severe side effects she suffered from. Despite the harsh treatment, the cancer returned three times. By the third time it was metastatic and terminal. Three years after the diagnosis my daughter died. She was only 36. I saw her suffering and chose not to undergo such treatment".

The days were tough and the nights even tougher, yet Rachel, the activist by nature, conducted her own research on the computer, reading hundreds of online studies.

"I wanted to decide what's going to happen with me. I decided to go for a bilateral mastectomy and breast reconstruction, but opted out of the chemotherapy my oncologist recommended. I thought my body was smart enough to know how to deal with diseases. In addition, I saw that despite the previous radiotherapy my cancer had returned in the same place, as was the case repeatedly with my daughter, despite the chemotherapy she

---

[2] BRCA 1 (breast cancer type 1)/ BRCA 2 (breast cancer type 2)

underwent. As a result, I lost faith in conventional treatment. I felt as if getting the usual treatment would be like betraying myself to the doctors. I wanted to decide what happens with my body. The sense of helplessness and my body's betrayal frustrated me greatly. I heard about Sara Hamo, who was cured by the Kingston Clinic method and turned to her for guidance. Sara guided me through a dramatic change in lifestyle. I followed the method for a year. The external results were clearly evident:

I lost ten kilos. To avoid poisoning my body, I rejected chemotherapy and pills that inhibit hormonal activity in the body. **I repeated my mantra that 'the cancer can't kill me', and thus managed to overcome my fear of cancer.** During this struggle my daughter died, and it was very difficult.

Today I do yoga and meditate twice a week, take a walk every morning, eat a lot of vegetables, attend conferences of the 'Ta'atzumot' Association[3], where they present holistic information on coping with cancer and lectures by cured patients describing how they did it. Once every three weeks I undergo lymphatic drainage to improve drainage by the lymphatic system. I keep doing things I love, such as painting, sculpting, and traveling. I got rid of friends who weren't good for me. I received psychological therapy to cleanse myself emotionally. And I decided that in order to protect myself, I will avoid anger, not make a big deal of things, and just roll with the punches. I avoid things that might be difficult and just walk away.

I believe everyone has "their time". My mother is a holocaust survivor and my daughter died at a young age. I believe it was written in the stars. Maybe this gives me peace. I am optimistic and see the bright side of life - maybe that helps me survive".

Rachel's daily schedule:

- Wakes up at 6 in the morning and takes a walk
- Drinks wheatgrass juice
- Eats a banana every day
- Carbohydrate + goat cheese only. No cow's milk.
- Lunch - salad, cheese, and cooked vegetables
- Goat milk yogurt and ground flaxseeds – every day
- Last meal of the day at seven in the evening
- Low intake of sugar, including fruit sugar

---

[3] http://www.taatzumot.com website of Taatzumot

- Doesn't eat industrial foods
- Doesn't take CT scans
- Paints as therapy and a way to disengage from the world
- Does yoga twice a week. Dietary supplements: Turmeric, magnesium, calcium, and vitamin B

What do I do now for my freedom?

My soul seeks freedom. When I was in high school I longed for the day I'd be independent of my parents, do whatever I want, and have money for my own decisions. I had a lot of spare time before enlisting to the army. I worked at the Vered Hagalil horse ranch. I traveled to the United States, where I worked in a restaurant, rented an apartment in Manhattan with a friend I met, made money, and had a good time. I was independent and happy.

When I joined the army I started keeping a binder with all the things I want to do when I get discharged. Two years after enlisting I sat in my parents' living room with the list and started realizing my dreams. And thus I set goals and achieved them. And now? I'm 50, I've got time. I'm already married with children. What do I do now for my freedom? I face a concrete wall six meters high that blocks the horizon, the view, and the ability to imagine the future. The sky is darkening, and I find it hard to set goals to fulfill. And my oncologist says that the only option left now for the metastatic breast cancer is chemotherapy. What does that mean?

I want to find solutions that will eliminate the need for chemotherapy. So the journey continues...

Ruth Bloch
Metastatic melanoma - Gerson Therapy – 3 years after diagnosis

"The Gerson Therapy is not suitable for most people. You need to start strong and adhere to all elements of the method"

- Ruth Bloch

During my morning walk my shadow waves at me from the sidewalk. My left hand rises and waves goodbye to me. I pass by the houses near my home of sixteen years and I can't tell what their residents look like. I ponder about what I should do. I make plans. Another part of me is asking me to come back here, to the present, to this street, to the many images I'm facing now. A little boy wearing a helmet comes riding alone on a bicycle, panting heavily as he pedals up the hill. A man wearing a black yarmulke sits on a stone wall talking on his mobile phone. A single vehicle drives by him, its wheels quivering on the interlocking stones, and different types of shadows shade the houses, the sidewalk, the cars. I push the garden gate and rush into the house. Without slowing down my pace, I instinctively start moving around kitchen objects, sorting each item by category. Moving, removing, sweeping. Everyday tasks are getting over me... In one hour I'm going to see Ruth Bloch.

Ruth Bloch is a great woman, though small in dimension, who creates massive sculptures and makes big changes in her life. Ruth is a professional sculptor. When faced with melanoma for the first time Ruth was 25, a young mother of two children. At the time she was diagnosed with stage 2 melanoma. Ruth underwent experimental treatment for two years, receiving injections of weakened tuberculosis. She recovered from the treatment and even gave birth to a baby girl six years later. Four years ago she discovered the cancer had returned. The disease metastasized and spread to the lymphatic system. In a complex surgery, the lymph nodes in and around her armpit were removed. Several metastases were found in the lymph nodes, so the oncologist suggested starting a series of interferon treatments to slow down the disease. The selected protocol was to include a month of daily treatment as an outpatient, and then reduced doses for a year. Already in the first treatment at the hospital severe side effects started appearing, and after ten treatments Ruth and the doctors decided to stop the process. "The oncologist suggested that we resume the interferon treatment after a week of rest. During the break I decided not to go back to conventional treatment at this stage", Ruth recalls.

"Immediately upon receiving the diagnosis I became an internet master, checking every available information online, speaking with research centers around the world which responded to me politely, but weren't very optimistic... I remained deeply committed".

Initially Ruth started treating herself with the Budwig Diet, under the tutelage of an expert from England. This method was developed by Dr. Johanna Budwig for the purpose of reducing levels of inflammation in the body. An important part of the method is the consumption of omega-3 fats. The method is complex yet logical, but Ruth's investigation found no evidence that the Budwig Diet cures metastatic melanoma. She turned to Dr. Pnina Bar Sela - a well-known expert nutritionist and Ruth's homeroom teacher in high school. Pnina suggested that Ruth try the Gerson Therapy.

"After talking to Pnina I looked up the Gerson Therapy. During this time, I heard others mention this method and even happened to see a film documenting various cancer patients (including some who had metastatic melanoma) who were cured with the Gerson Therapy". (See box).

The International Gerson Center is located in Tijuana. There's also a branch in Hungary, which Ruth decided to visit in order to learn the method. Ruth says: "I went to Hungary for two weeks when I was still very weak from the surgery and the interferon I was taking. I learned the therapy and applied it religiously. If you're committed to life, you do whatever it takes, no shortcuts. I was committed then and remain so now. For a year and a half I followed the protocol of the Gerson Therapy, eventually making adjustments, reducing and adding elements from Ayurvedic medicine.

During that time, my journey intersected with that of my older sister. A week and a half after I underwent the surgery, my sister was diagnosed with advanced colon cancer. We went through this wonderful journey together. These were separate yet overlapping journeys that stimulated and fed off each other".

Eighteen months later, Ruth's sister died.

"Ever since then, I've been approached by people who heard that I cured my cancer and wanted to talk to me. I listen to them and try to help them find the right path for them. The Gerson Therapy isn't suitable for everyone, but there are different ways to get cured."

Ruth still makes sure to drink a lot of vegetable juice every day, and maintains an organic diet based on foods that are "allowed" and "not allowed" under the Gerson Therapy. Those wishing to apply the Gerson Therapy must undergo a period of training, accompanied by doctors and experts on the subject.

"Nutrition is a very important element in my lifestyle", says Ruth, "but it's only part of a comprehensive regime. Among other things, I also practice yoga every day; go to bed early and get up early; find time to work in the garden; and continue to sculpt every day. My life is blessed with a rich family life and a lot of love, above all".

---≪•≫---

Gerson Therapy

The Gerson Therapy was developed by Dr. Max Gerson, a German physician (1959-1881) who introduced a vegetarian diet focusing on the intake of potassium, juices, and coffee enemas as a "metabolic method" for cancer treatment.

Dr. Gerson claimed that cancer is a degenerative disease that requires tough dietary measures. He used nutrition as a means for generating internal biochemistry that allows a maximum release of healing resources. Gerson's diet method was designed to increase the discharge of toxins and waste products; "fill" the body with fresh, concentrated, and available nutrients; and help dissolve tumors.

The method includes processes that cleanse the body of toxins, improve metabolism, and stimulate the function of the liver - the most important organ in processes of cleansing, filtering, sanitization, and rehabilitation. The diet itself entails a special balance of sodium (little salt) and potassium (a lot of potassium from vegetables and special supplements), vegan-organic foods, and freshly squeezed vegetable juices. It also includes enemas of coffee and liver extract (squeezed from young naturally grown calves). During the first six weeks of the diet there is no intake of proteins, to allow the cells to emit oxygen and enable rehabilitation. That is, no fish, eggs, butter, milk, or dairy products. Then we add nonfat yogurt and cheese and drink 12-13 glasses of juice a day immediately after preparing them. Especially notable is the combination of carrot with apple. There is no drinking of water. Coffee enemas are done when needed, sometimes even four times a day, which helps remove waste from the body. We eat thee vegetarian meals a day of fresh and cooked vegetables without adding water. Restricted ingredients include salt, hot spices, tea, coffee, cocoa, chocolate, alcohol, sugar, white flour, ice cream, cakes, nuts, mushrooms, soy products, cucumber, pumpkin, strawberries, pineapple, canned foods, frozen foods, smoked foods, salty foods, and baking soda. Gerson also prohibited hair coloring. In addition, we take dietary supplements according to the protocol. In his book "Cancer Can Be Beaten", Shlomo Guberman notes the types of cancers for which Gerson's protocol is most effective: melanoma, lymphoma, colon, ovarian, lung (small and large cell), pancreas, prostate, and early stages of breast cancer. It is not recommended to follow Gerson's protocol during chemotherapy. Participation in Gerson's workshops and treatment centers around the world will provide precise guidance for proper treatment. It is not recommended to attempt the therapy alone. The said details of the diet are partial and one should not rely on them solely.

---≪•≫---

Halima Ben Neria
Non-Hodgkin's Lymphoma - Budwig Diet and treatment by aliens – 8 years after diagnosis

Halima, who runs a cat boarding service in the rural community of Aviezer nearby Beit Shemesh, has kept away from the modern rat race and ensured her health the best she could. Nevertheless, for over 17 years she was tempted to smoke six cigarettes a day, drink beer from cans, three cups of strong coffee every day and sometimes a few glasses of wine to lighten up the mood.

"Until the age of fifty I ate chicken and fish, feeling considerably guilty about it. I took an impressive amount of vitamins and dietary supplements. I used to go once a year on my own initiative to take blood tests in order to reassure myself, like getting a 'health certificate'.

I lived in a condominium in Jerusalem and was writing a novel. Many residents in our street had cancer. This was actually reported in a piece on the investigative TV show 'Fact'. They claimed that it had occurred due to the proximity to the UN antenna, other cellular antennas mounted on nearby local houses, and a powerful transformer of the Electricity Company located in the street. I thought my house was far enough from the antennas and yet most tenants in our building who passed away during the 18 years that I lived there died of cancer".

Halima, who used to feed the cats outside the building, faced constant harassment by neighbors who even resorted to puncturing her car tires. The tough experience of living in that building increased her desire to make a major change in her life and move to the countryside.

And so, at the age of 53 she found a home in the community of Aviezer and moved there.

"I was breathing as if I was back in my natural setting and felt I was getting healthier. In the first days I lay on the bench outside and watched the wind and the sun play with the crests of the tall pines. I swept the road in front of my house and knew it would stay like that. When I hanged laundry in the sun I imagined myself in a movie, a woman running a farm on her own in the Wild West, making the desert bloom. New expanses for endeavor were revealed before me in the garden. I woke up at dawn, eager to discover what's new in the garden. The smell of soil and vegetation brought me back to similar moments in my childhood. It's weird, I thought. Had things not been so bad for me, I wouldn't have ended up being so happy.

I started a new and exciting life. I trusted my health and the forces directing me from within to the right path, drawing my strength from a sense integrity and inner peace that I achieved in my efforts to nurture the life around me. I turned the decrepit yard into a blossoming garden and grew organic vegetables. I had a column in "La Isha" magazine for women, where I wrote my thoughts on life and presented gardening tips. I replaced my walks on the treadmill at the gym with strolling at dawn through the woods and fields. The days ended too fast. I'd be sipping a glass of wine, basking in the hammock, looking at the orange sky in the west, following the sun disappear behind the hills, and I'd already want it to be dawn again. Every day I thanked God for guiding me through my decisions. This year I kept postponing the blood test from month to month.

In the following year the blood tests showed a decrease in white blood cells. The doctor felt my spleen and said it was enlarged. The ultrasonography showed an enlarged spleen and enlarged lymph nodes in the hepatic portal. I was struck with worries invading my healing space. I predicted the worst - cancer!

The thought that I might have cancer seemed like slamming the door on everything familiar in my life and opening the door to another life. As far as I could imagine, my new persona would be as one would expect after chemotherapy: bald, yellow, wrinkly, ill, and weak".

The rest of Halima's story includes a painful biopsy on the hepatic portal, without anesthesia, and a sense of urgency to find out what's going on. Halima felt she can't afford to lose a single minute, and every day that goes by without treatment the cancer spreads through her body as she stands idly by. Although it takes many years for cancer to form in a person's body, this is the approach held by most cancer patients and doctors.

I remember that feeling. Today, eight years after my first diagnosis, I realize that stress is unhelpful. It weakens the immune system and causes a lot of damage. I'm also familiar with the liver biopsy. I will never do that again without anesthesia, and I hope I never have to repeat it. To me this test is like severe torture.

Halima says her shrieking was heard well in the hallway when she underwent this procedure. I'm sure mine was heard well too...

Halima's liver biopsy found a stage 1 follicular lymphoma.

The CT scan found multiple lymph nodes behind the peritoneum, in the hepatic portal, in the mesenteric root, and all across the abdomen. The following was concluded: "enlargement of lymph nodes in all stations. Enlarged spleen. Potential disease with uncontrolled spread of cells belonging to the lymphatic".

"I have all these things in my body?", Halima asked.

Later on she had a bone marrow biopsy that showed additional manifestations of the disease in the bone marrow. "So I guess I really have the worst of all", she thought.

Then they sent me to a PET CT scan in addition to the CT scan. Today I know what I didn't know back then, that before any kind of CT scan you should swallow an impressive amount of antioxidants: CoQ10, Vitamin C, and Vitamin E, to help the body handle the amount of radiation it absorbs.

After they removed two nodes from my armpit, the final diagnosis was made: I have grade 2 stage 4 follicular lymphoma.

Despite the diagnosis I refused to undergo chemotherapy and follow-up CT scans every three months. At home I had a few books on alternative cancer treatment that I collected in the course of my life. Something inside me knew that one day I might stand in front of this hurdle so I better be prepared. I read Sara Hamo's book on the Kingston Clinic method, and reread Yossi Sidi's book "Cancer, the Gift of my Life". It was actually my cat's veterinarian, well-versed in alternative medicine, who recommended the Budwig Diet to me.

Despite all the bad news I got, I felt healthy and alert. I couldn't imagine going through chemotherapy with all its side effects. I was ready to die rather than go through that torture. My doctor is a sympathetic person. He was attentive to me and his tone of voice was calm. I told him I decided to try the Budwig Diet. He hadn't heard of it. I gave him a general description of its approach to curing cancer and the specifics of the diet. "This requires a great deal of preoccupation with food," he mused aloud, "isn't that difficult? The alternative methods don't always help", he added.

"Neither do the conventional ones", I replied, "and they are hard too". I invited him to read about Budwig online, and he said he would do so. The doctor was satisfied and gave me a test referral for three months later. I left his office knowing that nothing in my life will remain the same. "Hasta la vista, baby". Since then I am only willing to do blood tests and an ultrasound of the spleen to know if the disease is spreading or in remission".

What does Halima do?

- Goes to sleep at nine o'clock, wakes up at sunrise.
- Eats organic vegetarian food. Grows her own vegetables in her garden and then buys the rest from good, fresh sources.
- Does physical exercise, including walking in areas with rich vegetation and clean air.
- Jumps on a trampoline.
- Sunbathes an hour a day, with almost her entire body exposed.
- Prepares a mixture of organic cheese with flaxseed oil and adds ground flaxseeds to her food.
- Takes dietary supplements: Q10, Vitamin D, turmeric, selenium, zinc, digestive enzymes, friendly bacteria, B complex, folic acid, magnesium.

It's been eight years since Halima chose the Budwig Diet, and she continues to read, catch up on the latest updates, and find out what else can help her. For years she saw her spleen and liver diminish and expand in ultrasound scans, reflecting her level of adherence to the diet.

Two years ago she lost hope due to the instability of the tumors and decided to start treatment with aliens, whom she's believed in since the age of 12. She turned to Tovy Be'ery, who communicates with aliens telepathically.

"My situation is chronic - my body lives with the cancer, and to avoid a constant battle, I turned to the aid of aliens. Their treatments are amazing. In the past year there has been no change in the size of the tumors, unlike before their treatment. They wrapped the affected nodes in a silicon balloon to separate between them and the healthy cells. They inject their own chemotherapy in there, which doesn't cause the side effects we're familiar with. The process isn't painful at all, though you can feel the treatment. For example, when my nostril trembles I know the aliens are putting in or taking out my catheter. They planted a 'black box' in my stomach to see what and when I eat. After analyzing the results the instructed me how to change my diet.

"In every session they run a body scan to see if anything has grown and where. The answer is given immediately. They cut slices 1.5-mm thick from the infected glands and inject into the tumor a substance that kills it. Then they smash everything and the body removes it on its own. When the removal is completed, they plant healthy tissues in there".

In Halima's blog you can read in detail about the Budwig Diet and find out more about her experiences.

www.budwig-Israel.com

---✧•✦---

Essentials of Budwig Diet for Cancer Patients

Dr. Johanna Budwig (1908-2003), a German biochemist, was nominated for the Nobel Prize for her work in the field of cancer.
Based on her research findings, she added a mixture of skim milk protein and hemp oil to the diet of advanced cancer patients, and studied the changes in their blood. According to her, the tumors receded and disappeared, and some patients were cured. At the same time, other symptoms of the cancer had disappeared.

Budwig Protocol

Foods
Homemade pickled juice. Raw or steamed vegetables, namely green and cruciferous. Herbs, legumes. Sweeteners: stevia, unpasteurized raw honey, dates, figs. A lot of flaxseed, medical marijuana, hemp oil. Medicinal herbs in their natural form. Seeds and nuts except for peanuts (unroasted). Raw cocoa.
Grated coconut.

Materials for making cottage cheese and oil smoothie
Flaxseed oil or hemp oil stored in the refrigerator (up to 12 months in the freezer)
Organic cottage cheese or organic goat cheese
Electric hand blender

Preparing Smoothie
Mix two tablespoons of hemp oil with 3 tablespoons of cottage cheese in a blender until you get a uniform texture. You can add a teaspoon of raw honey (unprocessed), cinnamon, vanilla, hazelnuts, walnuts, rose hips, a pinch of sea salt or rock salt or cayenne pepper. Add freshly ground

flaxseeds (don't buy ground flaxseeds because their fatty acids are released when crushed and they start a process that makes them more harmful than useful). After a week you can increase the amount to 2 tablespoons of oil and 6 tablespoons of cheese. You can replace the cheese with goat milk yogurt and then multiply the amount of yogurt relative to the amount of cottage cheese. It is recommended to make this twice a day.

Drinking
Small quantities of natural red wine. Carrot juice, apple juice, and beet juice. Berry juices, herbal tea, black tea. Distilled or reverse osmosis water.

Exposure to Sun
It is recommended to get 20 minutes of daily exposure to the sun - not in the afternoon.

Forbidden foods
Sugar, animal fats except for yogurt and cottage cheese mixed with flaxseed oil. All types of meat, all commercial salad dressings, preservatives, and processed foods.

It is necessary to follow this protocol for three to five years. Keep in mind that not every reduction or remission of tumors necessarily signifies the end of toxicity in the body. To implement the diet fully and seriously, I suggest reading a book on the method and finding an alternative therapist who is familiar with it.

---≪•≫---

Tova Be'eri works with aliens

Tova Be'eri, a healer, works with aliens and defines herself as a "current connecting between alien and man". In a small home enveloped by a large courtyard full of potted plants and animals, behind a locked gate (because the dogs run away) I met a woman who seems quite average. The house is full of expressive paintings drawn by her, gemstones glued on the paintings, fairy dolls on every shelf and desk, religious books, books on Kabbalah and awareness, gems and more.

Tova tells me she's been able to see aliens and talk to them since she was a child.

"They're medical doctors," she explains, "from other worlds and galaxies. They're fully involved in the treatment I perform. It's a collaborative effort in which we touch the psychological aspects. Every disease has a mental aspect. We get sick because of unresolved emotional issues. There are ways to circumvent the emotional place and reach places that were blocked. We make mental corrections".

I lie on Toa's treatment table. She puts her hands above me and I feel warmth spreading below my hands. She moves her hands over my body and the warmth moves with them. I feel shivers.

"Your problem is technical, not emotional," she says. "You need to fix it so that it won't come back. I am the conductor, the link between you and the aliens. I place my hand over you so they can connect with you. They use their own equipment and medicine. They put a substance to soften the rigid material that formed in your gallbladder. They also did some cleaning in your liver. They took your DNA and ran other tests on you. Since this was your first time with us, the treatment was delicate so as not to create unnecessary tension in the body. They live above my home in a spaceship. They're always here..."

I felt completely overwhelmed on my way to the car after Tova's treatment. I sat in the car and it didn't even occur to me to start the engine. I spent a few minutes in thoughtless gazing. It found it difficult to talk. I wanted to be alone with myself. I had no doubt that something had just happened on Tova's treatment table, be it due to her strength or the aliens - something that affected me deeply. I then started the car and began driving without looking sideways. I snapped out of it when I heard the squeal of another car's brakes to my left. That night I couldn't sleep. I scheduled another meeting. My kids laughed at me when I told them about it. I laughed too, but I put aside my skepticism in the meantime. Even after the second treatment I couldn't sleep at night. A few days later my eldest son came up to me and gave me a business card. "This person sat next to me on the train and told me to give this card to anyone in my family who is sick. He says he can help. You believe in such things, so maybe you should call him".

In my typical curiosity, I look up the name online. I find his website and read letters from patients. It says there that he even had success with metastatic cancer. The letters from his patients impress me. If I went to the aliens, why not try practical bioenergy, especially in light of my stomach condition.

I call the therapist with the business card and asked him to scan my body remotely, as he usually does, and tell me about my situation.

"Your condition is excellent. I wish everyone was like you", he tells me.

I am tempted to believe him for a moment.

"You have gallstones in the liver, which doesn't look good, and a mild intestinal infection. The stomach problem is no big deal. I can help you solve it... In the last two weeks you've been in a situation of simulated pregnancy. Do you want to be pregnant?"

"I'm 51".

"So? That doesn't matter".

"But I don't have ovaries".

"You don't have any ovaries?" he marveled.

By now it was clear to me that I won't go see this therapist. The conversation with him reminded me how important it is to consider carefully who you go to. How does one check? Ask to speak with the people who were treated by him, or hold an introductory talk on the phone. Dare to ask questions, even if you'll come across as a nag. What's true when choosing a doctor is also true for choosing an alternative therapist.

CHAPTER 2

Arguing with the Doctors

Looking for freedom, for a place that excites me.

A place where I'd want to wake up every morning.

Friday morning. A lawnmower upsets the morning silence. To my right, the to-do list fills up on a white piece of paper. Urgent, important, general. I intend to consciously create the feeling of freedom today. Last night I disconnected the phone. I look at it, but I don't turn it on. It feels a bit like an enemy of freedom. I'm used to wanting, answering, doing, caring, sharing. I have a headache. There will be no freedom here until my study is tidy. It's as if I didn't clean the place a week ago. Surrounded by notes full of scribbled phone numbers of people I want to talk to. A box of to be digested medicine doesn't belong here and will go straight to the medicine cabinet.

As part of my current journey, I'm touring the country, absorbing landscapes into my body, examining the effect of the various expanses on my spirit, until I find a place where I'd want to stay, a place that excites me. A place where I'd want to wake up every morning.

This morning I went to Givat Ada to meet Rafi Mintz at his studio. Rafi is a painter and sculptor who years ago cured himself of a skin disease with the macrobiotic diet. Since then he's learned the method and he now treats others with it. I went to him in the hope that he has some insight on how to help my stomach. Macrobiotics is a philosophy of life based on the wisdom of the East, and the balance between our masculine and feminine forces - our Yin and Yang. Diseases, according to Macrobiotics, occur as a result of imbalance. See the box for Rafi's suggestions on the macrobiotic diet.

The house in the plot above Rafi's used to be mine. We built our homes at the same time, and in between them we planted a meter-wide buffer zone of shared fruit trees. My husband at the time refused to live there. My soul would wander to the expanses we could see from our living room, to the vineyards and the tender hills. When our marriage ended we sold the house. My soul still wanders to the space of that house. For me the trip to Rafi was a quick stroll down memory lane. I met Rafi for the first time over two decades ago. I was a reporter on vegan issues for the "Adam and Eve" newspaper, and I went to his home in Jaffa to interview him about his recovery.

Rafi is sitting on the other side of the table, his eyes analyzing my features: "You desperately need freedom", he states. "You study all the time, you feel the need to be secluded, but you're hurting yourself creatively. Something about your creative development is holding you back. And instead of going with the flow and saying 'everyone can wait, I need to live first', you try too hard and waste your energy attempting to control others. This is hurting you. Go back to the place where you're not angry or blaming others. When you blame others, it comes back to you. Remember that everyone always tries to do their best. Everyone tries hard like you.

Although you have leadership skills and aspirations, you can't use them against others. You're already done with raising your kids. After the age of 5 there's not much we can teach. The most we can do is set an example. Save your energy and return to your inner child, the little girl who deserves to live a full life. The girl who lives by her inner emotion and feels satisfaction. Go dancing, go singing. Forget the guilt, you don't owe anything to anyone and no one owes you anything either. Let me ask you a difficult question: What are you afraid of?"

"Emmm..." I delay my answer. "I made stopping cancer my life purpose and I'm afraid of not succeeding because that means I failed."

"Great answer...", says Rafi. We both smile.

"Well, listen to this answer," Rafi continues, "it's all in your hands, you're on the right track. The more you insist... you can trust yourself completely. You're hurting yourself by maintaining that you need to get rid of the cancer first", Rafi raises his voice and continues passionately, "You say: I've been chasing the cancer for five years? Ten years? I should grab it by the tail, cut it off and eradicate it once and for all. Nature doesn't do anything against itself. The divine entity - the cosmos, doesn't go against you. This problem poses a hint for you. The messages from the universe were subtle at first: headaches, runny nose, insomnia, poor vision. When we don't listen to hints, nature gives us even stronger hints: for example, a headache will develop into a migraine. The body creates problems to signal that it needs help. You have the power to go back a few steps to a point where everything was ok; to the mental state where you weren't yet blaming others or feeling so angry and the physical state where your body was still stronger.

The cancer cells attack the strongest system in the body. When milk ducts and lymph nodes are attacked, there's an emotional link to femininity and sensuality. I'm afraid you denied that and remained alienated from your femininity. Do you know why you did that? How is it your fault?"

"First of all, it's all my fault - this is a central theme in my life," I say. "Whenever my name is called out I wonder what I did wrong."

"If you took the trouble to come here and this encounter is important," Rafi tries to explain, "then when you walk with little Dorothy again – you'll feel the difference already."

"Wait, tell me - what do you mean by little Dorothy?"

"She's the little girl who deserves to live a full life, but as she got older she thought she became a grown up who has to act differently from what her soul wants.

As long as you have a lust for life you will return to self-fulfillment through art. What suppresses your creativity? You need new and exciting things, good exhibits, culture" (but I just want to be alone). "To be excited!!!" Rafi cries out. "What are you reading?" What's your view?"

I look out the window of his studio and see two large statues in the garden and the familiar green hills in the distance.

I've already heard about the desire to live. I'm trying to remember where. Oh, yes. Dr. O. Carl Simonton, an oncologist specializing in radiation therapy and his psychologist wife Stephanie, who together founded the Cancer Center for counseling and research in Dallas, USA, begin their book "Getting Well Again" with what they see as the main cause of recovery: the desire to live. Simonton found that patients whose condition improved, for whatever reason, had a stronger "lust for life than those whose condition deteriorated faster.

Rafi continues:

"Go dance finally, so your lungs will fill up."

"I know I should live with a sense of freedom but I feel this concept is out of reach for me at the moment – I'm all dead inside."

"Are your parents alive?"

"My mother is alive, we are pretty close."

"Why does that make you cry?"

"Because of the knowledge that there's something out of my reach – I don't know how to get it. Sometimes I try to be alone. I don't get excited about anything."

"Look around you for something that will enrich your life: books, movies, good exhibits – that's where you'll find something that excites you. Even the choice of people you associate with is important. I can tell you're very strong even though you say you're shattered from the inside".

"Last night I thought about giving up."

"Go along with that - say: Guys - world – I'm giving you my heart. I don't care if you give me yours back, 'I feel good giving my heart'."

"My heart is drawn to live here."

"You are the one who chose not to live here, but don't rule out any option that comes to mind - you have time. That kind of attitude actually affords the most time. Go at your own pace. On the other hand, take the step now – and your body will lead the way. Your body knows you better than you do and you just have to listen to it. Not all at once, any kind of extremity brings about another extremity. Things are within your reach - do what enriches your life."

My meeting with Rafi made me think about my lifestyle, my happiness, and how much I express my femininity in life. It would be easier for me to apply the principles of the macrobiotic diet than the other recommendations. In any case, I follow his recommendations in addition to other nutritional methods and adjust my diet based on the state of my stomach.

Rafi's recommendations for macrobiotic food span over four pages.

Below are the main points:

Foods to avoid: animal products, especially meat, animal fat, dairy products, processed sugars, simple sugars and foods prepared with them. Fruit juices, sweetened sodas, and soft drinks. Artificial sweeteners, coffee, and tea. Food coloring and preservatives. Any industrially processed foods. Refined oils and strong alcoholic beverages. Don't store food in the freezer and don't heat or cook it in the microwave.

Rafi recommends the following composition for your diet: 30%-60% cooked grains, 10%-15% legumes, 30%-60% vegetables, and seaweed (half tablespoon to tablespoon per day). It is recommended to eat anticancer foods like miso soup, which has been found to reduce gastric cancer when consumed on a daily basis; kumbo seaweed, cruciferous vegetables such as broccoli, cauliflower, cabbage, Brussels sprouts. It is better to eat organically grown produce. Rafi recommends diversifying the food and its form of preparation. These recommendations are personal and this list is only partial. I strongly recommend seeking the assistance of an experienced therapist when composing your own menu.

What do I need to change in my life?

I'm at Alonei Aba with friends. I came to breathe the green pastures. I walk through the fields sprawling outside the house. Vast, green, mountains, sunset, pleasant breeze. I return to the house. From the shower and I can see the cypress trees enveloping the house, and the crow waiting at the top for something interesting to happen. I smile. The windowsill is at the level of my chest. I enjoy the cold water on my skin. Yesterday I spoke with Susana Marcus, who changed her way of life sixteen years ago to cure her body of cancer. One of the main aspects of her new approach was emotional work. My conversation with Susanna stresses the need to release old angers and pain, to let out my old song. Is it possible that I focus too much on my life's drama than on the things that make me happy?

I ask myself the key questions she asked. Where am I stuck? What do I need to change in my life? What can I do to be happy? Difficult questions to answer. I can meditate for an hour on each question and raise possible answers, hoping one of them will feel right for me.

In the morning I walk through the small village, mentally photographing the homes and their styles. Some of them have a great view. I peek in to check what they see... Fields, oaks, pastures... Perhaps I want to live here. Perhaps this is the change I want/need? Is this some old dream waiting to come true? Here, to live in this house with the iron gate and the vine with purple flowers. With a winding path embraced by rosemary, sage, lavender. How different would my life have been had I lived here. What would my daily routine look like? Where does all this quiet come from? The inner view or the outer vista?

I return to the Templar home where I'm staying. The smell of the adjacent cowshed fills the spaces of the house, denying me of the inner peace I need. My friend gave me a small, cozy room, separate from their home – one bed, a simple wooden bookcase with four shelves, and a fan. The asceticism is pleasant for me. I exit the room and go up the stairs embedded with fragments of colored porcelain, done by the woman of the house. I push a blue wooden door and enter a hallway leading to the kitchen. In a large room, old cabinets are painted in bright green, and a large fan on the wall reduces the heat and tempers the smell of the cows. While smelling this scent, I am exposed to the theory of Dr. Candace Pert on molecules of emotion. I dedicate the morning to this theory. Dr. Pert - an American researcher who discovered that chakra points - through which energy flows in the body, according to ancient teachings - are located in the same places where scientists discovered concentrations of nerve cells that can produce and secrete neuropeptides. Neuropeptides are complex, small molecules composed of amino acids. They are found in all parts of the body and facilitate communication between nerve cells. Some neuropeptides can function as hormones secreted into the bloodstream and affect various distant cells.

After many years of research, Pert discovered that the nature of thoughts affects the type of protein produced in cells. "If negative and burdensome thoughts can cause the body to get sick," says Pert, "then positive thoughts can make it get better - by healing the cells." Pert talks about programming the subconscious and about therapeutic musical frequencies. I find an audio file of Pert online: "I take a deep breath and relax completely... As I exhale, I remove stress from the body... I forgive myself and others and the forgiveness gives me more energy and focus... I relieve myself from criticizing myself and others...". And thus it goes on for twenty minutes. I do exercises, imagining new and good proteins. The body relaxes, the mind quiets down. In recent days I've been listening to music at high volume whenever I get a chance - during walks, in the car. Music affects my mood, improves it, elevates it and makes me happy. Does it stop the cancer cells from spreading? Will I be able to write that I was cured by music? That prospect makes me laugh.

Saying goodbye to the heat and flying to Sweden

I woke up today in Ra'anana. It's late and I don't have much time to walk and make juice. I decide to skip meditation again. I look for something which will make me feel good. I will offer my son, Nadav, to choose a European country where he could practice the sport he specializes in: Jiu Jitsu. I'll spend a week in a European city and pretend to be a local. I'll realize a little dream of mine.

Thankfully, Nadav chose Sweden.

In early August, we say goodbye to the scorching heat and fly to a country where autumn has already begun. My cousin Adi lives with her family in a town not far from the city where the training club is located. Nadav practices every day and I go for walks in the woods, sitting on rocks and looking at the lakes. "Don't rule out any option that comes to mind," Rafi Mintz said.

I'm in Sweden. I continue reading materials about cancer treatment. The most obvious conclusion from my recent readings is the need to stimulate the immune system to be at its peak. I'm sure the forests surrounding this small town are good for the immune system, as is the love within me. My morning qi exercises help me open my heart. That's good. Now is a good opportunity to talk a bit about the life energy called qi. According to Eastern philosophy, this energy exists in the universe and in every body. It is the basis for mental and physical health. According to this theory, the qi's effects on health are clearly evident. Qigong exercises strengthen this energy.

In the morning I felt the tumor - it seems small. I went out for a bike ride through the forest in the rain, like the locals. I thrive in the outdoors. I need at least an hour a day in nature.

Do you want to live here? I ask myself as I face of the large lake in front of all this green. The tranquility is phenomenal. It's like a large kibbutz with well-kept lawns and houses without fences. A month ago I was in Mitzpe Ramon, walking along the cliff overlooking the spectacular view. Do I want to live here? I asked myself. It seems that both living as a nomad and returning home are good for me. The possibility of moving from one magical landscape to another. The renewal, the ability to move around in nature. Not wasting energy on moving apartments - just moving from house to house, from nature to nature, from the desert to Alonei Aba to Sweden.

I am not ruling out any option.

The forest here is pure happiness. It's raining on me. I choose a path. The smell of fertile soil full of humus. The forest envelops a small lake. The roots of the trees are filled with moss and escape holes for fleeing animals. I get off the official path and enter the woods. I am alone. A few people walk along the path. I am surrounded by nature. All this beauty is my great love. I am thrilled. At this moment I'm living exactly like I want to.

Awaiting the blood test results

We returned a week ago. This morning I took a blood test and I'm waiting to see the state of my immune system in the hope that I can continue taking the new biological drug that I now get as a compassion drug. A compassion drug is one that is not part of the standard medical protocol. Sometimes it's still experimental, not yet approved for marketing in Israel and or sold normally. The doctor needs to contact the pharmaceutical company directly to get it, and the company requests a special permit from the Health Ministry to import the drug. I found this drug thanks to my friend Estelle who had sarcoma four years ago. She sent me an article about the experiments conducted on this drug in Europe and the United States. I saw the results achieved so far and felt hopeful. The data shows an average three-year life extension for women with metastatic breast cancer. I contacted the drug company Pfizer and asked to participate in an experiment in Europe, but they declined. Gadi had an idea. Since he is familiar with the high-tech world and its networking culture, he suggested that he contact the drug's product manager. The minute he raised that idea, my friend Yael remembered that one of her colleagues once worked for Pfizer and knows the people who work there. And thus, after a long, bureaucratic process, I got the drug. Had I not received it, I think my hopes would significantly diminish. I have trouble overcoming abdominal pain and can't eat all the good and nourishing things I want.

My kitchen becomes a laboratory

Estelle comes over to help me prepare extract from the cannabis I have, which is approved by the Ministry of Health. The protocol of Rick Simpson, which cures cancer according to some accounts, is posted online. The Health Ministry won't allow me to prepare the extract the way Rick describes. Estelle is excellent at reading in English and happily willing to help me, despite her own cancer. She comes to me with a large heating plate. We crush the cannabis flowers in a small blender, put them in a jar and fill it with 95% alcohol. We mix the jar, transfer the substance to a pot, and place it on the heating plate outside the house to let the alcohol fumes evaporate. The product is thick, black, and bitter. It should eliminate cancer cells, and help me sleep.

Get rid of guilt. How do you do that?

It's my stomach again. The phone rings. It's Ilan, the film director, on the line. He wants to discuss the concept with me. He's talking about timing.

A month ago I suggested that he make a film about "my heroes." Ilan liked the idea and helped me promote the issue.

I figure that by the time we start shooting the film about survivors, it might turn into a film in my memory. I conclude the conversation with Ilan and type "radical remission" on Google. I need inspiration. Or maybe not. In fact, who cares if I'm gone anyway? Why make the effort? What good do I have in this life? I am constantly aware that I am choosing between giving up or letting go - generously spending the money that's left and saying: I am ready to die. Am I indeed ready?

I return to the bedroom. "Gadi, I want to talk to you."

I sit down on the bed in front of him. He has a serious face. "Gadi, I'm going to die".

Gadi bursts into laughter - "again with this?"

"Are you relieved? What did you think? That I'm going to talk about money?"

"Dorke", he calls me gently, "there's no bucket list of things to do. You know exactly what you need to do. You already know everything".

I say nothing. After a few minutes of looking at him, he falls asleep. I go back to the computer. Noa Sehayik wrote intensely for a year. I want to write all night. I go down to the kitchen and take eight drops of cannabis in a cookie. I hope this gets me high quickly.

I lost faith in my ability to self-heal.

"Dorke", Gadi calls me, "come over here, I want to tell you something."

I get up from the computer. He's lying on the bed and I lie down on him, keeping my left chest in the air to avoid pain (the chest metastases cause sensitivity to touch). I place my head on his shoulder socket and feel his bones sticking out against my body.

"You need to stop feeling guilty."

"How does one do that?" I rush to ask.

"I do not know, you need to figure it out yourself".

I repeat our conversation in my mind. You have to stop feeling guilty, but how is that possible? You need to figure out...

I open my eyes and see his neck. His hands are on my back, caressing. I enjoy lying on top of him, feeling like a baby, protected. I can fall asleep like this. He brings his head closer to mine and when I open my eyes I see nothing. My eyes are glued to his neck.

Sometimes I think I know nothing...

Semi Routine

Today was the opening of an exhibit of book illustrations at the Givatayim Library, where I presented a children's book about coping with ALS. My brother Shai wrote it and I drew the illustrations. My friend Yael picked me up and we went together. I felt horrible. After presenting the book to the audience, I got off the stage and went to the bathroom to throw up. I felt a slight relief from the nausea and pain. Being accustomed to this vomiting, I wiped my face and quickly went back to what I was doing.

12:20 AM. I can't fall asleep. I remember my old friend, A. I go to the computer to check if she is still alive, but can't find any information. I search on WhatsApp and find that she was last seen on September 2013. I search on Google and her date of death comes up. I feel sick.

Today Gadi told me his graphic designer has metastatic breast cancer (damn, so many people get cancer) and was sent home by her doctors because there is no treatment that can help her. She asked Gadi if she could talk to me and perhaps seek my assistance. I look up her name on Google, find her email address, and write to her.

The next morning she calls me and we arrange so I come visit her.

I am excited towards the visit - perhaps because I think I may be able to help. I jot down on a note the things I want to discuss with her. Gadi drives to Tel Aviv and I join him for the trip. As soon as I enter the car I spill my drink. Damn, this is starting out badly. I get off near the graphic designer's building. The doctors ran out of ammunition against the metastasis in her lungs and liver. Surprisingly, our meeting is mentally draining and difficult for me. My stomach starts aching and I want to go. I hail a cab and go to my sister Tal, who treats me with Japanese acupuncture. She balances my body, boosts my immune system, and relieves my pain. After Tal removes all the needles, I go vomit. Today I only threw up twice.

Even when I'm hurting, it's pain, not suffering

If there's something I truly hate, it's bumping into the doorknob, or getting my shirt caught in it as I keep walking. I instantly get filled with rage all over my body, and I don't stop. I continue forward to the task, moving along, acting like it's no big deal. Slowly the anger dissolves inside my body on its own, without my intervention. Maybe it's the same with the disease – I don't want to let it stop me. I want to pull off its doorknob...

"You write melancholy posts, so I wanted to ask how you're doing", said a message I received from a childhood friend.

"I'm not sad," I replied, "I'm glad I'm here. Survivors are those who were told there's nothing that can be done and yet are still alive many years later."

I didn't understand why he decided that I'm sad or how my writing suggests sadness. An hour later, a friend told me that people are asking what happened to me and inquiring about the severity of my condition. So in light of these questions, I have a confession to make: Except for when I bump into doorknobs, the situation is pretty good. Even when I'm hurting, it's pain, not suffering. And the pain is a result of radiation I underwent last year. Yesterday, for example, I had a great day: I spent the afternoon at the beach and saw an amazing and totally corny sunset. The sun practically melted into the water. I put on a bathing suit and I enjoyed my body, which shed many pounds this year. I am pleased with my body.

Writing makes me very happy. Every time I post something on Facebook related to the book, I get comments, feedback, dialogue. The world interacts with my writing, with me - what fun. "No," I hear some of you screaming in my ear, "that's not what we meant. It's great that you're optimistic and happy and active, but what about the cancer? Is it back? Is your condition severe? Why are you writing? Give us more details. How many tumors? Where, when, why, how, what? And how much longer do you have to live? "

Hey, friends, relax, please. Tone down the panic. I realize the big gap between how we perceive this disease and how we live with it. Many of those I met as part of my research for the book told me that this disease made them live. "You're more alive than me," a friend said to me. "I see you and forget you're even sick." This is true. I don't look or act sick. I continue to live my life, adjusting to the evolving physical condition. According to my current research, it turns out that it's possible to live with cancer for many years. It's even possible to be cured of difficult conditions that seem hopeless.

The same childhood friend wrote to me about Erez Waxman, a healer who claims that your health begins to deteriorate as soon as you believe you are sick, because this belief influences the mind and weakens you. Since I decided to leave no stone unturned, I called Erez.

"As far as I'm concerned you are healthy," Erez told me at the beginning of our conversation, "and I don't really care what conventional medicine claims. Cancer exists in everyone and the body knows how to fight it.

It is the medicine that suppresses the soul. I believe that there are many people around you who feel pity for your situation. About 70% of them 'have' cancer, but the difference is that they don't know it. Their body acts to reject the cancer even when they're unaware of it. This is a natural process that occurs in the body all the time".

I remember a theory I read about recently that opposes early detection of cancer for this very reason. The argument is that some of the tumors discovered at an early stage will naturally disappear if not treated. Many studies explore the phenomenon of tumors spontaneously disappearing. This is a rare yet known phenomenon. When the tumors disappear, we can't tell if it's a spontaneous incident, which occurs in one out of every 80 thousand cases, or if it's a result of the cleansing of toxins from the body and changes in lifestyles.

"You, however," Erez continues, "were solicited by the medical system so you need to thoroughly understand how you can bend reality and start a new, unsolicited life. Do you realize that you're in the midst of a biological healing process?"

All those who understood, raise your hand. The researchers say we all have cancer cells in the body all the time, but our immune system usually knows how to handle them. Sometimes something goes wrong and then the cells multiply to the point where we can feel them. Sometimes they multiply and the immune system destroys them, without us even knowing about their presence. This is a natural process that occurs all the time. Nevertheless, we are so afraid of this word. Of this disease. Why are we not so afraid of diabetes? Or heart disease? "Cancer has excellent public relations," my friend once said to me. That is true. This disease benefits the pharmaceutical companies wonderfully. And I read more than once that since the invention of chemotherapy the death rate among cancer patients has not changed significantly.

Once we eliminate the disease, having learned what the strangely cured patients did to stay alive with cancer and even cure it and having spread this gospel to others - what will the pharmaceutical companies do? How will they go on scaring us? Perhaps they'll have to start doing PR for another disease, say shingles. Have you noticed those commercials lately? I told two young doctors some stories of recovered patients that I collected for this book. One of them answered immediately, only half jokingly: "Oh, and what about us? We won't get any patients anymore." I'd like to say: "I wish", but what I really pray for is a combination of medicines, conventional and alternative, in mutual respect and understanding.

Nightly Research in Search of a Surgeon

I am determined to find a surgeon who can operate on me and remove one of the metastases located behind my sternum (chest cavity). I start asking everyone I know if they can refer me to a chest surgeon. Naama, a fellow member of the playback group I act in, is a pediatrician. Occasionally I consult with her about finding information on specific topics. This time she jots down in English what I need to look up: Minimally invasive thoracic surgery for retrosternal metastatic lesions.

I send emails to several surgeons, asking them if there is any point in proceeding with this. I also get references from friends and crosscheck the information.

Dr. Ben-Nun from Tel Hashomer tells me that the surgery is possible. He needs the approval of the oncologist, who's on vacation in Greece, so I wait for him to come back. In the meantime, I take the biological drug. When the oncologist returns from vacation he approves the surgery, even though he thinks the metastasis behind my sternum isn't life threatening. I set an appointment with Ben-Nun, who explains to me the risks and prospects. In the meantime, I file the information. If I eventually have to undergo this surgery I will be prepared. I go on to examine other options. According to my to-do list, it's time to check the option of a hyperbaric chamber for treating the radiation damage. This is my next subject of inquiry.

"Those who took responsibility extended their lifespan and beat the statistics."

-Results from a study on prolonging survival of cancer patients.

As I meet more people who experienced a dramatic remission or managed to halt the disease, I understand that they have a significant common feature: the ability to take responsibility for every aspect of their lives and thus reduce the feeling of helplessness in the face of the disease and the doctors. All the cured patients I met took on an active approach in their decision-making process.

A study by Watson and Cunningham from 2004[4] - "How Psychological Therapy May Prolong Survival in Cancer Patients: New Evidence and a Simple Theory"- compares between people who took responsibility when they got sick and those who didn't, with respect to quality of life and longevity. The results were clear: those who took responsibility extended their lifespan and beat the statistics.

They tell us that taking responsibility is a crucial part of recovery, and this is where things get quite confusing. The term "you gotta" is repeated in every other conversation. There's a therapist in the North of Israel, a healer in the Center, an expert in the South. There are even health centers in Australia and India that you gotta try!!! How is one supposed to know where to go? You can't consult about complementary and alternative medicine with conventional doctors. They don't learn it in their university training and don't have time to add this knowledge to their protocol. Most doctors just say that if it doesn't help, it can't hurt. My treating oncologist at Tel Hashomer occasionally gets emails from me with links to studies I found online which may be relevant to my case. He takes the time to read them and shares his opinion. I know from the stories of other cured patients that he's not the only one, but there are not many like him.

How do you choose what to do?

Many patients seeking more information do research independently, starting almost from scratch. The amount of information is growing by the day and needs consolidation. Eventually every recovering patient chooses their own path, not without experiencing considerable confusion along the way. One of the difficulties they face is deciding what to do, out of the variety of recommendations and therapists.

This book may be confusing too. It mentions various diets and methods that helped people heal. As you will surely notice, some of them even contradict each other. I made a shortcut for those exploring this topic by compiling the stories. The question now is what to do with all the information gathered. At first, this information encourages action, instilling

---

[4] How Psychological Therapy May Prolong Survival in Cancer Patients", A. J. Cunningham and K. Watson Integrative Cancer Therapies": New Evidence and a Simple Theory .3, no. 3 (September 2004): 214-29

hope that it is possible to get better. I understand that some areas are repetitive, but necessary: conducting an active search for a solution; understanding the disease and the implications of the prescribed medical treatments; looking up information in forums abroad on common conventional treatments around the world; nutrition and herbal medicine; sports, emotional cleansing, guided imagery, or meditation. I personally also like the idea of happiness in life and fulfilling dreams. Each of these categories encompasses many options. I would recommend finding one therapist for each area. It's best to find someone with proven success whom you feel comfortable around. From my experience, I also recommend asking to speak with their other patients.

At a panel on innovation in medicine and healthcare at the TEDMED conference held in Jerusalem (2014), Yishai Knobel, founder and CEO of HelpAround, discussed the two major revolutions in the medical world in recent years - "Dr. Google" and Dr. Facebook": "Not only do we come to the doctor after consulting with Dr. Google, we can now also tell all our friends on Facebook which doctor to go to and which drug to use." Judging by their latest TV ad, Clalit Health Services are not too happy about it.

The panelists at the TEDMED conference talked about the proliferation of "non- filtered" medical information and its availability to the public. One doctor noted that many people make crucial decisions about their health based on irrelevant information. "It's important to educate patients to filter this information and trust the medical system," he explained. And yet, a large number of the cured patients in this book recovered thanks to information they found online too.

A Facebook group of women receiving the same compassion drug that I get was recently opened. I joined it. Most of the women there are participating in a study on the drug. In the group they share the side effects they experience after taking the drug. This information disrupts the drug company's research because those receiving a placebo (a dummy drug used in studies for control purposes) realize they're not experiencing the drug's side effects. According to online reports, Pfizer, which invests large sums in these important studies, doesn't like this collaboration, but for now can't stop it either.

Estelle Baranes made some fateful decisions thanks to Dr. Google and non-filtered medical information. It seems this actually saved her life. With good English and common sense, she was able to choose the relevant information.

Estelle Baranes
Estelle - Sarcoma - insisting and searching for information –5 years after diagnosis

Estelle Baranes sings in a choir, attending the dance festival in Karmiel every year and raising three sons. Her strong desire to live, combined with determination, perseverance, responsibility, and the ability not to be intimidated by doctors, led her to pursue completely different treatment from what was offered to her at first. Five years have passed since her illness was first diagnosed and she is now clean, working, singing in the choir, traveling, celebrating life, and feeling good. The expected survival time for the type of cancer Estelle had is two years.

"In 2009, after two days of pain, my gynecologist suggested that I remove my uterus, 'because you have fibroids growing and causing pain and we also need to make sure you don't have cancer," he added. I went to three doctors for consultation. The first was in favor of surgery and noticed that one of the fibroids was outside the womb. The second doctor said without checking me that there's no need to do anything. The third doctor was also in favor of surgery, but he said there's no need to rush because it can't be cancer. I went back to the first doctor, who tested me and found that the fibroids are still growing. In the time that passed - a month and a half – the doctor, who I appreciate greatly, forgot that he had suspected I have cancer. In retrospect, I realized that had the doctor remembered his suspicion, he would have prescribed an open abdominal surgery instead of the microscopic surgery he ended up performing on me. When we got the test results on the material surgically removed, it turned out to be an ectopic cancer named Leiomyo sarcoma, or in short - LMS. It's a rare type of sarcoma that only four out of a million people suffer from. Not so pleasant. Despite the scare, I summoned the courage to search for information online. I stumbled upon an American website with a forum of sarcoma survivors. After reading the materials, I realized that my survival depends on the cleanliness of the edges of the removed tumor. I called the surgeon, who laughed at me on the phone: "judging by your question, you don't understand anything about this. I'm the one who urged you to undergo surgery and now you're mad that I forgot the suspected cancer?' I did not get an answer from him.

I went looking for an answer. It turned out there is no protocol for my condition. I met with professors at Tel Hashomer's sarcoma unit, with gynecologic oncologists at Meir hospital, with a professor specializing in sarcoma at Ichilov hospital, and a gynecologic oncologist at Tel Hashomer. All the doctors agreed that I should be treated with internal and external radiation. I continued reading posts and articles posted by patients in the American forum, and realized there is another treatment practiced around the world today, offering a new type of chemotherapy that yields relatively good results, without radiation.

At the same time, I kept preparing for radiotherapy. The preparation at the hospital was a difficult and unpleasant experience in itself.

I brought an article on the new chemotherapy mentioned in the forum to an appointment with the professor specializing in sarcoma. I wanted to check if I could get it. He responded dismissively, citing the small number of participants in the study in question. Still, he jotted down the name of the article. It seemed to me that my knowledge and questions annoyed him. Three days after the meeting I was scheduled to begin radiotherapy. I was very nervous about it. In a kind gesture, despite my feeling that he dismissed the information I brought, this Israeli professor suggested that I contact the head of the sarcoma department at MD Anderson in the United States. He even gave me his email address.

I sent to the American expert a summary of my story, including my intention to undergo radiotherapy. I got an answer the very same day: "Radiotherapy is a bad idea, you should undergo chemotherapy." I managed to get a hold of the American expert on the phone. He was amazing and talked to me for half an hour. He convinced me to give up radiotherapy and undergo a series of chemotherapy treatments. On Sunday morning, I sent a fax to the hospital announcing that I am not coming for radiotherapy.

At Tel Hashomer I consulted with a gynecologic oncologists, who spoke on my behalf with the sarcoma expert in the US, and the latter persuaded the doctor from Tel Hashomer to give me the chemo. Now I had to find a way to get the chemotherapy, which wasn't covered by my health insurance for this specific disease, but was covered for other conditions. The drug costs 40,000 shekels if bought privately. I used all my contacts and sent letters wherever I could to get my healthcare provider to approve my treatment. Time was of the essence, as I had to start treatment within eight weeks, but I still didn't get approval for receiving the drug. I was rescued by my doctor friend from California, who collected money from friends and bought the first dose of the drug. Later on, I ordered it directly from the pharmaceutical companies. The two following treatments were already funded by my healthcare provider. As the treatment proceeded, I kept on reading articles and information. During the third round of chemotherapy, it was reported that in the United States they're adopting an anti-hormonal treatment for sarcoma. I initiated another test on the surgically removed tissue, and asked them to check the tumor tissues' sensitivity to hormones. The result showed that the tumor is 100% sensitive to hormones. I realized that the anti-hormonal treatment can save me. The gynecologic oncologist refused to accept that. "This isn't a grocery store," he said, "you can't just choose what you want. You will not get this unproven treatment here." I completed the fourth round of chemotherapy and debated whether to continue. I went online to consult with the Dana-Farber Cancer Institute and the medical school of Harvard University in Boston about the anti-hormonal treatment. Despite his initial opposition, my gynecologic oncologist in Israel wrote the letter for my correspondence with the hospital. In their reply the hospital confirmed that the anti-hormonal drug treatment is commonly prescribed for sarcoma. Thanks to the response from the Dana-Farber hospital, I managed to get the drug in Israel. This drug too is not covered for my disease, but with the assistance of "Friends for Health" and "Ezer Mizion" I was able to obtain it. Two years later my gynecologic oncologist in Israel contacted me to find out where I get the drug, because he started prescribing it to his patients. At the same time I took dietary supplements for three years, which strengthened my immune system immensely.

It's been five years now – and I'm clean", concludes Estelle.

I Yearn for the Outdoors

Estelle taught me to never give up, keep seeking solutions around the world, read studies, join online forums abroad, and continue to seek consultation both in Israel and abroad. Yes, it's tiring and difficult. I realize it's important. No doctor, no matter how nice he or she is, will do it for me.

On Yom Kippur I decide to take a break from reading material on cancer and look for someone who needs a house sitter. There are Facebook groups for that too. I find an offer that stirs my senses. A house in the rural community of Even Sapir of a couple whose dog needs care. My heart races in excitement. Gadi agrees. He always does. On the eve of Yom Kippur we arrive at the house, which was built inside a chicken coop. We unpack the heaps of my special food and are enchanted by this simple, rustic place. Just what I wanted. A crow cries from the burnt forest to the left of the house. Inca, the dog, basks in the sun. The birds chirp. We brought along our computers and many books, as if we're staying here for a month. I read about "grounding" and the importance of staying connected to the ground, about walking barefoot and absorbing the electrons the earth releases. Even walking with shoes made of natural materials can help you absorb the electrons from the earth, from the ground. This creates the action of grounding. I remember an old book my grandmother had that urges its readers to wear as much ventilated clothing as possible, without rubber pressing on the body, and if possible, sunbathe completely exposed. I have no doubt that this can strengthen the immune system. Grounding can mean other activities in addition to eating properly and exercising. From now on I will work in the vegetable garden barefoot. I'll go out to the yard more often, and do yoga and meditate on the lawn. Grounding calms the sympathetic nervous system and supports heart rate change. Negatively charged ions enter the body through the feet. It takes the electrons about eight minutes to reach from the ground to the blood stream and dilute it. Grounding has an anti-oxidative effect and can alleviate infections in the body while the excess molders from it into the soil.

Now I have another list of things I want to do all day long. The trick will be to integrate these habits into my normal life.

When we returned to our home, I put the list on the refrigerator, citing the date I began these activities. I took the yoga mat to the porch and cleaned the meditation corner so that everything would be ready for tomorrow's activities.

Shuka Eliezer
Prostate cancer - independent research –
9 years after diagnosis

"The purpose of natural cancer treatment is to restore the body's balance and health"
- From the site of the Israel Cancer Association

Meanwhile, those around me continue to search for strangely cured patients to introduce me to. I find Shuka through a friend of my mother. My mother gives me a vague description, with terms like Omega-3 and flaxseed oil. "You know, all those things you do..." she tells me.

At a shelter-turned-study-and-library in a new apartment building in Holon, I found him crouched over a computer screen, checking, investigating, reading, gathering, and processing all the information needed for the theory he developed.

Eight and a half years had passed since Shuka Eliezer was diagnosed with prostate cancer, with a PSA index of 10.4 and a Gleason score of 8. The cancer is aggressive and the prognosis is not good, said the urologist. Shuka underwent a radical prostatectomy procedure, complicated by damage caused to the rectum and requiring a colostomy procedure[5]. Three months later he underwent another surgery to repair the problem. As a follow-up treatment, Shuka also got hormone therapy for another year and a half. When it turned out the cancer is coming back at a faster pace (PSA 21 2 times higher in 5 months) Shuka was told that in light of the high aggressiveness and the history of his disease and treatments, it is highly probable that the disease is metastatic and therefore the only available treatment is hormone therapy. The oncologist recommended waiting a few months until the PSA will rise further before resuming the hormone therapy.

---

[5] Surgical procedure in which part of the colon is transferred through an incision in the abdominal wall, creating an artificial opening (stoma) that allows excrement to drain into a bag.

Shuka refused to accept the decision, and being that he has a degree in Applied Mathematics from the Technion, he decided to apply his skills and experience in performance research and mathematics to study the illness.

"When I started researching the topic I realized I was totally ignorant and didn't know anything tangible about my illness and true condition. After 8 months of intense research, during which I read hundreds of abstracts, nine books, and dozens of articles, I found the solution and devised a diet, which I called CUNC- Cancer Under Nutritional Constraints. This diet focuses primarily on reducing fat from the menu. One month after starting the diet, I already noticed a change in the PSA and after two months I already had highly convincing results since the rate of increase in PSA dropped dramatically. I concluded that this approach is much more effective than all the medical treatments. However, I never dismissed the conventional treatments, since it was clear that the diet doesn't kill the disease, but only hinders its development. Therefore, we must also use all medical means that can help us.

After starting the diet, I looked for tools that would help me monitor the results of my activities. I developed amazing mathematical models that clearly vindicate the approach I chose to take and can make predictions about the cancer's behavior. Later on this helped me understand what I see. For three years I developed the small model followed by the expanded and comprehensive model I published, along with many other articles on my site.

The diet gave me time to examine my condition calmly and patiently. It turned out the cancer is not metastatic, but is adjacent to the original area of the prostate. I tried ultrasound treatment called HIFU[6], but within a month it turned out to be ineffective and the cancer returned to its rapid growth. After a few months I decided to undergo radiotherapy, which lasted three months, but didn't help either. As a result, I decided that my only choice at this point is to combine the diet with hormone therapy, alternately".

---

[6] HIFU - an acronym for High Intensity Focused Ultrasound - this technology generates ultrasound waves with a transducer vibrating at a much higher frequency than the human ear can pick up. As they pass through the body, the ultrasound waves transfer energy to the tissues. In my ultrasound (like an abdominal or gynecological ultrasound) I found that this energy is low and negligible. By increasing the frequency significantly it is possible to increase the energy transferred to the tissue. By focusing the ultrasound waves on one a single point, it's possible to concentrate the energy at very high intensity and thus destroy the tumor tissue.
From the website titled "Living with Prostate Cancer."

Rationale for Shuka's Diet

Shuka found many studies indicating that metabolic products of arachidonic acid are essential for building cancer cells and encourage the growth of blood vessels around the cancer (angiogenesis). Arachidonic acid is a fatty acid received from the consumption of animal fat and omega-6. Therefore, avoiding it will reduce the supply of food necessary for building the cancer cell, and in addition will cause less infections in the body that lead to a growth in blood vessels that feed the cancer. In light of this understanding, Shuka devised his diet (which also includes dietary supplements), which he still follows today.

"The doctors I met after starting the diet had different opinions about what happened to me. One admitted that the aggressiveness of the disease had significantly decreased; another claimed that low-fat diets have been tried in the past and that they stop working after a few months. But when I went back to him several years later he said to me: 'You are your own doctor."

What Shuka Does

Shuka eats food containing 2% fat, avoiding meat, poultry, and egg yolks. Since nuts, seeds, and avocados contain more than 40% fat, he avoids them altogether. The only oil he used in the past was flaxseed oil, of which he added about 10 grams per meal. In the recent year he avoided flaxseed oil too, because it contains about 27% Omega 6. Instead of that he consumes two capsules of Omega-3 per day.

Shuka takes the hormonal medicine inconsistently, whenever he decides to - whereas this treatment tends to last one to two months, after which he takes a break of six or seven months, and then starts over again.

Shuka does the following:

A. Dietary supplements and anti-inflammatory drugs:

- Mega Resveratrol
- Turmeric Extract (curcumin)
- Loxin-5
- Omega-3

- Aspirin – 81 mg per day (prevents infections and slows down the growth of blood vessels that feed the cancer)
- Celecoxib - about 200 mg every three days (minimal, to avoid serious side effects). This anti-inflammatory drug is effective in combating cancer, since it inhibits angiogenesis.

B. Dietary supplements for general health: Vitamins E, D, C, B9 + 6 + 12, selenium, zinc, magnesium, lutein, calcium, and CoQ10.

C. Walks, especially during the winter - two or three times a week, 12-13 km every walk.

Shuka is convinced that the main thing that helped him was the combination of the diet and supplements with the anti-inflammatory drugs. In his view, the diet bolsters the medical treatments. Shuka's website[7] is called "Playing Chess with Cancer", and in it he elaborates on the diet and the various studies.

---

[7] Shuka's website: http://survivewithcancer.wordpress.com

Nurit Tzadok
Esophageal cancer – changing the conventional treatment – 4 years after diagnosis

*"I see the good in my life and in the people around me...
I constantly thank God".*

-Nurit Tzadok

Nurit Tzadok was a preschool teacher, a special education teacher at a junior high school, and later worked with youth who dropped out of the education system.

Nurit goes out every morning to nurture her vegetable garden outside the housing project she lives in, in Holon. There she grows herbs and fruit trees: lemons, oranges, tangerines, mango, fig, and pomegranate. "I see the good in my life and in the people around me. I love my garden. I do a lot of work on it every morning. I constantly thank God and appreciate everything in my life." Nurit says, emphasizing that this was not always the case. At the age of 67, she experienced a dramatic shift in her life after undergoing some tests in October 2010.

"The tests at Tel Hashomer discovered esophageal cancer the size of three to nine inches. Two of my sisters had cancer, were treated with chemotherapy, and eventually died of the side effects. I witnessed their suffering and had a hard time agreeing to accept chemotherapy into my body. I sat down to study the disease, researching information online and reading lots of books on the subject. After much deliberation, I decided to not undergo chemotherapy. I wanted the biological drug given for esophagus cancer, as long as I'd I get it without chemotherapy. I couldn't find a doctor who'd agree to treat me this way. I told my treating doctors I'd take 'vegan chemotherapy', and explained how plants have a chemical capacity to cure the cancer and how I intend to take medicinal herbs and dietary supplements. They laughed at me. 'What,' they doubted, 'there is chemotherapy in nature?' 'Of course,' I replied, 'There's mugwort, turmeric, mushrooms, green tea'. The amused doctor absolutely refused to give me the biological drug only, and I was declined in another hospital too. Among the many books I read was a book by Shlomo Guberman – 'Cancer Can Be Beaten'. I consulted with a friend who's been a patient of Guberman for years and turned to him for advice, somewhat desperately. 'Wait', Guberman recalls, 'There's a department director in Jerusalem who's always interested in these methods, Prof. Reuven Or at Hadassah Ein Kerem. "

Professor Or welcomed me gracefully and accepted my request to get the biological drug only, but he added an ultimatum: 'If the tumor does not disappear within a year and a half you will take whatever I tell you'. I accepted.

With the help of Prof. Or, I got the biological treatment only, avoiding chemotherapy, and added dietary supplements, which I called 'chemotherapy of nature'. I was not alone. Professor Or monitored me and believed that I could possibly restore my immune system. Two months after starting the treatment, there was a TV program featuring interviews with doctors who claim that vitamins are false, that turmeric is nothing but a rip off, and that people die from taking these supplements. I got cold feet, and immediately called Guberman. 'Do whatever feels right,' he said, 'I won't tell you to stop or not. Follow your heart.' I sat in the garden and I asked myself whether I want to undergo chemotherapy like my sisters had? I decided to keep doing it my way. Luckily, my family supported the path I chose and now I was at peace with the direction I was taking.

At the same time that I was taking the biological drug, I underwent a detox procedure with Dr. Pnina Bar Sela. I cleansed my body and made sure not to put any toxins in it. I took anti-cancer dietary supplements and nourished my body with vitamins. I was convinced I would get better since the Ann Wigmore method and the supplements were strengthening my immune system. Shortly after I got sick, my third sister got cancer. I tried to sway her to take my approach, but she absolutely didn't want to hear about vitamins, dietary supplements, or body cleansing. She didn't think she could handle it. I proceeded with the alternative treatment, doing everything that's alternative and harmless. I underwent bio-ergonomic treatment once a week with Rina Orenstein, who for a whole hour would transmit energy to me. Every morning I strolled along the beach and breathed the fresh air.

After six months, the tumor diminished by two inches, but there was still an outline and I wasn't out of the woods yet. However, a year after it was detected, the tumor was gone entirely, and after three more months even the outline disappeared.

There was a lot of joy at the hospital, and they spoke and gave presentations about my case.

It's been four years since then and I'm still being monitored by Prof. Or. Every time he meets me at the hospital he is very happy. He says I am a hero and recommends my approach to other patients.

I make sure to spend time outside every day, in the open air, walking along the Jaffa promenade and breathing in the sea air. I continue to take all the supplements to reduce the risk of the cancer returning, though the doses are smaller. When I was sick I took 9,000 mg of turmeric per day, and gradually lowered the dosage to only 1,000 mg.

Although many people ask to consult with me and hear my story, I find that most of them heed the warnings from conventional medicine and have trouble mustering the physical and mental strengths to make the necessary change. I can understand them. I remember how the doctor laughed when I told her that there is chemotherapy in nature. I think that reflects incredible ignorance. Even the doctor at Tel Hashomer warned me that within a year I'd come back to him in a wheelchair, begging to receive chemotherapy. I did return to him after a year, but not as he expected. He was rather indifferent to my most amazing results. Still, I hope that my case moved him in some way".

What do you think allowed you to dare?

"My sisters' experience with chemotherapy was the main catalyst for the path I chose. My first sister who got sick underwent chemotherapy, which damaged her liver, and she eventually died as a result. In the case of my second sister, the chemotherapy caused a systematic organ failure, and she too died as a result. I decided not to take the same path. At the time when I was sick, my third sister also got lung cancer and her lobe was removed. I suggested that she try alternative treatment. I'm convinced that had she gone to consult with Guberman she could have recovered. But she was firmly against it, even though she could already see the positive effects it had on me. The cancer spread through her body and she died two years later. "

Nurit's Daily Routine

Nurit wakes up at seven in the morning; goes for a walk; practices yoga; works in the garden, and meditates. She maintains a strict natural diet, drinking wheatgrass, vegetable juices and shakes. She avoids sugar, white flour, and white rice. At the beginning of the recovery process she made sure to eat organic foods. Now she only make sure to avoid vegetables that are more heavily sprayed than others. She continues to take supplements, which she orders from abroad.

Three times a week she goes to a country club in the morning. She continues to dance, sing in a choir, and attend lectures at the Avshalom Institute.

"I was helped by so many people in my struggle to defeat cancer: Dr. Pnina Bar Sela helped me with my diet; Shlomo Guberman with the supplements; Prof. Reuven Or with the biological drug; Rina Orenstein with the bio-ergonomic method. I believe my success can't be attributed to any one of them, but to the all these actions together along with my optimism and happiness. I worked on my immune system, ate well, took supplements, and walked a lot. Besides the fact that the cancer is gone, I feel much better today than I did before I got sick. In my case, the disease made me change for the better".

"What do you dream about?"

"Being healthy and dying on my own two feet as an independent person."

What I learned from Nurit

Nurits story highlighted for me the need to take responsibility for the types of treatments I'm willing to undergo, whether conventional or alternative medicine.

Now I look at the mirror and smile at my reflection. "It's possible," I tell it. The biological drug will help eradicate the tumor. I will have the patience and determination. A wave of excitement rises inside me – yes, it is really possible, I don't have to die. I already visited Guberman and got the list of dietary supplements from him. I did it but gave up when the tumor doubled in size. Later on, I quit taking the supplements completely due to stomach pains. Now, after my conversation with Nurit, my emotional roller coaster is soaring. I am motivated to take them again. How did I forget Guberman. Well, time to work. Morning, body cleansing, walking, trampoline.

Ahuva (alias)
Breast cancer - Kabbalistic meditation and nutrition by Nissan Morgenstern - 5 years after diagnosis

"I realized I got the tumor in response to my 'request'"

- *Ahuva*

At a conference of cancer survivors, behind a table laden with self-help books on health, she stands wearing a blue, flowery, long dress. Her hair is short and not dyed. My friend Ruth Roi Weinstein suggests that I approach her. "She has an interesting story," she says.

"Yes," she answers my question, "I have a tumor in my chest", her soft hazel eyes rest on me, "and I have not undergone any medical treatment. But I'm not available to talk right now," she says. "Call me and I'll tell you. I come to every convention like this by bus from the Jerusalem region, because this is important to me. What do I mean? Call me, and I'll tell you. If possible, call on a Sunday when I have time to talk to you. Call only after 10:00 AM. Before that I'm busy with my healing activities. "She certainly knows how to set boundaries. I wonder if she was like that before the disease.

I called.

"The first question I asked myself," says Ahuva, "was why I had cancer in my body. After a previous experience in which I cured myself of a digestive disease, I was sure I was protected from illness, certainly from cancer. Before my cancer was diagnosed I went through some rough experiences, including a grueling period with a family member. Six years ago, when I was 57, I reached the point where I wanted to say goodbye to the world, like my father who died suddenly at the age of 58. Later on I realized I got the tumor in response to my request. After discovering the tumor, I never repeated that request again.

When I discovered a lump in my breast I went to the hospital for diagnosis. The doctors urged me to do a biopsy. I wasn't keen on having them insert a needle into my breast, but eventually I heeded their call, so that I could understand what I'm dealing with. Two weeks later the doctor informed me gently that I had a malignant tumor in my breast.

My previous experience with health issues was a severe ulcerative inflammation in the colon, which overwhelmed me and made life very difficult for my family. After many years of suffering and effort in search of a remedy, I found my way and managed to cure the disease! As a result of this 'experience', I reached two clear conclusions. Firstly, that the path to health involved taking responsibility for my recovery process and that my will and resolve throughout the process will lead me to recovery. And secondly, that conventional medicine doesn't always have an answer. I had promised myself I'd never be in a hospital bed again. Now I faced the moment of truth.

Despite the pressure from my family, I knew I didn't want to undergo conventional treatment, which I believed would not cure me. I promised my children I'd try the approach of natural healing for three months, and if I see that it's not useful I'll opt in for surgery.

At first I didn't know what to do. After all, this is a difficult situation, and it's safe to say that I wasn't steeped in serenity at the time. I knew I had the tools, both professional and experiential, but I had to find the right path. My faith and knowledge that I'd find a way led me to it. As the sages say: 'Man is directed to the path he wants to follow...'. The more I learned and read, it became clearer that one of the things that saved me was that I didn't touch the tumor. I learned that by removing the primary tumor in the breast, the cancer is allowed to develop, spread, and metastasize. Maintaining the original tumor prevents it from spreading.

I found the right path for me: Initially, I learned from Michal Boker about the Kabbalistic meditation 'Ana Bekoach' (Please with Strength), which I practice every morning (and evening, if possible). I use guided imagery, positive thinking, and optimism for the process. Through Michal I reached the 'Ta'atzumot' Association and got to know more wonderful people such as Prof. Gershom Zajicek, and Ruth, and many others who work laboriously for this important association. Prof. Zajicek strongly supported my approach to 'suppressing the cancer', providing validation to the insights I already had from a sober medical source.

In terms of physical healing, I used a method I was already familiar with – 'diet by type of grain' by Nissan Morgenstern, a Jerusalem therapist I highly appreciate. His nutritional method, precisely tailored for each patient, is based on the notion that every person has a different type of grain suitable for them. Eating wheat is suitable for a handful of people; for others barley or rye are suitable, and for others it's spelt. The 'grain type' is also indicative of the type of personality and it influences the method of treatment. Morgenstern monitors me closely and is very supportive, and thank God, the results speak for themselves.

Twelve months after diagnosis I noted to myself that a year had passed and 'the sky didn't not fall in'. Then another year passed and another one, and after three years I told myself that I can start to relax. My worried family also felt reassured, which truly encouraged me. Today I continue my professional career, in addition to my intensive daily activity to 'suppress the cancer' through meditation, nutrition, exercise, and fun activities such as learning, hiking, yoga, and laughter, which I like especially. Since the day I promised my kids I'd try natural healing for three months six years have passed".

Therapist Nissan Morgenstern is convinced that eating wheat is one of the causes of the disease. "All diseases," says Morgenstern, "are related to wheat. After the Second World War Europe started eating wheat. Before that meals consisted almost entirely of grain porridge, and the common breads were made of rye, barley, or oats. At the same time during the switch to wheat, there was an increase in cancer, morbidity, and many other diseases". Morgenstern also prohibits intake of sugar, various fruits, cow dairy products, as well as the use of oil for frying, cooking, or baking.

---≪•≫---

At a conference of the Israelis Society for Complementary Medicine, held in November 2014 at the Maccabiah Village, Dr. Uri Meir-Chizik spoke about the history and politics of nutrition. Fascinating subject. Chizik described a process that occurred during the last five centuries, starting in Europe and gradually spreading to the entire world - Urbanization and industrialization have completely changed what we eat. The food economy has changed dramatically in those years, with these processes pushing us away from local traditions. From a historical perspective, one can see the processes that contributed to and encouraged this process, and try to learn from them. In the past, wheat, rice, and corn were rather negligible foods among hunter-gatherers. Relatively little meat was eaten and processed sugar and milk didn't even exist. Today these are all major components in our diet. All of these changes are related to culture, politics, economics, and human health. Did I already mention how fascinating this is?
One way or another, most diets mentioned in this book are closer to the diet of the hunter-gatherers than the modern diet.

---≪•≫---

CHAPTER 3

Living a full life with cancer

A chance to be with my son

My stomach asks me to go downstairs and make lunch. Life here is starting to follow a regular schedule – quite a revolution. Lunch is at one o'clock. I go down to the kitchen, which has already become a temple of food, and remember to bring along the notebook I keep to document the action. It features the list of supplements to be taken in the afternoon and the food I plan on eating today. I'm lost without the list.

At five o'clock Nadav asks if I can drop him off at the bus stop. He wants to go to another Jiu jistsu practice this week in Netanya. Which stop? The one where the bus to Netanya stops. But where is that? Don't know. At the Kfar Saba-Ra'anana junction. Which side, north or south? Don't know. Find out. OK. Can you drive me? Yes, I can. Nadav looks it up and I drive him to the bus stop, wondering how long he'll have to wait for the bus now. There's the stop, but I'm not dropping you off, I'm taking you to Netanya. Really? Yay! Thanks, mom! My pleasure. I have the book "Living with Cancer" in my bag. I drop Nadav off, find parking, and walk towards the sea. I hear a lot of French and English. The scene at the large fountain built on the boulevard leading to the sea is lively: Kids in bathing suits splashing water and shouting in excitement. In the adjacent lily pond a small brown dog is swimming while his owner stands by the pool, waiting calmly for him to finish his dip. Netanya. A thousand stairs lead me to a piece of soft sand. In front of me, the sun is fleeing into the water. I sit on the sand and dive into my own quiet bubble. The voices from the outside don't penetrate my veil of my silence. The words in the book fascinate me. In my notebook I summarize the important points. Dr. Block recommends taking blood and saliva tests I haven't heard of and adjusting the dietary supplements based on the results. I read again that regular and early sleep is important to my health just like avoiding sugar. When do I go to bed every night? Well after ten. Add to that my daily hour of exercise, which is strongly recommended to do every day five hours before bedtime in order to fall asleep more easily. Outdoor exercise early in the morning also induces regular secretion of melatonin and provides beneficial exposure to light in the morning. I write down my daily schedule, which includes a physical exercise that will reconfigure my metabolism. My hour of waiting for Nadav's practice to end passes by quickly and I go back to the club where he is training. The smell rising into the street makes it crystal clear that I'm at the right place. Men soaked in sweat going in and out the door to the practice room. "Your son is very special. He's made of the right stuff", I am told by one of them. "Really?" I say to the sweaty man. "You don't have to drive him over", the coach remarks, "there's a bus that comes all the way here. A lot of my students come from Tel Aviv by bus. "Yes, that's true, but I have a chance to spend time with my son all the way here and back. That does not happen a lot anymore. If he takes the bus, how will I hear all the compliments about him, and what will bring me to the beach in Netanya?

First post – searching for recovered patients

My first Facebook post about the book I intend to write, and my request for help in finding strangely cured patients, attracts many reactions. A friend of mine refers me to Susie Dvoskin. I look her up on Facebook, she writes to me. I find Susie's page and learn that she is a triathlon champion. Her numerous photos in running gear don't reveal a hint of her illness. I send her a message telling her about my project.

She answers immediately: "Hey Dorit, I too learned to live with cancer, enduring stage 4 thyroid cancer for six years now. At first, I thought this guest would leave, but I realized I was wrong and must live with it and not let it bother me. The basis for my health is doing sports every day, in every situation.

Susie Dvoskin
Thyroid cancer spreading to the bones - sports training - 6 years after diagnosis

"Breast cancer patients who don't do enough exercise might hurt their quality of life and reduce chances of survival".

-New research from the University of North Carolina

Towards the end of the week I get a hold of Susie a few hours before she flies to China for her summer vacation.

Susie found out she had stage 4 thyroid cancer six years ago. I present her story not because she managed to beat the cancer, but because she lives with the limitations caused by the disease as if they're just setbacks along the way. Her life doesn't revolve around the cancer. It exists, but with true determination she's able to put it aside and not let the physical limitations deny her of one of her great loves: sports, triathlons in particular. Even though Susie has thyroid cancer, which is considered more mild and less violent than other cancer types, by the time she was diagnosed it had already spread to the hip joint.

"That's rare for this type of cancer." Susie says, "it must have been there for a long time, growing very slowly, relatively speaking. Thyroid cancer can be treated with radioactive iodine until it reaches the bones, after which it doesn't respond well to the iodine, or like in my body, stops absorbing it".

Susie is 68. She grew up in Los Angeles and now lives in Ra'anana. She refuses to be defined by cancer. "This is not the essence of my life, this cancer is not who I am. What defines me is the empowerment of women in sports, my sports activities, and my work: my activity in synagogue, training new teachers in the Bar/Bat Mitzvah program for the special children of the Masorti movement, and setting up a website featuring all the 'haftarahs' and their readers for B'nai Mitzvah studies".

21 years ago, Susie made her first steps in the world of triathlons, along with her daughter Tamar. They participated together in two full triathlons for women and a few "trios" before Tamar was killed during cycling training when she was 21 years old.

"After the disaster, my husband and I found a way to continue living together. The Israeli Triathlon Association asked us if we would like to have the triathlon named after Tamar. We agreed and even became its organizers. Since then we've been organizing the triathlon throughout the year." Susie and her husband Danny organize the annual Women's Triathlon in Herzliya in memory of Tamar.

Twelve years after losing Tamar, Susie completed a half "Iron Man" competition, suffering from severe pain in the hip joint. The tests results diagnosed cancer, resulting in a hip replacement surgery.

Susie is a fighter. "After I recovered from hip surgery – I crossed the Sea of Galilee, swimming 21 km, at the age of 64. It was amazing."

When one of her two vocal cords was damaged in another surgery and she couldn't talk, she worked with a speech therapist and a vocal coach for six months to learn to speak and sing with one cord only. Since then Susie feels the cancer is struggling for its place among her intensive pursuits. "But even when it succeeds, it doesn't define me", Susie says. Susie does every day exercises adjusted to her changing physical abilities due to the surgeries and treatments she undergoes: swimming in the sea twice a week in the morning; an hour and half of Pilates; stretching; biking outdoors and on a trainer at home. One to two hours of exercise every day.

"I make adjustments. I've been training with triathlon coach Ran Shilon for eleven years. For every physical condition and after every surgery he finds a way for me to continue training and devises my training program accordingly. I don't give up. When I couldn't participate in a full triathlon, I did what I could: I swam with the help of a friend who assisted me in getting in and out of the water, and walked with crutches as much as I could.

There was a period when I could only do ballet exercises. Recently, before the Israeli triathlon championship, I couldn't walk more than 400 meters, whereas I had 5 kilometers to walk in the competition. Ran suggested that I do some stretching, yoga, pilates, and cycling. This way I'd strengthen my body and muscles without causing pain. And I did it! I completed all the legs of the race. I can't run since my hip replacement, so I taught myself to walk faster. I continue to enjoy a lot of swimming in the sea and the pool.

As part of the triathlon named after Tamar, I talk to a lot of training teams before the competition, telling them about the history of the triathlon, our daughter Tamar, and myself. I talk to them and share my story. I don't hide the disease. I show the participants that life can go on even with disabilities and illness.

The motto of the women's triathlon is: Everyone wins! So do I!

My goal is to empower women in sports and encourage them to include sports in their daily life in the long-term. In my personal life I rely on sport, a healthy diet, and an optimistic attitude."

Perhaps it would be good for me too, to do a lot of sports. Its ten minutes to four. According to the new treatment plan I wrote yesterday, it's time for a walk, followed by a swim. Second round of exercise today. There is no choice. I need to reconfigure my metabolism, as I said earlier.

According to Dr. Peter J. D'adamo, people with blood type O, like me, should do half an hour to three quarters of an hour of aerobic exercise at least four times a week. I don't do it. D'adamo also tells me to do physical exercise whenever I want to eat something sweet.

The decision to include physical exercise in my daily routine gets more and more practical manifestations. For several days straight I've gone on walks, during which I pick some seasonal fruit and macadamia nuts that fell from a tree on my trail. When I get back, I practice qigong. Twice a week in the afternoon I do yoga with Miri and Nachman, a couple which retired from the high-tech industry and plunged deep into the world of yoga. They offer yoga practice for cancer patients free of charge. I do my best to attend classes, where I meet Ruth, the lovely woman who now helps me navigate through the dozens of possibilities. Ruth manages the activities of the "Ta'atzumot" Association and has close ties with therapists and patients. Ruth's embrace is a good reason to go to yoga class.

Nir Malhi
Brain tumor - martial arts weapons
12 years after diagnosis

"The mind is much stronger than the body...
First you win and then go out to battle.
I applied physical combat to a mental challenge.
I realize it is limited in time, but it's been over 12 years already".

-*Nir Malhi*

At the end of the summer I go south to meet Nir Malhi. After coordinating it with his wife Efrat, who manages his meetings and phone calls, I find two hours when he too is free to meet and feels well.

Twelve years ago, at the age of 47, one of Nir Malhi's doctors gave him a number: 80 days. You have 80 days to live. No more, no less. The first thing Nir said was: "I am not not giving up."

The diagnosis was: GBM - glioblastoma, a very aggressive tumor that grows rapidly, increasing pressure inside the skull and causing headaches, vomiting, and drowsiness. This relatively unusual tumor is rarely eliminated through surgery. Moreover, the tumor contains cells with various mutations and therefore different substances are needed to affect it. Life expectancy is less than a year. Three to five percent of patients survive more than three years, for known reasons. In 2007 Dr. Kirk and other researchers in Germany tried to identify parameters that could be associated with longer survival. They studied 55 survivors, examining demographic information, treatments administered, environmental conditions, as well as other diseases, and occupations. All the survivors underwent radiotherapy and chemotherapy. But besides the fact that they were all of young age, Kirk didn't find any common denominator among the enduring survivors.[8]

---

[8]. http://brain.oxfordjournals.org/content/130/10/2596.article-info
2007 2596-2606 http://dx.doi.org/10.1093/brain/awm204

The man sitting in front of me wearing a black yarmulke tells me he grew up in Kibbutz Hatzerim. He served as a fighter in the Navy Seals, including diving with his comrades in the Kishon River. Around that time, towards the end of his service, he started becoming more religious, got married and had a child. Upon being discharged, he worked at the central unit of the Israel Police and served in other positions in the security system. When he completed his service to the country, he separated from his wife and set out to find a martial arts teacher.

We sit on the porch of his house, smoking cannabis. Each with our own individual pain. The fellowship of cancer patients is evident.

"16 years ago I went to look for bargains in the martial arts market," says Nir, "It was my journey. I went from teacher to teacher in Europe and the United States, but couldn't find what I was looking for. Eventually I went to Japan, where I found a Chinese teacher, who I stayed with for six years."

In Japan he met a young woman from Israel who had won a free trip to Japan, and they quickly fell in love. They stayed in Japan for six years before returning to Israel, where Nir opened the Israeli Center for Tai Chi. After another six years, he turned to the business world.

The website of the Tai Chi Center says: "practicing soft and internal martial arts (Tai Chi, Qigong, Chan Chuan, Xing Yi, and Pa Kua) balances the body and treats many medical problems. The exercise activates the body in a calm and peaceful way, without effort or use of force; developing posture, agility, inner strength and coordination; enhancing concentration, awareness and introspection, and therefore it is also called 'meditation in motion'".

Nir, a warrior at heart, summoned the internal forces to cope with the tumor. The doctors in Israel advised him to operate on it. Rabbi Firer also tried to persuade him to undergo surgery. Nir chose to opt out of surgery because of the expected results: paralysis in part of his body. Nir found that unacceptable. He went to Germany, where he received weakened chemotherapy. Then he found a medical center in Houston, United States, where he goes twice a year to get a chemotherapy cocktail that keeps the tumor in its current state.

Nir is in constant pain, but he's most frustrated by the inability to hold small objects - he keeps dropping them. "There's no way I can even send a text message, so I don't use a cellphone anymore. I got a chance to have more peace and quiet in life. It reached the point where I realized I was the phone's slave, constantly checking what happened, who wanted what, or what others wanted from me. I switched to another method. On my computer I see my office and pass every room, talking with the employees.

The coping entails detachment, not because of the radiotherapy but as part of my way of achieving the peace that allows me to do what I need and like. Coping without actually coping, simply by living my life.

Wait, before you interview me, tell me about yourself. Any kids? How old? Last name? This is quite an interrogation...".

I have no choice, I'm being pressured now and I need to answer him.

"My eldest is 18 and a half years old, a great spirit. Soon he'll be joining the army. The little one is 17, European champion in jiu jistsu...", I tell him.

"I have children who were national champions in street defensive fighting" (Israeli combat method.) says Nir, rubbing his hands not in pleasure but in pain.

"I can't explain what it is exactly that protects me, be it my mental strength or combative spirit. I know I'm not ready to be defeated. I am decisive, serious, focused, willful, and never liked to lose.

I heard about survivors who played guitar every day for an hour, and that's what might have helped them. For me it is something internal. I don't think of myself as a sick person, even though I am sometimes confined to a wheelchair. I just go on living my life and slowly return to my normal self.

(I too am theoretically sick, but I live, work, function – whether or not I'm in pain. I have missions in life. The pain envelops my life, while the others get scared and don't understand that it's part of my life - I know the pain will subside soon.)

Nir lights another cannabis cigarette.

"Mental power is much stronger than bodily power. You make an internal move, and just like in a street fight, you know you're going to win. In his book The Art of War, Sun Tzu says that first you win and then go off to battle. You do something and then you win. I applied the principle of physical combat in my mental struggle. I understand it is limited in time, but it's been 12 years now.

I don't eat sugar because cancer likes sugar, but I do drink alcohol, especially beer which alleviates my pain and even contains anti-cancer elements. In general, I eat very little. I eat healthy, unprocessed food once a day. I don't feel hunger. I don't take dietary supplements.

I struggle by staying alive, getting up for morning prayer, working, teaching, studying Talmud, doing tai chi. I smoke cannabis mixed with tobacco so I can remain focused and continue to work. I read a study claiming that those who maintain their regular routine despite the difficult prognosis have a much higher life expectancy, as do those who drive their doctors crazy.

I am treated at the Burzynski cancer clinic in Houston. Specializing in brain tumors, this clinic offers familiar drugs in compositions that don't kill or significantly reduce the tumor, but rather retain its condition. The idea is that a violent tumor will reappear much more aggressively if you kill it, so we don't try to eliminate it, just maintain its size. This clinic has high survival rates for patients with brain tumors. When detected, the tumor was three centimeters large. Over the years it grew to eight and a half centimeters, and it now ranges from seven to eight centimeters. I've been living with it for 12 years now. They do not want it to diminish too much, because the strong cells survive and continue to develop.

On the holiday of Hanukkah I go there again. Until now I went twice a year for a period of a month and a half each time. This year I'm going only once. Some doctors I met had qualms about this clinic. Firer called them charlatans. I don't think they treat me, I think they help me, like a squad providing covering fire to help me overpower this terrorist."

Nir is a sharp and fascinating person. It's a pleasure to talk to him. The conversation flows and the time passes quickly. As we're talking, his wife Efrat is at Tai Chi class. He tells me he expected to meet a weak and ill woman, and was surprised by my vitality when he saw me. The suffering doesn't show on me. Even the gastroenterologist who treated me didn't see it on me - perhaps that's why they didn't realize how much I am suffering.

"You can even smoke with cancer. It's not contagious," he laughs. "Besides, we're already immune".

I am persuaded, but I inhale too quickly and start coughing right away. Although I've been smoking for a few months now, I am still untrained.

"In Germany I underwent a low-dose chemotherapy. For this treatment, you are placed in a kind of oven for 24 hours. This treatment, funded by the Ministry of Defense, exhausted itself relatively quickly. Don't you think it's a bit eerie to go to Germany and be placed in ovens and even pay ten thousand euros a week for it?" he asks with a smile.

"I think we have a personal responsibility to change our situation, and we have the power to do it. I can't define what I do exactly, but I know we have the power to win, to make a difference. You don't have to be passive.

In martial arts the objective is not the fight itself, but its outcome - the goal is to make life an art form through combat. Through training you develop your personality and learn how to solve problems with minimal effort. I apply these principles in life, relationships, at work, and in my struggle with the disease.

I don't rely solely on doctors. I am a warrior at heart. I've never accepted defeat, I can't separate my life from the fighting".

"Do you have any thoughts about the cause of your cancer?"

"In the two decades after my service, a high percentage of Israeli naval commandos got sick. It's probably also related to the Kishon River. I didn't dive much in the Kishon - maybe a few dozen times. There are some whose illness was clearly caused by the Kishon, but half of the patients had never seen the Kishon. Their illness is a result of high stress. I once had three missions in one week. You are constantly under pressure. It's not exactly a healthy lifestyle."

When we say goodbye, I ask if we can shake hands. Nir smiles and says he doesn't shake hands with women.

What's special about Nir? What allows him to live 12 years after detecting a disease, whose rare survivors usually live an average of four additional years? How can his story help others? This is actually a question I'd like to ask about each of the people I met. What helped them besides the chemo and radiotherapy?

"So there's something we're able to do and we do it", says Nir, "The question is how to get everyone to do it - it seems to me that what we do is also suitable for healthy people".

Zalman
Pancreatic cancer – doesn't give cancer a chance– 6 years after diagnosis

"I think that anyone who finds out they have cancer should drop everything and commit themselves entirely to getting cured, in order to save what's most precious to them".

-Zalman

Despite the biological drug, I feel the breast tumor is still growing. At night I lie in bed and examine it by force of habit. Quietly, alone, just me and the tumor, and it's growing. I swallow my spit and remain silent. I don't tell Gadi.

I haven't taken all my supplements this week. Most of the time I feel nauseous and I can't eat, let alone swallow all the dietary supplements. I drink very little during the day. I have a feeling that a visit to Zalman's might help me collect myself. I look forward to this visit.

We're scheduled to meet on Wednesday at nine in the morning at his home in Talmei Menashe. "I want to spend time with you this morning," I ask.

- "I walk through the field at a pretty fast pace," he says.
- "Okay, I'll walk with you."
- "Are you in shape?"
- "Pretty much".

Before going out for the walk, Zalman made himself a concoction of the dozens of extracts that fill the kitchen and dining room: Vitamin B, D, and E, six fungi, pot marigold, astragalus, sheba, bindweed, pao de arco, green tea, milk thistle, omega 3, liquid selenium, a mixture of Chinese herbs recommended by therapist Sharon Bar-Gil, lecithin and pollen in a spoon.

He read a lot of material on each of them, consulting with several therapists and choosing the most convenient extract for him. "I must be convinced that the supplement or drug I am taking should help me significantly. I don't take everything I'm offered."

As much as he could, he replaced pills and capsules with drops and liquids for better absorption. This morning ritual takes nearly half an hour. Before he gulps the concoction, I get a taste. It's not tasty.

Zalman finishes the cup of bitterness and health in one gulp, measures his blood sugar level, and gives himself an insulin injection. Before leaving the house, he takes a teaspoon of honey mixed with mushrooms, black cumin, and black sesame prepared by his herbal therapist Shelly Cohen, to get some energy for the walk. I too take a spoonful. Zalman takes off his shirt. "I love the sun, it has a life force, so I walk shirtless and hope to break a sweat. It's good for the body and it airs out my lungs". Zalman waves his arms sideways and I mimic him. The house sits on a plot in this rural community and we start walking toward the field bordering the yard, passing by an impressive orchard of fruit trees and a large section for growing vegetables awaiting the season to begin.

Zalman told me in advance that he doesn't talk during walks, but rather does guided imagery. He constantly cleans the body and fills it with the energy of nature. Zalman quickly plows through the clods in the field. I lag behind and the gap between us grows. Breathe, you're not breathing, I can't hear you breathing. I take a deeper breath and try to make a sound but can't close the gap. I consider going back and waiting for him. "No," he protested, "I'll adjust my pace, but you can walk faster. The plan is to walk for 40 minutes and even run some of the time." I breathe loudly now, my hands folded as instructed, swinging back and forth to energize the legs and massage the thymus gland. "We passed a third of the way" Zalman cheers me up. "You see the curve over there, give everything you got until we reach it." I hit the gas, but I'm out of fuel. "No, you're not giving up. If you want to deal with cancer - you must not give up." Zalman sounds like a coach. Later he'll tell me he considered starting a training group for cancer patients. "I'd like to do basic training with them and teach them how to adapt to the lifestyle of a cancer patient. I don't use warlike terms. After all, the cancer is inside us, part of our body. We don't want to fight our body." We didn't have time to develop that theme. When we reach the curve I tell Zalman that the white spots I see in my eyes have intensified and now I can't see anything. Even though we just met half an hour ago, I put my hand on him and keep walking fast at his side. "Feel the wind, let the energy of the wind and the sun wash over you. You're not breathing, I can't hear you breathing". The blurriness in front of my eyes increases, and even though he thinks I can make it, I announce that I am sitting down. It's more important what I think and feel – as I slowly realize. I sit down and try to get up after a minute. The world spins – isn't that what it's supposed to do? I am the center and everything revolves around me. I sit down, then lay down and raise my legs. Zalman supports them. "Probably low blood pressure," I tell him.

"Tell me," he asks, "What is your health situation?"

A new pain in my skull, I update Zalman. I detect on his poker face that he is concerned. At the same time I see us from the side, in the middle of a plowed field – a woman lying on her back and a shirtless man holding her legs as they swing upward.

I get up and we continue slowly. Consumed with shame, I make it to the armchair on the balcony of his house. Zalman brings a cup with a drink concocted by his therapist. As soon as he found out he was sick, he hired a therapist to help him organize the journey to recovery. She sorts the dozens of dietary supplements, prepares the special drinks, squeezes juices, prepares the food according to the special instructions, and massages him every day. All the concoctions, powders, and vegetables are stored in three refrigerators. When he was recovering from back surgery, still relying on crutches, he started walking in the fields with his therapist at his side holding a chair. Whenever he got tired he would take a break and sit down.

Slowly but surely, he went back to walking normally. Six years ago, in 2008, Zalman, a 64-year-old businessman who owns hostels in Jerusalem and Jaffa, was diagnosed with a very aggressive type of pancreatic cancer - adenocarcinoma. "At first it was impossible to operate on me. I had to undergo chemotherapy to reduce the tumor.

As soon as I realized that the chances of survival after five years with pancreatic cancer are 4%, I quit my job and started looking for a solution frantically. I entered a state of emergency, working only on my recovery from seven in the morning to midnight. I searched online; read all the cancer literature published in Israel; went to healers, nutritionists, supplement advisors; did hyperthermia - heating the body through a special procedure that attacks cancer cells; and got into intensive sports activities. I examined anything I found that could possibly help me. I still constantly check for new possibilities. I have a hot tub in my backyard and I warm my body in it twice a day at a temperature of 39.5 degrees (Celsius). At first I walked twice a day, but now only once a day. For a year and a half I didn't work, just committed entirely to taking care of myself. After six months of chemotherapy the pancreas did indeed diminish and I found a surgeon who was willing to operate on me. When they opened up my stomach it turned out the entire pancreas was inflamed and in a pre-cancerous condition. So they removed it entirely, as well as the duodenum and gall bladder. I spent a month and a half in the hospital recovering from the surgery. I couldn't take supplements or resume my program. I told myself I have to get better. I became diabetic due to the removal of the pancreas and now I give myself an insulin injection three times a day. At this point I was recommended to undergo radiotherapy because pancreatic cancer usually returns after surgery. I remembered well how my mother, who had cancer, passed away due to a bowel obstruction as a result of radiotherapy. Aware of the potential harm and benefits, I checked the data and decided against radiotherapy. I even decided not to undergo the recommended chemotherapy after surgery. Now that there was no sign of cancer in my body, I didn't want to weaken my immune system through chemotherapy, which was only supposed to extend my life by a few months. The doctor didn't insist, and in each visit with her I came healthier and more energetic. I told her she is welcome to refer other patients to me. But that didn't happen.

I heard about one person who survived for over five years. A good friend of mine also survived five years with pancreatic cancer before dying a few years ago. It was clear to me that I was fighting for my life and nothing is too difficult or expensive for that purpose. Even today, six years after the surgery, I am totally committed to my health. I don't know anybody in my situation. **I think that anyone who finds out they have cancer should drop everything and commit entirely to recovery, in order to save what's most precious to them.**

Even today after fully recovering, I still work on all fronts, both physically and mentally. I maintain a clean, almost vegetarian diet of unprocessed foods and a lot of fruits. I exercise an hour and a half a day to warm the body. I take eighty (80) supplements, green juices, camel milk, green tea, and various powders. I do acupuncture, attend any workshop on the subject of cancer I can find, and practice circular breathing as part of my journey. I'm also subscribed to blogs on the subject of cancer. Anything I hear about that could possibly benefit me and won't cause harm - I take. This area fascinates me.

I spend half a day treating myself before going to work. Every six months I take blood tests and meet with my doctor, who tells me: "Whatever makes you feel better - go with it."

On the kitchen counter there's green juice containing wheatgrass, vegetables, liquid aloe vera, pectin, five apricot seeds, and other concoctions. I get a small cup and only manage to drink half of it. Zalman finishes it all in one gulp. That's how he deals with the bitterness. Then some more supplements, a glass of camel milk with protein powder, and a large amount of enzymes, following the Gonzalez school of thought[9]. We start lifting weights on the lawn to strengthen muscles. Having recovered from the walk, I join in on the exercise.

"Now go to the hot tub, massage the lymph, liver, and feet. Just don't pass out on me over there. Only fifteen minutes. Want a sip of this concoction? It's an herbal extract I got from a traditional Chinese medicine therapist. The first one I went to was Prof. Yaakov Shoham, an internist who specializes both in oncology and complementary medicine. He instructed me on nutrition and vitamins. I still visit him once every six months. While you're in the hot tub, I'll take care of the orchard."

He eats his first meal for the day at 1:00 PM. The therapist serves Zalman a tray with two drinking cups, a bowl of dietary supplements, and a salad plate on which he generously pours lemon juice, mixed nuts, a mixture of six healthy oils he orders especially, and tahini.

After dinner, Zalman goes to work in Jerusalem, not before packing the food for the rest of day in a lunchbox: lots of fruits and frozen food.

Determination and perseverance are the key words that describe Zalman's conduct. "It's not necessarily the supplements or the diet. The spiritual and mental aspects have a bigger impact. I can't believe I was cured and this disbelief helps me persist. Since it protects me, I keep doing everything at high intensity."

---

[9] Dr. Nicholas Gonzalez's healing method has three main components: diet, additional nutrients, and removal of toxins from the body. In his cleansing method, Dr. Gonzalez also uses coffee enemas. Each patient must eat additional nutrients religiously. The method includes vitamins, minerals, trace elements, amino acids, and so on. Dr. Gonzalez adjusts the diet personally for each patient. There is a strong emphasis on treatment with proteolytic enzyme supplements, produced from the pancreas gland, for the purpose of halting the cancer. From the website - Cancer, a Practical Guide to Natural Healing.

Camel milk

Camel's milk: one of nature's most powerful healing materials!!
Similar in composition to mother's milk and significantly boosts the immune system.
Declared by the UN as a "superfood" that helps treat the most difficult diseases.
Clinical studies indicate that it has unusual anti-inflammatory qualities that help suppress inflammatory processes associated with most human diseases.
According to the studies, drinking milk is suitable for the following diseases: diabetes, cancer, colitis and Crohn's disease, skin problems, most autoimmune diseases, and more (from the website "Halav Bereshit" - Research and Development Ltd. - Developing medical applications from camel's milk).

My friend who died of pancreatic cancer also did a lot of meditation and guided imagery, but not with the same determination. My commitment is very strong. I am particularly worried about becoming complacent. I'm not sure it won't happen. It's possible after ten or twenty years. In the meantime, I lead a full and active life. With all my commitment, I am an optimistic person who lives life happily.

Zalman has a regular routine. He doesn't have to make new plans every day. His therapist helps him, undoubtedly, but in my opinion the fixed regiment helps him even more. It turns out that my meeting with Zalman is very significant for me. His determination is contagious. I return home and place all the supplements on one shelf. I hang my list of morning activities on the refrigerator and make a phone call to order camel's milk. Then I set one appointment with Prof. Yaakov Shoham and another with naturopath Sharon Bar-Gil.

Zalman buys the mushrooms from Shelly Cohen. I decide that this will be my next destination.

CHAPTER 4

Faith, prayer, mushrooms, and strengthening the immune system

"I believe that healing can take place only out of tenderness and compassion. When there is an illness in my body I don't fight it, I listen to it. I listen until I understand what it came to tell me. Only once we listen to the illness with an open and compassionate heart can it can be released from the body, and with the generous help of the Great Spirit, the healing process can begin".

-Shaun Efraima

Shelly Cohen – Mushroom and plant farmer

On the phone she sounds amazing, nice, and open, as Zalman described her. She intrigues me and we decide to meet in her home in the rural community of Beit Hanan.

I enjoy my travels across the Land of Israel that lead me to places and people I wouldn't have met otherwise. Shelly's farm and house seem as if they're inhabited by people absolutely unwilling to surrender to civilization. Something about her look reminds me of myself as a little girl trying to set up a plant nursery in my parents' backyard and collecting potted plants and branches to replant from anywhere possible. I planted the seeds of the papaya fruit that grew in our yard. I recall that my grandmother was like this too. In her home in Tiberias she grew various plants, which she used for treating itself. Especially aloe vera, which she used for making healing creams. She made meatballs and soups from malva.

"For every material in the world there's a mushroom that breaks it down", Shelly explains as we sit on a large swing in the yard. "I read a lot about the treatment of people with mushrooms, but I don't treat people, I treat plants and the soil. I grow plants, I grow and collect mushrooms and make them edible. In the last three years there has been a dramatic increase in the number of cancer patients who come to buy my mushrooms.

No matter the type or location of the cancer, it is programed to survive. Unless the person changes his mindset and nutrition, chemotherapy will only weaken him instead of helping him. The mushrooms are smarter than the cancer. Their effect is proven very quickly on a body free of toxins. Some of the mushrooms I grow myself and the others I import or gather from the fields during winter. Friends from around the country call and alert me where they've spotted mushrooms, and then I go out early in the morning to gather them. I prefer gathering wild mushroom to growing them. I found out that the active ingredient in naturally grown mushrooms is much stronger than that of those grown artificially.

Every mushroom has different qualities. Studies have shown that caterpillar fungus, lingzhi mushroom, and hen-of-the-wood have been used in East Asia for thousands of years to strengthen the immune system and treat cancer patients. The lingzhi mushroom kills bacteria and viruses, lowers blood cholesterol levels, prevents tumors in the body, and increases the level of interleukin, a protein that stimulates the immune system to action primarily by increasing the production of T cells. The mushroom also contains very strong antioxidants and relieves pain in arthritic diseases."

Shelly grinds some black cumin, sesame seeds, milk thistle, and a mixture of mushrooms. She adds all that to a jar of honey and mixes it thoroughly. Thus, she claims, their absorption capacity in the body increases tenfold and has a stronger impact. I plan to take a teaspoon of this splendid honey every day – just like Zalman.

In an article from 2014, Dr. Susan Percival and other researchers note the following: "Preliminary evidence suggests **that mushrooms may support the immune system** by interacting with gut flora, enhancing the development of adaptive immunity, and improving the immune functionality of the cell."

The constant mentioning of mushrooms in articles attracts my attention. In a gathering of "Ta'atzumot" I meet naturopath Dr. Amit Henin, who studied the mushrooms and chose to use them.

Feeney MJ, Dwyer J, Hasler-Lewis CM, Milner JA, Noakes M, Rowe S, Wach M, Beelman RB, Caldwell J, Cantorna MT, Castlebury LA, Chang ST, Cheskin LJ, Clemens R, Drescher G, Fulgoni VL, Haytowitz DB, Hubbard VS, Law D, Myrdal Miller A, Minor B, Percival SS, Riscuta G, Schneeman B, Thornsbury S, Toner CD, Woteki CE, Wu D. Mushrooms and health summit proceedings. J Nutr 144 (7): 1128S-36S, 2014

Dr. Amit Henin
Brain tumor - mushrooms –
6 years after diagnosis

"The cost of treating myself with mushrooms was 12,000 shekels a month for a period of eight months.
Expensive, but it got the job done

-*Amit Henin*

Amit is a handsome woman. Working as a therapist for 25 years, she wrote a large part of the curricula on naturopathic medicine and supervised the naturopathic colleges in the country. "One day I felt an intense pain in my toes, followed by a serious edema. Nevertheless, I tried to keep working, remain a functioning wife and mother, and maintain the household. I moved on. But when I gained ten kilos in two weeks I realized I have a systemic problem that must be examined. My situation did not impress my doctor. But I continued to search for an answer. I could no longer move my foot and thigh, and could only walk by pushing my leg with my hand. No one knew that something was wrong. I managed to hide it all the time ".

In September 2008, Amit – a naturopath and chairwoman of the Israeli Association of Naturopaths – discovered the cause of her physical condition: a rare and aggressive tumor in her brain four centimeters large, which necessitates that she undergo two surgeries.

"I didn't panic or lose my cool. For years I supported cancer patients. I'm very familiar with this. So we looked for the best surgeon. I realized I was facing a complex operation. Uncertain about how I'd come out of surgery, I asked for a two-week postponement so I could go traveling with my daughters. Despite the plan for a reassuring trip, I was very frustrated, preoccupied with myself, and very unpleasant to be around. It was a terrible trip. When we returned I decided to be alone for three days in the attic. For three days I didn't eat and only drank water - asking myself what I want to do in life, what I am satisfied with and what I'm not. I questioned whether I want to live or give up on this life; whether I want to ascend and meet my mother who was murdered randomly five years earlier. After those three days I decided I want to live. I chose life.

The surgery went well, but a few months later an inflammation appeared, along with 'water on the brain', and I had to undergo another surgery. After the second operation I started feeling a constant, excruciating pain that made me want to give up on life," says Amit. "I was given morphine and opium, but the pain persisted insufferably. The pain caused an indescribable burning sensation. As a therapist, I'm considered a pain medicine expert, and I couldn't find a therapist or treatment that could help me. At night I would cry, talk to my mom, and ask her to take me to her. I couldn't sit, stand, or sleep. Life became unbearable for me. I flew to Milan to see a pain specialist I knew, hoping that he would help me, me, but he couldn't either. During this entire time, I continued to work and teach.

One day a friend of mine talked to me about mushrooms. I don't just take anything that's given to me. I have to make sure it's backed by scientific research. I do not rely on rumors. I didn't know much about mushrooms. But after trying everything, the mushrooms were the last drawer I hadn't opened yet. In my condition, I couldn't lose anything except for a lot of money. I studied the active ingredients in mushrooms and the mechanism of action, and once I was convinced of their effectiveness I started taking large amounts of lingzhi mushrooms and cordyceps. After a month and a half the pain subsided. For eight months I took large amounts, which restored the nerves damaged during the removal of the tumor and reduced the cerebral edema.

The results of the MRI test conducted eight months after I started taking the mushrooms surprised the doctors. According to the analysis, my head appeared to be in precancerous condition. The body repaired the brain tissues damaged during surgery. The cost of treating myself with mushrooms was 12,000 shekels a month

for a period of eight months. Expensive, but it got the job done".

Amit's story inspires me to learn more about mushrooms. Through Amit I also reach a therapist in the north of the country who worked with Maria, a woman who was surprisingly cured of sarcoma, as I had heard. I call the therapist and to my surprise I discover that the woman I'm looking for also took mushrooms.

Can prayer save me?

"What's your mother's name? We'll pray for you", told me a religious woman I met. Since then, every time I meet her daughter she reminds me that her mother prays for me every day.

Okay, I say and smile. Thanks. But I'm not exactly sure what to say about that. Someone is thinking about me, wishing the best for me, but I don't believe it has any power to heal me. As far as I'm concerned, until now it was no more that a quirk.

In the same context, I heard an interesting story from a girl sitting next to me at a conference on nutrition: eighteen years ago her mother-in-law was rushed to the ER due to seizures. The MRI revealed a 2.5-cm increase in the size of the cerebellum. Three different doctors recommended removing the tumor surgically. Her son, a man of faith, called her every day for two months and for half an hour he would say to her: "It's no big deal, you are healthy. Trust in God". In the meantime, he prayed for his mother every day. Two months after diagnosis, another MRI scan showed no sign of cancer. Since then it's been eighteen years, as I mentioned.

In the United States prayer is considered the most common alternative treatment, as shown in a study examining thirty-one thousand people in 2004[10]. When I begin to explore this subject, I find that the link between prayer and healing is the subject of many studies. The Medical Center at the University of the Pacific in California held a study with a control group consisting of AIDS patients who were prayed for. The number of survivors in the group that was prayed for was greater. At San Francisco General Hospital they claimed that patients who were prayed for showed better clinical results. In a study held at Duke University in the United States, thirty patients with heart disease who had a group of believers pray for them, showed results twice as good as the patients in the control group, for whom no prayers were said. But it turns out there are also studies with opposite results. Cardiologist Herbert Benson of Harvard University in the United States conducted a study examining 1,802 patients with heart disease, divided into three groups. The results showed that patients who were prayed for and knew about it - suffered from more complications. Perhaps the knowledge that people were praying for them made them believe their situation is dire.

---

[10] nih newsletter http://nccam.nih.gov/news/newsletter/2005_winter/prayer.htm

The idea that prayer can save me doesn't really fit with my life experience. Is it possible that believers are less ill? Following my current research, I choose to see faith and prayer as additional tools for strengthening the immune system. I don't think it matters which god, higher power, or angels one believes in and worships. What matters is the inner conviction, the strong desire to be cured, and especially the attitude that faith instills in people. As a child I was impressed by the stories of the sages who at times of crisis called "Shema Israel" and were saved in the last minute.

I found a fascinating and similar story in Dr. Sanjay Gupta's book "Cheating Death", published by Armchair Publishing. Gupta tells the story of a 16-year-old boy who had four malignant tumors in his body developing rapidly and there was no conventional treatment available. The boy asked his father to enlist anyone who could come to the hospital to pray for him. His father, a doctor, scientist, and rationalist, accepted his son's request. Hundreds of people packed the hospital auditorium in a public prayer. A week later the result was amazing – no tumors were found in the MRI scan.

Maria (alias)
Sarcoma – prayer, faith, and mushrooms - 1 year after diagnosis

"Every time I pray, I feel calm and confident."

- Maria

In March 2013, 44-year-old Maria from Usifiyeh, mother of two children in elementary school and science teacher at a junior high school in Haifa, arrived at Ichilov Hospital. Her complaints of pain and a swollen ankle led to the diagnosis of a cancerous sarcoma tumor. "I tried chemotherapy but it didn't help so the only remaining treatment was to amputate the foot. They said it was very urgent. It was a disaster for us" says Maria.

Maria and her husband sent all the documents and test results to America for a second opinion, but they received the same answer - only amputation!

When she realized there's no choice, she scheduled a foot amputation surgery at Ichilov. After waiting for hours to be picked up and taken to her operation, it was decided to postpone the surgery to the next day. And the next day – it was postponed again.

"After the third postponement I decided that it was a sign from above and I must trust my instincts. Despite the concern of those around me, I chose to opt out of this surgery", says Maria.

"I'm a believer. At home, I prayed all day while I searched the internet for other solutions. I added to my daily diet supplements like turmeric, flaxseed, and poppy, and received treatment from a therapist in Beit Keshet."

Maria worked with therapist Dafna Meshulam, who administers Integrated Physical Emotional Clearing (IPEC) - a treatment method that focuses on the body, mind, and energy. (See box)

IPEC method

Dafna explains the method: "Every illness also has an emotional source. Under the IPEC method, we diagnose the disease through applied kinesiology (muscle testing) and uncover its cause relatively accurately and quickly. After diagnosis, we will balance the body and clean all energetic, emotional, and physical blockages. The process includes changing your diet and strengthening your belief and emotional systems. The body has an innate, built-in ability to communicate and cure itself. Cancer cells can resume communication between them and restore their strength after chemotherapy." By healing what's broken and unnecessary in the patient, Dafna restores the body's innate abilities of balanced communication, which helps it heal.

"Treatment as a whole releases and opens blockages at all levels and improves the general physical and mental situation. Emotional processes are very important in curing cancer. Together with processes of forgiveness and emotional balance, we move from a state of 'illness' to that of 'compassion' and 'healing'.

When treating cancer patients, Dafna also uses supplements, most of them based on caterpillar fungus of the FOHOW Company. These supplements enhance the immune and nervous systems as well as communication between them, resulting in a natural healing process of the body.

"Thanks to Dafna I learned to be calmer, not only on the outside as I was before, but especially internally. In addition, following her advice I included caterpillar mushroom extract in my treatment. It's a Chinese formula containing the active ingredient of the three mushrooms: Chinese caterpillar mushroom, lingzhi mushroom, and shiitake".

Two months after cancelling the surgery, a bone scan analysis revealed a spot in an area where the tumor was growing five months earlier. I was shocked by the results. I asked Dr. Jacob Bickels, director of the orthopedic oncology department at Ichilov Hospital, who just two months ago was convinced I would die without surgery, to check the results again. "What did you do? " he asked, "What treatment did you take?" I told him I prayed.

In a TV interview, Dr. Bickels said the following about Maria's case: "I think we hardly understand anything about the effect a person's mental state on his body. We haven't even started to scratch the surface of this issue and I think that's Maria's story".

Another test held two months later showed unequivocally on the computer screens that the spot was still diminishing. A biopsy revealed that what appears on the screens is not an active tumor.

"This is unprecedented. Cancer remission is very rare, and I've never seen it happen with sarcoma", Bickels told reporters." This phenomenon is unlikely and undocumented."

Stunned, Maria attributed the recovery to her prayers: "God helped me. I prayed more than ever. Every minute of the day I spoke with God. I continue to pray and want to always be in touch with God."

I asked Maria what message she would like to convey to cancer patients: "Have faith in ourselves and our strength to overcome any difficult situation. Those who overcome such situations become stronger."

Maria's case was so unusual that a team from the hospital ward decided to visit her at her home to see and hear what she had done from up close. She showed the visitors her prayer book and the dietary supplements she took, including the Caterpillar fungus formula.

Maria added: "Every time I pray, I feel calm and confident. Of course I was afraid, but despite the fear I always felt at peace."

Prof. Bickels admits: "She was not treated with conventional medicine. Medicine supposedly has a very clear scientific element, but in the end of the day you treat people. If there's anything unscientific – it's people".

Mushrooms and the immune system

The stories of Mary and Amit motivated me to further examine the relationship between mushrooms and the immune system. I wanted to find studies that substantiate the claim that mushrooms strengthen the immune system.

I found a Japanese study[11] in which extract of the shiitake mushroom was given to mice ill with sarcoma. Six out of ten mice experienced a complete remission of the tumors, and when the dosage was increased - all ten mice showed complete remission.

---

[11] Cancer Res 1970; 30: 2776-2781
Life Sci. 2006 Dec 23; 80 (3): 205-11. Epub 2006 Sep 6. Goro Chihara, Junji Hamuro, Yukiko Y. Maeda, et al edodes (Berk.) Sing. (an Edible Mushroom) Marked Antitumor Activity, Especially Lentinan, from Lentinus Fractionation and Purification of the Polysaccharides with

The lingzhi mushroom has been used in Asia for thousands of years. One of its popular names is the "immortality mushroom", which speaks for itself. A study examining its active ingredients found that it inhibited the spread of metastasis of lung cancer cells in mice.

Caterpillar fungus is also known as cordyceps or tochukaso. This mushroom is used both in Chinese and Tibetan medicine, and is known for protecting the liver and kidneys and having anti-tumor properties.

It seems that mushrooms are very effective in strengthening the immune system. Japan's health system includes in its treatment coverage substances from medicinal mushrooms for cancer patients. I find a mushroom that can restore myelin in damaged nerve cells. I ask in the Mycolivia Company, which grows and sells mushrooms, for information on this mushroom's effectiveness on nerves damaged by radiation. The solution for my abdominal pain and damaged digestive system might come from that direction. Mycolivia doesn't conduct studies, but rather consolidates information from many studies published around the world. The Company's naturopath sends me two articles on the lion's mane mushroom and its impact on nerve cells. I file them in the 'gastrointestinal treatment' folder. I'll get to that later.

Mycolivia's website features a few abstracts of studies on the effectiveness of mushrooms in cancer treatment. For example, a study conducted in Japan from 2004 to 2010 examined the effect of incorporating lentinan mushroom with chemotherapy for patients with gastrointestinal cancer on the survival of patients for one, two, and five years. Survival rates were better in the study group than in the control group: 1 year - 91.3% compared to 59.4%; 2 years - 45.7% compared to 32.7%; and 5 years of survival - 10% compared to 0%.

Guided imagery - rational or insignificant?

Dr. Carl Simonton, an American oncologist, found that guided imagery inhibits the spread of cancer cells and causes their remission. He wrote a few books on the subject and even set up support groups. Simonton called patients who practice guided imagery 'very special patients'. The number of studies on the effects of guided imagery on the body and on various diseases is increasing. Even rationalists are willing to admit there's a connection between body and soul. Guided imagery is no longer considered witchcraft. Hundreds of essays support this theory.

American professor Sandra Levy studied the link between emotion and cancer. In her book "Behavior and Cancer"[12] from 1985, Levy presents a comprehensive review of various behavioral factors that contribute to cancer risk, both directly and indirectly. Levy, who is now a pastor in Virginia, shows how stress and other mental states can affect the growth of cancer. Research databases feature hundreds of studies that show a link between stress and the weakening of the immune system, by damaging natural killer cells (NK). These are cells in the immune system that are supposed to attack cancer cells. Even in the medical community there is no doubt that meditation and guided imagery reduce the level of stress and strain.

Ta'atzumot Gathering

In the afternoon, Gadi and I look for parking in the small and charming streets of North Tel Aviv, in the area of Yehuda Hamaccabi Street. The signs in the entrance to the street are confusing and inconsistent. Another round and another round. There's one... No, you can't park there. Here on the right. No, I won't fit in here... Over there, on the left... Finding a vacant parking spot in the street brings us great joy. We found a spot where we're allowed to park. We check the signs again. Yes? Alright!!! We park. We're late. It's alright, we know the material. Cured cancer patients tell us how they did it. We actually go there just to absorb the atmosphere, and meet Ruth, the heart and soul of these meetings, who was cured of cancer herself.

A staircase leads up to the second floor of the Bnei Dan hostel. Walking up stairs is good – it strengthens the bones, back, hips, and legs. Inside the Reform synagogue a meeting of the Ta'atzumot Association is being held, with about 70 participants sitting in a semicircle. I scan the audience, trying to distinguish between patients and therapists. That woman with the blond wig at the end has a funny hairdo, as if it's real hair. And there's Billy Shaked, the guided imagery instructor, in a white shirt, and Alan the healer in a black shirt. I've been treated by both of them. Over there on the right is that woman who once told me she cured herself with turmeric and black pepper. She still comes... very nice. (That is, she's still alive)

At the center of the circle, Prof. Gershom Zajicek advises participants on how to behave during chemotherapy. Prof. Zajicek is a cancer researcher

---

12 Percival, SS. Nutrition and Immunity Balancing Diet and Immune Function. Nutrition Today, 46 (1), 2011 doi: 10.1097 / NT.0b013e3182076fc8

who founded the Ta'atzumot Association over five years ago. He believes wholeheartedly that guided imagery and meditation prolong patients' lives dramatically due to their effect on the immune system and carcinogenic processes in the body. In his opinion, the cancer is not a fatal disease, but rather a 'plot twist' in life. "If you get cancer," he says, "know that you can live with it in harmony for years". Or in other words: "Living with cancer in perfect health. Curing cancer is a multi-step process," he explains. "First you halt its progress, that is, put it to sleep. Only then can it be removed". For that purpose, Professor Zajicek and the Ta'atzumot Association recommend additional medical tools that were tested and found most effective for enhancing the medical process.

The main theme of the meetings is 'building healing powers', just like building muscles. The healing powers are achieved through holistic practice – addressing the person as a whole. Zajicek argues that man is born with a capacity to deal with cancer, just as he is born with the ability to speak. Healing powers grow stronger when the person discovers he is ill. The reaction to cancer differs from person to person. According to Greshon, those who can effectively summon their healing powers will live in harmony with the disease. He calls them cancer yogis. In contrast, those who have a hard time summoning the strength need the support of the "cancer fitness club". The Association's gatherings are part of that club's activities. Recently, the organization started providing volunteers, just like personal trainers, who help patients mobilize their inner resources to cope with the disease. Initially, this training aims at strengthening the body and slowing down the spread of the disease, rather than weakening the tumor as practiced in modern medicine. Zajicek views guided imagery and meditation as the top methods of complementary medicine. For those who fail to do it, he suggests going to a healer who will do the work instead of the patient. But getting help from healers doesn't eliminate the search. As Zajicek says: "Everyone must do research. Everyone must take their fate in their own hands. That's the purpose of cancer yogis. They examine the various methods for suppressing the cancer and determine which one is right for them."

During the break somebody plays the piano, as Zajicek holds the hand of the woman standing next to him, leading her to dance the waltz. He laughs, she laughs. He knows how to live, I think to myself. The others look at them, but no one joins. Everyone smiles. Have fun, have fun, my mind tells me.

Avner Shilo
Thyroid carcinoma, metastatic - Guided imagery and emotional work
–31 years after initial diagnosis

"The purpose of our actions is to keep us away from the pain and suffering".

-Epicurus, Greek philosopher

The story of Avner Shilo from Kiryat Tivon, who stopped his cancer on its fifth recurrence twenty years ago, is inspiring. "I had the privilege and the pleasure of getting cancer and curing myself of it entirely on my own", Avner writes in a booklet he published. "The path from illness to the spring of health was and still is fascinating, delightful, partly prickly, sometimes elusive, occasionally winding, but mostly fun and exciting."

It's surprising how many few cancer survivors welcome their disease and their new approach to life following the journey to recovery.

"I was fourteen and a half when I was diagnosed with cancer for the first time", Avner recalls. "It started with a routine visit to the family doctor at the healthcare clinic. The doctor, who already then was a head shorter than me, looked up to my neck, touched a bulge that I wasn't aware of, and asked: 'What is this?' I replied that I don't know and was subsequently sent to a series of tests at Hadassah Hospital, which at the time seemed endless.

Two weeks later I underwent surgery to remove the thyroid gland where the tumor was found, and it turned out to be cancerous. Later on, some metastases were found in my lungs and head, and I underwent chemotherapy to eradicate them.

The treatments were successful, but the cancer came back a few more times, and each time I underwent chemotherapy with iodine, which as very helpful... until the next time.

Each such treatment entailed severe nausea, vomiting, weakness, and one to two weeks of confinement to an isolation room at the hospital, as well as a temporary loss of my will to live.

When I was twenty, the cancer came back again. Once again I received treatment, followed by a ten-year pause. I thought the cancer had become a thing of the past. I got married, had three children, attended university, worked as a tour guide, and started an educational initiative that was very important to me.

Then all-of-a-sudden, at the age of 30, a routine checkup revealed that the cancer had returned to my neck, lungs, and head. Another session of chemotherapy with radioactive iodine was scheduled for me.

This time, for a change, I didn't automatically agree. I asked for a postponement, so I'd have time to try and deal with the cancer in alternative ways I had heard about at the time.

My request to postpone the treatment was denied, but I decided to take responsibility. I postponed the chemotherapy on my own, despite the doctors' objection.

In the next three months I started practicing self-healing methods on myself: relaxation and guided imagery. By the end of this period, the medical report said there is no change in the size of the metastases.

I was dismayed and disappointed. A date for chemotherapy was scheduled for me. Just before I left the doctor's room, in a flash of intuitive and oblivious insight, I asked for copies of the images from the test I had just taken. At home, a few hours later, my sharp-eyed wife Sarah studied these images and showed me something the doctors didn't tell me, perhaps because they didn't notice or found it significant: The metastases were actually considerably smaller.

That was enough for me to refuse chemotherapy. I was still skeptical but encouraged nonetheless, so I continued my search for a cure.

Meanwhile, I searched feverishly for a doctor who would agree to be in touch with me and treat me out of respect for what I was doing.

I didn't take another test until six months later. After a nerve-wracking week I got the results: the metastases are too small for chemotherapy. I was absolutely thrilled. I celebrated with my family and friends. This was a sign that my approach is working and that I should keep on looking for new ways to restore my health.

In the next five years I continued to work on myself. I learned two treatment methods of complementary medicine, and specialized in the "Jin

Shin Do acupressure" method. This alternative treatment method is based on traditional Chinese medicine theory, applying soft pressure on spots along the meridians[13]. I started treating other people and teaching Jin Shin. I got a new job, moved to a new place, and my fourth daughter was born.

In another comprehensive examination five years later, it was found that the tumor and all its metastases had completely disappeared.

I decided to use my personal story, the knowledge and experience I had gained, and everything I picked up along the way to help and treat other people, especially cancer patients. I guide them on how to heal themselves, give lectures and hold workshops for various groups. I also write and talk about my personal story. In doing so I feel that I'm continuing to heal myself too.

I feel healthy, as shown in the tests I take every once in a while. I continue to look for new ways to maintain my health, I treat people, and do my best to take care of myself, my family, and the world. "

The main aspects that Avner incorporated in the healing process

- Guided imagery with CDs he recorded. He continues to practice guided imagery while guiding patients and groups. "Every time I guide others I tap into my own inner forces of imagination. I teach in order to learn. I discovered that guided imagery is a wonderful, rich, interesting, fascinating, and free tool".
- Believing that the healing process relies on him and things he does internally, not just on the doctors and the medicine.
- Emotional change.

Avner doesn't focus that much on nutrition and supplements. Over the years he has lost patients who died while continuing to guide others for many years. He has no magic pill that cures cancer, nor can he predict who will survive and who won't. To strengthen his personal faith in healing, he sought to meet other cured patients who share his sense of destiny, action, and faith. Later, he contacted Prof. Gershom Zajicek and together they began to actively collect cured patients.

---

[13] A term in traditional Chinese medicine for the network of "energy channels" across the human body.

Avner's core beliefs:

A. Faith in the unity of body and soul, and their mutual influence on each other.

B. Faith in the human spirit and the human capacity for self-healing.

C. Faith in the healing power of love.

Avner treats people and teaches in Kiryat Tivon.

His website: www.healcancer.co.il

---⋘•⋙---

Strengthening the immune system

As I advance with my own research, I am convinced that the immune system is the key to our health, to the remission of the tumors, and to curing infections. I didn't invent anything new - but I put a much greater emphasis on this than on anything else.
How to strengthen the immune system? Every cured patient has their own answer. When I know all the options, I am able to choose between them. So far I've learned that living a happy and satisfying life, doing sports, adjusting your diet, taking dietary supplements and specific herbs, holding a strong belief, practicing guided imagery and emotional cleansing - all strengthen the immune system. This extended list actually covers all aspects of our lives.
MD Anderson Hospital in the United States, like other research institutes, run experiments on the link between strengthening the immune system and cancer. Dr. Elizabeth Mittendorf (MD Ph.D.) says: "We believe that more and more patients will enjoy the benefits of therapy on the immune system. The challenge will be to identify the specific approach for each patient. When doctors can do that, treatment of cancer, especially relating to the immune system, will be more individual."
Dr. Susan Persiol from Florida, United States, looks for links between aspects of diet to the strengthening of the immune system. Her research focuses on strengthening the immune system with nutrients, especially T cells. Her lab examines ingredients of fruits and vegetables and tries to study mechanisms of the immune system affected by food. The goal is to improve the functioning of the immune system while minimizing chronic infections.
In an article published in 2011, linking between balanced diet and the immune system, Dr. Persiol writes: "The T cells of the immune system

develop in a situation of balanced diet. Several studies have shown that specific plants induce T cells (of the immune system) to reproduce.

All nutrients are important for maintaining the immune system and providing adequate amounts of protein, fat, carbohydrates, vitamins, and minerals that protect us against diseases. More nutrients are needed if there's an infiltration of a pathogen.

To keep the immune system at its optimal state, the best thing to do is eat fruits and vegetables and drink tea. Folic acid, Vitamin D, C, U, phytochemicals, and fiber foods.

I'm going back to teach painting

> *"In the end of the day, when we face death, what will matter is not what we amassed in life but what we gave. Not what we learned, but what we taught".*
>
> *-From the movie about the Gerson Therapy*

Today I went back to teaching my painting group after taking a year off. A large inner smile stretched in me as I opened the door of the club where I teach. Just recently I thought I wouldn't be able to teach anymore. And yet, I recovered after all and I am now here with my students. Teetering between optimism and fear. After the painting lesson I rushed to Tel Hashomer hospital for an ultrasound check up and mammography. It turned out that what I had mistaken for a single lump is actually five lumps in my left breast. I received the news with indifference but later in the day the fear started gripping me and I lost my calm. It's been two days since the check up. I find it hard to wake up in the morning. Gadi enters the room and urges me to get out of bed.

I slept poorly last night again. I've got two hours until I go to another ultrasound check up, this time to examine the uterus. My friend Hani will come pick me up. There's a lot I can get done in the two hours until she comes. Before putting on my gym clothes, I lie down on my back on the bed, and reach my hand out to the tumor. I manage to feel one of its four members. The rest must be deeper. I can't wait for the moment when I'll feel it diminishing significantly. The test on the uterus came out normal.

In the afternoon Anat comes to take me to the beach. After no more than twenty minutes we arrive at the beach for the disabled. We brought clothes and shoes for walking and left the water bottles and towels next to one of the sheds scattered along the beach. We walked to the end of the boardwalk, which was quite a distance, bought lemon popsicles and sat on chairs facing the sea, staring at the sunset.

"I'm looking for a dream," I said, "something that will move me deeply."

"I'm in the same exact situation," Anat responded.

"For me, you're a collector of adventures." I told her.

Anat laughed, "That's exactly what I think of you," she said.

"What do you say? Shall I look for a dream for you to fulfill and you will find one for me? Something that will move us both."

I think that Anat was pretty excited by the sea. I wasn't. It was pleasant, but not more than the other places I go to. Yes, it's nicer than being at Tel Hashomer, where I visited twice this week, but no more pleasant than the Ra'anana Park or my backyard. It seems we sat there for a few hours. All the way back I twisted uncomfortably because of my abdominal pain. I still feel it, and again I'm suffering from an irritating nausea and belching most likely linked to the gall bladder. The abdominal pain is relentless. I haven't eaten anything today that could cause this. Maybe I didn't eat enough. I don't know what to eat.

At my age can you enroll in medical school?

In the morning I met the neighbor's son who had just returned from his long post-army trek around the world. Now he's moving to Be'er Sheva for pre-med studies. I looked at him, a young man starting out his life, and as he described his plans, I wondered if I am past the right age to study medicine. Perhaps this way I could help myself. I remembered the movie "Conviction," in which the protagonist studies law to prove the innocence of her brother who was accused of murder and sentenced to life in prison. She succeeds.

On Friday afternoon we went to the beach again. As I faced the stormy waves and warm sand, I was occupied with one thought – to enroll in medical school. I tried to look up information on age limits on my cell phone but couldn't find anything. In the evening we went to see a movie with a couple of old friends. Then we went to the cafe next door and I was tempted to order ice cream. On the drive back home I asked Gadi to pull over and I vomited all the ice cream on the sidewalk. Only then did I start feeling better.

As soon as I got home I sat down at the computer. I'm curious about the admission requirements, perhaps for biology instead of medical studies, so I could better understand the material I engage with and explore it academically until I find a solution for myself.

Efforts to resume my normal routine

I suddenly remember places around the country that were off my radar, like Akko, for example. I like to find in them special spots for painting, small and unknown hotels, special restaurants. And when I find such places I get excited and tell all those who are interested in my painting workshops that soon we'll hold an entire weekend of painting at the magical place I found.

A year has passed since the last weekend activity I organized at the Church of the Beatitudes overlooking the Sea of Galilee. I thought I wouldn't get to organize such trips anymore. But as part of my efforts to resume my normal routine, I suggested to Evie - a painter friend of mine, to join me as a partner and organize this workshop together with me. Evie accepted the challenge and we took the train to Old Akko for a day of preparation. We started out full of energy but by the afternoon I was exhausted. I felt embarrassed for my weakness and realized how hard it would be to teach these workshops alone.

The responses to my announcement of the next workshop were quick and warm, and the list of participants filled up quickly. None of them is aware of my exact medical condition. On Friday morning, the amateur painters, Evie, and I meet at the visitor center in Old Akko. Our excitement and joy are staggering. The place is shaded by tall tropical plants and sycamores. Evie leads the way and I support her. We have a busy program from Friday morning to Saturday afternoon. Evie's presence allows me to walk away when I cringe from the abdominal pain and when I want to throw up. I have no doubt that I can no longer do this alone. At least as long the problem with my digestive system can't be solved.

At night, in the same hotel room where former president Shimon Peres stayed a few months earlier, I have trouble sleeping, and not because of the previous guest in the room. I would only find out the next day from the owner of the hotel what distinguished room we're staying in. This month I ran out earlier than usual of the cannabis drops that help me sleep. My body is restless and not even Loriva pills for relaxation and sleep induction can help. An hour passes by as I lie on my back and try to sleep, unsuccessfully. I get up to write and feel chills through my body. I wonder how long I can go on with this nightmare, and how I'll endure the next day.

On Saturday morning the group of painters settled in a beautiful corner, under a large shed next to the beach, facing the view of the ancient port of Akko. I gave instructions for the painting and by the time I was done my body was spent. Tired and disappointed in my body, I went back to the hotel to recharge, leaving Evie alone with the participants for a few hours. In the afternoon I managed to recover and teach another workshop. This effort to resume my normal routine did not improve my blood counts, which were low again the next day.

Now we have to strengthen the immune system. But how?

The biological drug inhibits the enzymes responsible for dividing the cells, without distinguishing between cancer cells and other cells in the body and thus affecting the immune system. This results in great weakness, low blood counts, and infections anywhere in the body. Due to the low counts, I can't continue taking the drug. I am momentarily stricken by weakness and despair, which awaken dormant monsters within me. A part of me is convinced that I will die in the coming years. The image of me dying in five or seven years is in my mind now. I know this is bad. I know I have to remove this image from my mind, but I can't seem to do it so far.

For a moment, it's pretty discouraging and depressing. But I recover and decide not to give up. I worked hard to get this drug, which I have high hopes for, and now I am setting a goal for the coming week: to strengthen the immune system. I read, search, and prepare a list of everything that can affect the system and improve its functioning: going to sleep earlier, preparing for sleep at eight o'clock and being in bed by nine; giving the body the rest it needs and allowing the immune system to strengthen during sleep. At the same time, it's good to wake up early and go on walks. That's a bit more difficult for me. Other ways of getting stronger involve my faulty digestive system and I must find a way to ingest foods that are beneficial. I know the Astragalus plant can help boost the immune system, but I have trouble swallowing it in capsule form. At the store I find an Astragalus root that can be used for making tea. The taste is terrible. I come up with another idea - I make soup from the roots and throw in some seaweed and a little root of ginger, which is also known for enhancing and strengthening the immune system. I add a few pieces of Astragalus and shiitake mushroom. Indeed, the soup contains substances that are good for me. Due to the inflammation in my body, Shlomo Guberman offers to increase my dosage of omega-3 to 6 grams per day. I comply. I also know that joy and pleasure can raise blood counts. So despite the physical exhaustion, I attend a three-day dance festival in Givat Haviva. Gadi initiated, organized, packed and we went. I was weak, but I loved being there. On Friday, at the festival, I received exceptional treatment from Irit Mor, a body and soul therapist. The treatment included a massage during which Irit kept talking to me, pressing the painful spots and asking me to breathe. Irit read my body and soul and told me what she saw. At a certain point, when I was nauseous but couldn't throw up, she threw up instead of me. That impressed me very much. Irit said I had not completed my mission here on Earth. I agree with her. She says I must demand of the higher powers, the angels watching over us, to give me more time to complete my mission. The books I write are my mission. Sending off my children to an independent life is also my mission, as is being there to teach them and learn from them.

The next day I regained my strength. My blood counts were higher than ever before, allowing me to resume taking the drug. I succeeded. I have to remember that once I stick to a method I regain my faith, and the more thoroughly I do it the stronger my faith gets. My talks with the survivors help me muster the strength.

Naturopathy is medicine too

I want to study medicine. This field fascinates me. I know that at my age it defies logic. Studying naturopathy seems more realistic. I'm excited about the possibility of going back to school. My stomach pains don't lend any additional optimism. But I feel compelled to restore some kind of routine. School will be routine, especially since I'm interested in the subject. Encouraged by the ability to strengthen the immune system, I go to the Wingate Institute to enroll in naturopathy studies. I commit to four years of classes, three times a week. I wait with excitement and a little apprehension for the first day. Apprehension? Maybe because I won't be able to hold out for so many hours in class. Maybe I'll feel pain and get tired, maybe I won't be able to absorb so much material.

At night I tell Gadi: "You know, enrolling in the classes gives me hope, a kind of horizon. I can picture myself at a clinic in a few more years, consulting patients".

Gadi looks at me and smiles. I know he's glad to hear it. Sometimes it seems that he believes I'll succeed in this quest more than I do.

"I think it's great that you're going to school. You like this subject and the classes will be very interesting to you," he says.

CHAPTER 5

Deciding to Start Living

"Sometimes the fear of death causes people to die."

- Epicurus (Greek philosopher)

Today I am very sad. As I walk down the street I feel the sorrow filling my body from head to toe. I tug a large canvas to an area where I can paint. After I choose a thick brush and two colors - brown and white - I begin to fill the canvas with no plans or intentions, covering the drawing that was there before, just to spread the paint. I remind myself to avoid self-criticism regarding the aesthetics of the result. And yet, I notice a part of my painting that looks beautiful to me. "Don't stick to it, just move on", I tell myself. I play loud music, which makes my hands move quickly. "Enjoy the sadness, don't run away from it." I etch my death in the color of earth brown, painting and writing at the same time. The music motivates me. I get up and go bring the video camera in order to film myself painting and dancing. A smile stretches between my cheeks.

In the afternoon I drive to Beit Shemesh, to the most religious and the extreme part of the city. I dress accordingly. I normally wear a wig anyway, but now I have to wear long pants even though it's over 35 degrees outside. I choose a closed shirt with sleeves. I'm not used to this look. I change the sleeved shirt to a gray tank top. Now I am more satisfied. I put the sleeved shirt, which I've never worn, in the 'hand-me-down' bag. The clinic is only a few meters away from where I parked my car, but the number of eyes following me every time I go there is greater than the number of meters I have to pass. As soon as I drive into the neighborhood many eyes gaze at my bare shoulders. I take a scarf with me to cover them. As I wear flip-flops on my feet, I wonder if exposed ankles attract attention. I go to the health care clinic to meet Yona Luria, a medical psychologist, hypnotist, and guided imagery therapist. I sit in his room with the scarf on my shoulders and feel a hot flash.

The yarmulke on his head is knitted, which means he's not from the neighborhood.

"I'm feeling a hot flash, is it okay to take off the scarf?"

"Of course. I only work here, I don't live here."

"Do you have any experience with cancer patients? Any successes?"

"I work in the oncology department at Hadassah Hospital. I only work with people who combine conventional medicine with guided imagery, so I can't attribute any success we had to guided imagery alone. What I can say is that the doctors told me they witnessed some very unusual cases as a result of my work."

"I want to be an unusual case. I want it to work on me. I want you to help me. And I think you're the right person."

Luria smiles and asks: "What do you want to work on today?"

"I want you to help me imagine that I am reducing the tumor. Help me visualize the body's healing powers reaching the area of the tumor and reducing it".

Luria directs his blue eyes straight into mine.

"Is there a specific image you want me to address? Maybe something you especially like to do?" "I love working in the garden. I love dancing, eating, cooking".

I know from various articles that guided imagery can act directly against the hormonal effect of stress in my life and give me a sense of control over my thoughts. A friend of a friend recommended him and he even works with my health care provider. He manages to hypnotize me. When he speaks I sink into my body, aware of the fact that I can't get out of this conscious slumber without his guidance. I record our meetings so I can continue to practice at home. I close my eyes and he begins to guide my imagination. Within a few seconds I sink into deep, unfamiliar tranquility.

"You can take a deep breath," Luria instructs me, "breathe in through your nose and slowly breathe out through the mouth... find the right position... find a position in which the body is relaxed but steady. The back is straight, dignifying itself... excellent... In the exercise we can enter a pleasant state of relaxation, comfort, and tranquility. All the muscles are relaxed... All the muscles are released, calm, and loose, released, calm and serene..."

That's it. I'm already there, deep inside the body, or high up above it.

My hands and ankles are loose and relaxed...

Fifty minutes of magic pass by. Inspired by the environment, I thank the almighty for introducing me to this man. I put the scarf on my shoulders and leave the building. I get strong gazes outside. Nevertheless, I walk into a nearby supermarket, sensing the alienation. I'm in my own country, but I don't belong here.

The drive home takes an hour, but feels very short for me. On both sides of the road between Jerusalem and Tel Aviv, the nature bursts into my soul. This weekly drive takes me, even as I remain in the car, to nature, to the barren hills, the green mountains, the bushes dotting the exposed hills to the east. A large tractor collects the dried corn seedlings. On the radio, singer Yehoram Gaon chants the lyrics by Haim Hefer about Jerusalem:

"To you, Jerusalem

I go all my days...

"Have you noticed," Luria asked, "that you used the terms 'growth' (tumor) and 'the kids growing up' when describing your disappointment in the way you raised them and linked between the disease and your view of yourself as a mother? Our subconscious can grow tumors due to worry, and equally so, it also has the ability to reduce tumors", Luria told me at the end of the meeting.

I feel that I didn't raise my children the way I wanted to. I wanted to be perfect: quiet and relaxed about the kids and about life. This is perhaps the biggest disappointment in my life - I was not the mother I imagined I could be. In the end, I wasn't even the spouse I wanted to be. And what's happening now?

"The most beautiful and true ideologies get a little messy when they hit the ground", Luria says.

It is the days of Operation Protective Edge. I'm nervous, and at the end of the meeting with Luria we hear a "bang". I sit up. Did a rocket just fall? Luria remains calm, but any noise that sounds like the beginning of a siren stiffens my muscles.

My ears get clogged during the descent to Tel Aviv. The radio announcer requests that we pull over if we hear a siren, get out of the car, and only go back inside after ten minutes. This already happened to me twice.

In my father's final years, he loved Yehoram Gaon. The two forged a close and unusual friendship. They adored each other. Yehoram admired the pilot who taught him how to fly and overcome his fears, and my father admired Yehoram's sense of humor and love of humanity. There was very little room in this story for us family members, and after my father died of stomach cancer, the relationship with Yehoram dissolved and only the memory of love remained. Whenever I hear him sing or speak I remember the strong bond they had.

How badly do we want to live?

We are afraid of death. Do we want to live? How badly do we want to live? How do we live? The answers to these questions seem to have an impact on the arrest of the disease for long periods of time. Almost everyone I spoke to had 'something' important enough to keep them going. Susie wants to continue to participate in triathlons in memory of her daughter and was even willing to do it in crutches. 74-year-old Bracha also trains every day for the triathlon. When diagnosed with cancer, Susannah asked herself if she wants to live. Rachel Bornstein got out of bed one day and decided to start living, in small steps, day by day.

Beliefs May Become Biology

Towards the end of the last century, I came across a book that changed my view of the world and inspired me to ponder the possibility that there is more than meets the eye in this universe. At the time, my friend Nurit Levinson had just translated the book "Reinventing the Body, Resurrecting the Soul" by Dr. Deepak Chopra and gave me the Hebrew version to read. For the first time, I was exposed to what would one day become the path to my healing: the biochemistry of the body is the product of consciousness. This was a revolutionary notion in the early 1990s. Twenty years have passed since then, and although more people are open to these ideas, the vast majority still don't know who Dr. Chopra is or pay any attention to the link between faith and biology. Dr. Chopra has published several books about mind-body medicine, primarily claiming that beliefs can influence biology. Throughout his career has met Chopra cancer patients who were completely cured despite being considered terminally ill. Chopra believes that healing is a mental process, rather than a physical one. In his book Quantum Healing (Modan Publishing), Chopra writes: "If a patient can trigger the healing process from within, that is the cure for cancer." Chopra argues that the healing occurs when there is radical internal change, such that removes fears and doubts in addition to eliminating the disease.

If so, does it really matter what I eat? I met a few cured patients who didn't follow any specific diet or take dietary supplements and yet were cured or had lived for many years with the disease. My inner voice keeps whispering to me: Will one, two, three, or ten cookies really inhibit my recovery?

Will my nutrition cause the cancer to retreat or thrive? The cake in the refrigerator is speaking to me. Just one bite, how bad can it be? I placate its pleas and take it out of the fridge without letting it out of my sight. I start drooling already, excited for the taste I'm about to experience with my tongue. I eat one piece quickly, and then another, and another… as if the speed diminishes the sin… It's so delicious.

Is it possible, perhaps, or not, that my fate is predetermined? Could there be some master plan that I am a part of and the future is known or written somewhere? The only plan I want to follow is one in which I go on living, raise my kids, enjoy nature, enjoy Gadi, travel, work, read, paint, write, and so on. However, I can't imagine any future and that bothers me.

To advance my recovery, I still try to go to sleep early in the evening. But I still roll in bed every time and can't fall asleep before midnight. I read in several places that lack of sleep is one of the hallmarks of cancer. I must resolve the issue of sleep. And the ability to see a future… I write it down as a topic for my next meeting with Luria.

I currently face two challenges. First, I need to stop the tumor. Secondly, I must find a solution to the damage done to my digestive system. In both of these areas there is no magic pill for me and I search in different directions for solutions that will provide initial relief and eventual remedy. I don't rule out anything, including Chopra's suggestion that beliefs may affect biological processes. Just when I am convinced that my conversations with cured patients will soon expose me to something that could benefit my health, I come across the story of Rachel Burstein. Her story substantiates the notion that healing relies on faith. At a certain point during the harsh treatment she underwent, Rachel decided that she was getting better. She changed her inner belief and despite the doctor's gloomy prediction, she found the inner forces to announce the healing process. Could it be possible to recover by power of decision? Rachel's case encourages me to pay greater attention to my thoughts, beliefs, and feelings.

Rachel Burstein
Metastatic melanoma - mental strength and conviction –
40 years after diagnosis

"Every day I made one more step. I believed in my abilities and realized I know what's best for me".

-Rachel Burstein

Rachel Burstein had a beauty mark that developed into melanoma after spending many hours in the sun during her military service. By the time it was diagnosed, the melanoma had spread to the armpit lymph nodes. Rachel was only a young woman when she began chemotherapy, with no end in sight.

"I was slowly languishing. I stopped eating. I was twenty years old and all I could do was lie in bed", says Rachel. "I felt my immune system weakening by the week. I caught any disease I was around. Most of the time I lay in bed helpless. After three years of chemotherapy, before receiving further treatment, I suffered from kidney failure and had a fever of 104 degrees. I told the doctor I can't stand the treatments any longer and asked to postpone the coming treatment. The doctor explained that despite my physical condition I must get treatment, or else I'll have no chance of surviving for more than six months. But I knew I couldn't go on like this without any quality of life, so in spite of the doctor's harsh words, I made a unilateral decision to halt the treatment. I decided to stop lying in bed waiting for death. I told myself that from now on I would get out of bed every day and make even the slightest improvement compared to the previous day. Every day I would advance in one area. At that time, I vomited everything I ate and suffered from unbearable stomach pain. There was no internet back then, no online support groups or dietitians who could come to my home and guide me. By intuition, I started making shakes to drink and gradually, step by step, started walking again. I slowly regained the audacity that characterized me before the illness was diagnosed, and suddenly I started to enjoy life. I knew I was done with chemotherapy, no matter what. Forty years have passed since then. I think the decisive factor in my recovery was that I listened to my body and did what's best for it. Every day I made one more step. I believed in my abilities and realized I know what's best for me. It was a big gamble, but since I was in bed all day and enduring chemotherapy, life wasn't worth anything anyway. I was totally calm and kept repeating the following sentence in my mind: 'I must win' - because it's my nature. I had a strong conviction in my ability to heal myself.

It took another three years before I dared to say that I'm completely healthy. I realized that I have the strength to wage the battles I believe in. I recommend that patients trust their own abilities and listen to themselves. They should choose what's best for them from a variety of options, whether conventional or alternative".

I ask to see my future

At a meeting this morning with Luria I ask to see my future.

I take off my shoes and sit cross-legged on a chair in front of him. I close my eyes confidently. Luria guides me:

"You may sit comfortably for this exercise, which will provide release and help you find the correct posture... Easy, relaxed, and stable. At first you'll hear noises and sounds from outside. Slowly take a few deep breaths... Gradually focus inwardly. At this point, your entire consciousness is inside the body, cut off from the room and from where we are.

All the muscles are released, relaxed... Your thoughts are directed inward, more attentive and focused only on breathing. The air goes in and out... You see something in front of you that symbolizes time - a clock or calendar or anything else that represents time for you. When you see it with your own eyes, signal with a small nod... If you focus carefully you will notice that you managed to reach another time. Onward, to the future. Perhaps it's the same hour as now, but if you pay attention to the year and the month, you will see the progress of time."

I imagine it's the year 2024 and I am 61...

"Take a deep breath and let the air out," Luria continues, "for your own sake, you can focus on the new time you've reached... In front of you is the book you wrote. I wonder what title you eventually chose for it, and what design you picked for the cover. As you look inward you can retrospectively recall the mental strength and the persistence that helped you reach yourself..."

As he speaks, I see myself sitting in a large, bright studio in front of a large window facing an open view of the sea, or mountains, or fields. Transparent white curtains flap in the windows. The apartment is painted in white and sandy colors. I'm sitting at the desk facing the view. To my right is a pile of books I've written in the last ten years. One book each year. Now I have an image of the future.

---※●※---

In the year 400 B.C. Socrates said: "There is no disease in our body except for what's in our mind". According to an article from 1977on the major trends in psychiatric care, studies show that all illnesses have a psychosomatic origin*.

---※●※---

*Major trends in psychosomatic medicine: the psychiatrist's evolving role in medicine. Hoyle Leigh, M.D .; and Morton f. Reiser, M.D. ann internmed. 1977; 87 (2): 233-239. doi: 10.7326/0003-4819-87-2-233

---※●※---

Is love energy?

Newton claimed that everything has energy. Is love energy?
Dr. Candace Pert argued that love triggers and releases proteins that stimulate the immune system. How does one strengthen and develop his inner love? Ricky the therapist recommends that I be constantly thankful and see only the good in everything. In the Yamima classes I attend once a week, they talk about seeing the good inside me. The Ho'oponopono method from Hawaii recommends saying "I love you, sorry, and thank you" to your inner child whenever you experience stress and worry in life. So I make sure to feel love, which in turn releases the relevant proteins.

---※●※---

Who will help me? What else can be done?

"Anything that has the power to heal us doesn't seem too difficult or expensive."
-Michel de Montaigne (French philosopher)

Someone slammed the door downstairs. I immediately become alert. Should I go down and check? Why should I? They'll manage without me. Probably. I bet they will. Mom is busy. Mom has her own things she wants to do (it's important for my health to set boundaries).

Despite all the lists, walks, juices, and shakes, for some months now I've had a hard time trying to resume the lifestyle that would promote my health. The strong stomach pain and nausea have disabled my physical strength greatly reduced the hours of physical and mental clarity. For several months now I've been bearing the responsibility I took on myself in the quest to find stories of survivors. Every story I hear helps me collect myself again. Following my talk with Avner I've been gobbling up material on the subject, both online and through books. The book "Life Over Cancer" by Dr. Keith Block follows me everywhere now. It's the best book I've read so far that presents a holistic approach for cancer treatment. Reading it is better than many of the counseling sessions I had with alternative therapists. This book makes me think about those meetings and wonder what I got out of them. What new information did the therapists provide? Last week I went to a Chinese acupuncturist. "He's a world class professional" I was told, "you have to go see him, he's amazing". He greeted me but was unavailable to see me. Ten minutes into the meeting, he apologized and left to meet a visitor from overseas. I waited for him in the room for fifteen minutes, trying to meditate in the meantime. Eventually the therapist returned, apologized, asked a few questions, and checked my pulse. He prescribed a herbal mixture for me. Do you want me to treat you with acupuncture?

As if doing me a favor, he pricked me in two spots and sent me to his secretary at the reception desk to pay over a thousand shekels.

It took me a few days to realize that what I felt there was not random – why was I referred to a competent person who only sits and listens to me for fifteen minutes, doesn't say even one word of advice and only gives me some prescription for stomach pain? What about the cancer? Even the supplements he sells by the secretary can be bought by anyone, you don't need an appointment for that. So what do I do with this? To alleviate my bothersome thoughts, I decide to deviate from my habit (a very good thing to do as a cancer patient) and search for his email. I'll send him a letter. Okay. In my writing I am more guarded and protected than when talking on the phone. Unfortunately, I don't receive any reply to my letter.

For their treatments, the therapists I saw charged from 170 to 1,000 shekels. In the last week I've had internal discussions about the number of treatments and the sums of money. The expenses are piling up. A simple calculation shows that I have to spend a hundred thousand shekels a year on treatments and supplements: guided imagery, healing, Chinese acupuncture, Japanese acupuncture, yoga, tai chi, nutritionist, naturopath. If I were told there's a treatment that has a 50% chance of saving my life and costs a hundred thousand shekels - would I take it? I think it's easier to pay for such treatment than to decide to quit your job and invest in various treatments that aren't guaranteed to succeed.

What do the cured patients do? Some have quit their job to spend time searching for a cure and started savings plans for that purpose. Dr. Amit Henin said: "I had nothing to lose except for lots of money." Susannah Marcus told herself that unless she lives she wouldn't need the money anyway.

When the cured patients decided that they are determined to get well, time and money were not an issue. Quitting your job allows you to focus physically and mentally on your recovery, but hinders the financial capacity to support the process. This is certainly a difficult dilemma.

I search for another way, something that comes from within and doesn't rely so much on external consultants. Something that speaks to my inner instinct. There is knowledge within me, there is a cure within me. To get to this place I need to do something. The big question is – what.

I hear and read that those who transition to a lifestyle that makes them happier and more peaceful have greater chances of survival. I wonder what I haven't done yet. What part inside of me is so dormant, compressed within the body and wanting to be free? I have no idea. Will it help if I isolate myself for three days in the attic or the desert? Will it make things clearer?

I left all my therapists, packed the juice machine and yoga mat, and headed south to Mitzpe Ramon. A place for some time off in front of the open spaces, the hills, the caressing wind, and the sun disappearing behind the mountain curves. For five days, I did mostly nothing. The landscape seeped into my body, fostering a sense of inner space.

In Mitzpe Ramon during the afternoon, the wind tempers the heat as the sun makes its way to the horizon. The desert spans in front of me. I stare at the curves of the grayish mountains, my eyes looking outward, my heart looking inward, sitting cross-legged on the desert soil. I want to acquire new habits right here and now. Without any agenda, I look at the mountains. The sky is almost white. I'm waiting for an answer: what else should I do to improve my health and balance the energy of life. Habits, lifestyle. Based on my conversations with cured patients and therapists, and the books I've read, I realize that I need to find the healing power within me. I need to go inside to find my own path.

Five days in Mitzpe Ramon weren't enough for me. I was just starting to get a sense of the place. I came back feeling that I need something more extreme and secluded. I still haven't found what I'm looking for. I feel there's something out there that hasn't yet reached me. There is information that I haven't yet discovered, or hasn't yet surfaced.

Foods considered anticancer - some effective against specific cancers

This information is based on research and is reviewed in complementary medicine studies, but not taught in conventional medical schools. I present the information by types of substances found in the fruits and vegetables:

Substance	Found in Foods	Activity
Pectin	Citrus fruits and apples	Prevents communication between oxygen cells Prevents adhesion between tumor cells. Prevents metastasis
Rutin and Hesperidin	Citrus fruits	Natural antioxidant, anti-inflammatory and anticancer substances
Quercitin	Black tea, red wine, onions, tomatoes, apples, potatoes, grapes	Highly effective antioxidant that can reduce the incidence of heart disease and cancer
Limonene	Found in peels of citrus fruit	Known for its anticancer activity
	Apple peel	High intensity antioxidants and anticancer substances
Lycopene	Tomato, red pepper, cherry, watermelon	Reduces risk of prostate and breast cancer
Sulfur Compounds	Onion	Reduces risk of colon, esophagus, and breast cancer
Betalain	Beet	Protects the liver from damage. Effective antioxidant, and effective in combating heart disease and cancer

Cruciferous family	Cabbage, cauliflower, broccoli, Brussels sprouts, Chinese cabbage, turnips, kohlrabi, radish, Horseradish, mustard, and watercress	Special assortment of anticancer substances
Indole-3-Carbinol	Cruciferous vegetables	Especially helps to protect against breast cancer It has a unique mechanism that reduces the harmful form of estrogen in the body. **Those who have problems in the thyroid gland - must cook the cruciferous vegetables first**. The cruciferous vegetables contain goitrogens that may reduce the absorption of iodine, resulting in insufficient activity. These materials decompose when cooked.
D-glucaric acid	Cruciferous vegetables	Helps to neutralize carcinogens such as nitrosamines contained in sausage and smoked meat.
Carotenoids: lycopene, beta-carotene, alpha-carotene, lutein and zeaxanthin	Orange, red, and green vegetables	Prevent cancer through antioxidant activity
Beta Carotene	Carrots, tomatoes, beets, spinach, oranges, **red peppers** (also contains 20 types of carotenoids – antioxidants)	

Alpha Carotene	Carrots (strengthens the immune system with its high concentration of carotenoids. Fights against free radicals), bananas, beans, oranges	
Lutein	Lettuce, broccoli, spinach, beets, green beans, potatoes, oranges, buckwheat	
Zeaxanthin	Peach, potato, orange, spinach	
Flavonoids (also called bioflavonoids): Rutin, quercetin, hesperidin, spinacin	Onions, green beans, apples wood, green tea, broccoli, cherry and broad beans (high concentration in the vegetable's peel), cauliflower, eggplant, beets	Anti-carcinogens - anticancer
Selenium: consume small amounts. Not related to the Solanaceae family	Brazil nuts, not more than two per day	Powerful antioxidant - anticancer, anti heart disease

Or

Metastatic breast cancer spread to the bones -
Internal decision to heal – 1 year after diagnosis

"Within all this commotion, I felt my brain ordering my body to heal.

– Or

While still in advanced stages of pregnancy with her second daughter, Or found out she had breast cancer with numerous metastases in the pelvis and spine and a tumor 4.5 cm large in the right breast. "The PET-CT results showed a completely porous pelvis. It looked like I had faced a firing squad. At the time, the doctors weren't sure how I was even standing", she says. "I carried a pregnancy in very difficult conditions since my limp was misdiagnosed as an orthopedic issue. Though I'm accustomed to being in complete control, I started needing nursing already during my pregnancy. In an emergency procedure the baby was delivered a week early by Caesarean section. I couldn't carry her anymore due to my total physical collapse. A few days after the cesarean section I underwent 14 radiotherapy sessions that weakened me even more. I slept 14 hours a day for a period of six months, while my husband and my family quit their jobs for several months to raised our two daughters. During my waking hours I'd sit in the yard, overlooking the enchanting view from our small town. Within all this commotion and physical helplessness, I felt my brain ordering my body to heal, to recover mentally. I felt I had no other choice. I decided I was going to stay here and I had a strong sense that I would beat the harsh odds. But I also knew this would take a lot of work, persistence, and patience. Even though I am secular, I prayed and others prayed for me. I truly believed in myself and my ability to heal, perhaps because of my familiarity with the world of medicine and the knowledge that there are exceptional patients in every field of medical statistics, those in the edges of the normal distribution. I decided that I would overcome the illness. I had several visions, and in one of them I saw a master in China who could cure me. That was one of the reasons I started practicing qigong several hours a day."

Or quit her job as a project manager and medical equipment engineer and dedicated herself to recovering.

"I decided to channel all my skills as project manager to the healing process, making work plans and realizing that the deadlines may be flexible," she says with a smile. "I decided to put my analytical mind aside for a few months and let the body's magical healing powers take over for a change."

On the recommendation of therapist Sharon Bar-Gil, Or began taking dietary supplements. She also enrolled in qigong classes at the Broshim Campus, tried acupuncture, added to her diet green juices and pomegranate juice every day, and started eating organic food. Or goes on a walk four times a week and practices Pilates and yoga, each twice a week. She also jumps on a trampoline every day. Despite all the chaos and difficulty, she tries to live with her family as usual and makes sure to keep her sense of humor and smile.

Five months after diagnosis, as Or maintains the lifestyle described above, the PET- CT test showed a remission of all the tumors, with no absorption in the tumor in the right breast.

Or's story doesn't meet the Ta'atzumot Association's criteria for "specially cured patients" because it hasn't yet been five years since the metastases disappeared. Still, the disappearance of the bone metastases is unusual and remarkable, and everything Or does inspires and strengthens me.

CHAPTER 6

Dramatic Change in Lifestyle

"The doctor of the future will give no medication, but will interest his patients in the care of the human frame, diet and in the cause and prevention of disease".

-Thomas Alva Edison

Shaike Klein
Prostate cancer – nutrition, sports, and supplements – 4 years after diagnosis

"I returned home from the doctor's appointment depressed and discouraged, realizing I must do something to stop the cancer".

-Shaike Klein

Friday, eight thirty in the morning. I wait for Shaike at the entrance to the building where he lives. The building's glass door opens. I was wrong again – judging by the voice I heard on the phone, I pictured an old, slim man. But instead, I am greeted by a tanned, burly, and handsome man. Shaike quickly tells me that he didn't always look like this. Thanks to the diet and exercise he maintains, he shed twenty kilos from his body. I know how that feels. In the past year I too gladly got rid of twenty kilos. We walk together southward, crossing the bridge between Kfar Saba and Hod Hasharon, and arrive at the fields of Hod Hasharon.

"They just planted strawberries. Look how they separate and scatter the strawberries. In that field over there they were growing sweet potatoes, which were picked only a few days ago. I walk here every day, rain or shine. If it rains I take a raincoat. The farmers know me by now. I know the dogs. Feel the air and see the view. Here are the chicken coops, over there are the sweet potatoes. Every morning I see this landscape, and in the winter I can even see snow on the mountaintops of Samaria. The smells here - that's life - remind me of my rural childhood. This year summer is pleasant and I don't have to wake up so early."

"For years I would regularly check my PSA levels[14]", Shaike says. "Once a year I'd get results showing normal protein levels. But in 2011, there was an upward deviation. A biopsy I had undergone revealed cancer cells. The first urologist I met sounded like he was talking gibberish. I couldn't understand what he was saying. He didn't tell me that I have cancer, but rather sent me to consult with other doctors. I went to get a second opinion. In this meeting the doctor showed me the graph illustrating the rise in PSA levels and explained that this must be addressed. I became interested and started investigating my condition in order to better understand it. The more I read the more depressed I became. I wasn't happy about any of the treatment options. I thought it would be better to die than to experience the treatments and their effects on the body. When I said so to the doctor, his response was: Unless you get treated, you have ten years to live at most.'

We cross the fields and enter the neighborhoods of Hod Hasharon. We make a stop at the outdoor fitness park, where Shaike strengthens his muscles and does qigong exercises.

"I returned home from the doctor's appointment depressed and discouraged, realizing I must do something to stop the cancer. I continued my research online and read more books. I read about the many foods that are considered anti-cancerous. I went to Kibbutz Alumot to study the principles of healthy nutrition. For a whole year I faithfully applied everything I learned, but the PSA levels kept rising. Even after two years of nutritional asceticism, they continued to rise. I went to see the oncologist assigned by my health care provider - Dr. Ruth Laufer. She encouraged me to keep doing what I'm doing and then referred me to another urologist. I followed Ruth's recommendations and met this urologist. When I told him

---

[14] Testing the substance of PSA - prostate specific antigen - is a useful indicator for detecting prostate cancer.

what I was doing, he shouted and hurled accusations at me. I felt like a little kid being scolded. 'What do you think you're doing?' the urologist shouted at me, 'this is reckless. Do you want to die? You better do something quickly.' The doubts started surfacing after my encounter with this urologist. To put them at rest, I decided to undergo another biopsy."

We take the elevator up to Shaike's apartment, where his wife is waiting with breakfast comprised of fruit mostly. Shaike shows me the important spices and herbs planted in large pots on the balcony of his house. There's even a Moringa tree there.

"I awaited the results in great suspense," Shaike continues. "Despite the high PSA levels, according to the biopsy results I was cancer-free. I realized that what I was doing was actually helping me.

A year ago I changed the pill I take in order to shrink my prostate (a pill unrelated to cancer) and only then did the PSA levels drop. Just to be safe, I did another MRI, which showed that everything was clean."

What does Shaike Do?

Sports

He walks every morning for an hour and a half in the fields outside his home. Never goes to the gym. During the walks he takes breaks to do aerobic exercises. He practices qigong occasionally.

Diet

- No white foods diet – avoids sugar, flours, milk, cheese, meats, poultry, sweet juices, and fried food.
- Eats lots of fruits and vegetables - not necessarily organic.
- In the first two years he also avoided eating eggs and fish.
- **Dietary supplements**: Omega 3 and Vitamin D.

Haya Meron
Thyroid cancer - Kingston Clinic method and energy therapy –
12 years after diagnosis

"My goal is to turn the disease into a chronic illness that I can live with and still maintain a good quality of life. I make sure to be constantly aware of healthy and proper nutrition, keeping a relaxed mind and joy of life

-Haya Meron

They say thyroid cancer is hopeful. Once the thyroid gland is surgically removed, you undergo radiotherapy and then forget about it. Haya Meron thought so too, but ten months after her thyroid gland was removed, the PET-CT scan showed additional tumors in the base of the gland (the area from which the gland was removed), the lungs, and the spine. As the oncologist and surgeon fervently deliberated over the proper treatment for Haya, she sat at home feeling lost, but not for long. Haya describes herself as relentless. She contacted a spiritual communicator, who recommended that she change her diet with the help of Jerusalem therapist Eli Strauss and go to therapy, not with a psychologist, but in some alternative way.

Shortly afterwards she quit her job and found herself at home, at age 45, with 100% disability.

"I cut off ties with the hospital and persisted only in doing ultrasound and blood marker tests. Therapist Eli Strauss instructed me to follow the diet of the 'Kingston Clinic' method, and the spiritual communicator, whom I visited once a week in Yodfat, helped me with my breathing and provided emotional support. For three years I strictly followed the method and was committed to the treatments. Another test showed that the tumors in the neck remained unchanged while the other tumors diminished.

In 2008, after four years of strict diet, healthy lifestyle, and a lot of guided imagery, I did another PET-CT scan. The results revealed a 4-cm tumor in the head. I was referred to a conventional internist who treats cancer patients energetically. I contacted this doctor and she was determined that the tumor was not cancerous and that it would pass within a month. Hadassah Hospital urged me to remove the tumor because they feared it might be metastasizing. They prepared me for a long and complex surgery, but after the operation the doctor told me that when he opened the skull the tumor almost sprang up to him from the head. The tumor turned out to be benign.

My goal is to turn my condition into a chronic illness that I can live with while maintaining a good quality of life. I make sure to eat healthy and remain calm and joyful. This gives me the foundation to continue. I'll probably never be completely healthy, but who knows anything about health anyway... I try to eat as healthy as I can. Today I eat one fruit a day, usually an organic apple; a lot of vegetables, both raw and cooked; eggs (every other day); and hard buffalo cheese. I don't touch milk, yogurt, or soft cheeses. I occasionally eat tuna, nuts, and almonds.

My greatest sin is drinking coffee with soymilk once a day. It's very difficult for me to quit. I continue to follow the Kingston Clinic method with occasional updates suggested by the doctor who treats me energetically. And I still undergo enemas under the Gerson Therapy and take flaxseed from the Budwig diet. I sense what's right and best for me and act accordingly.

At any given moment I can choose what to think

Author and spiritual guide Louise L. Hay taught me that I can choose what to think at any moment. I can look at my thoughts, identify the ones that aren't good for me, and mechanically replace them. So I can replace a thought like "I will die soon and my kids will be left with no one" with "It is possible that I will get better. I want to get better and I'm doing everything I can to get better." The first time I replaced these sentences it seemed very artificial to me. But by the second and third time, I felt a pleasant sense of comfort spreading through my body. "It is possible that I will be cured". Wow... this is good news. For me the most revolutionary idea was born after I read Hay's very reassuring book: "You Can Heal Your Life", from which I took the sentence: "I deserve to be healthy". This sentence helped me get rid of the guilt I was feeling for tearing my family apart. This often led me to believe that the disease is my punishment. Another statement was: "I'm getting better, the liver tumor stopped". I started saying that before I could even stop this growth. Another sentence I memorize was: "What else should I know? Everything I need to know will be revealed to me." I consider these sentences a kind of mental programming. This way I programmed the brain to find a solution and stop the tumor in the liver. The solution came in the form of targeted radiation on the liver. This option wasn't even proposed to me. I actually brought it to my treating doctors' attention after searching for information in various sources. The phrase "What else should I know?" guides me all the time:

I listen, record, and manage my treatment program and my appointments. In fact, I conduct a private research, examining information from the internet, books, cured patients, therapists, conferences, and lectures. Any piece of advice I get is written down in a neat chart that gets updated periodically with new information. Here's an example of my chart from October (see next page):

1 – Finding Solution to Stomach Pain	2 – Stopping the Cancer
Pressure chamber for repairing radiation damage (echocardiography, chest radiography)	Examining tumor removal surgery - Dr. Ben Nun
Gallbladder removal surgery	Anti-cancer formula from Sharon Bar Gil and Shoham
Nutrition – gallstones treatment – Meirav Broshim Aromatherapy	Emotional work with Vered Gliksman
Hericium mushroom – restores nerves - two teaspoons per day for two months. Read articles	Mushrooms – strengthening immune system
Crowdsourcing website – ask about solution for stomach	Biological drug + Famera – every day
General Physical Maintenance	**Appointment with Oncologist**
Acupuncture - Tal - Motke – Complementary medicine from health care provider - set appointments	Show MRI to gallbladder expert
Sports, walking, trampoline, brushing body, hot/ cold showers, outdoor hikes	Increase cannabis dosage to 60 grams. Fax license to department. Set appointment for PET-CT
Meditation	Strengthening immune system with Neupogen and low dose of **Antonio bru** chemotherapy
Acupuncture - Tal – Shiatsu Motke – Complementary medicine from health care provider - set appointments	Show MRI to gallbladder expert
Doctors and therapists to contact	**Doctors to contact**
Gastro expert in Germany	Specialist stool and saliva tester
Dr. Dayan – colibiogen – for restoring flora damaged by colibiogen radiotherapy Samuelov – Guberman – Efrat Broida Form 29 C	
Eti Bracha – aromatherapy – for gallbladder	
Tests	**Tests**
Helicobacter – November. Intestinal parasites - none	Chest radiography

Candida celiac gastrointestinal disease	Echocardiography
Desirable Food	**In the Box**
Dietary fiber and lactic acid foods such as yogurt, sour milk, kefir, sauerkraut or fermented grain support and maintain healthy intestinal flora	Order Denosumab Prescription for Microlet Permission for special food
Consult with staff at hospice	
Foods I can and should eat	**Foods I can't eat**
Skim milk - goat – antacid that travels to the intestines Soured milk - goat Yogurt - goat Lean and soft meat Fish Egg protein Full grain Vegetables Artichoke + leaves – drink cooking water Jerusalem artichoke Boiled fruit Fruit juices, soft cheese - goats Almonds and walnuts	Fried foods Ice cream Spicy foods Alcohol Seasoned foods Butter - only a little cream cheese Yolk Avocado Olives Legumes – try every once in a while
Remedial Foods for Gallbladder	
Potato and cabbage juice - rehabilitates mucous membranes Sunflower seeds Bitter leaves	Chocolate Melon Watermelon Alcohol
Vegetables Cucumber Miso Root vegetable soup - Jerusalem artichoke, celery, parsley, beets, Astragalus root, ginger, turmeric powder, endive, leafy green vegetables Cook Astragalus, ginger, and cinnamon for 10 minutes Aloe vera juice	Fatty pastries
	Guberman suggests having lentil soup with sprouts, buckwheat, oatmeal and bone marrow

Beliefs and thoughts affect the bo

Our beliefs lie within us, setting the tone for everything that happens at the center stage, influencing our thoughts and actions. If I believe I'm no good at something, my chances of accomplishing it are smaller than when I do something with confidence. The last sentence is easy for us to accept. But does the belief that I will soon die of cancer actually hasten my death? Or alternatively, will my faith in my ability to overcome it strengthen my body and immune system? It's easy for me to accept that faith also affects my self-esteem and expectations, but impacting my chances of survival? Many curious researchers studied this field exactly. In the eighties, an American psychologist named David Spiegel examined 86 women with metastatic breast cancer who had exhausted conventional treatment. Half of the women received weekly psychiatric therapy, which included self-hypnosis. Although Spiegel wanted to prove that such treatment has no positive effect on the disease, the results suggested otherwise. The women who underwent therapy survived longer than those who did not. This was not the only study that yielded such results. Another study conducted at Yale University in the United States in the late eighties found that breast cancer spread faster among women who repressed their personality, had trouble expressing anger, and felt helpless.

Dr. Bruce H. Lipton, a biologist specializing in cell research, examined the mechanism by which cells control their physical condition. He discovered that the processes in the cell are governed by the physical and energetic environment, not by the genes in the cell. In other words, each cell has a consciousness and is influenced by its environment.

The biological study describes signals that prompt processes in the cell fluid and affect the cell's activity, survival, or lethality. Lipton sees this as proof that our thoughts affect the body's cells biochemically, and concludes that conventional medicine and physical treatment are insufficient for healing.

Lipton's study fits under the category of 'epigenetics'. The literal meaning of the word is - above genetics. Epigenetics is revolutionizing the perception of the role of genes. If previously the accepted view was that genes control all processes in the body, epigenetics examine how signals from the environment affect cell function. In his book "The Biology of Belief", Lipton described the effect of emotion, faith, and consciousness on the expression of the genetic code, thus concluding that changing our beliefs will lead to biological change in our physical body.

So I immediately wonder. Do I express anger? Do I feel helpless? Do I repress my personality? I probably do, in some cases. What can I do about it? It's time to take care of myself, and not on my own. It's time to find a therapist who can help me.

Michal realized this after seeing the PET-CT scan showing her body full of metastases. She turned to therapist Vered Gliksman and did this important work with her, along with all the other things she did, and the metastases disappeared. I read Michal's story several times and I speak with Vered. My conversation with her leads me to make a decision, even though she lives far away from me. I want to start working with her.

Michal
Metastatic Breast Cancer - self-healing –
7 years after diagnosis

"Today I know that it's possible to be fully cured of cancer and that my recovery is up to me. One of the major difficulties in the healing process was dealing with the doubt that it's even possible".

-Michal

Michal (alias) was 35 years old when she was first diagnosed with breast cancer. On her doctors' recommendation and in accordance with the medical protocol, she underwent surgery and was treated with chemotherapy, followed by radiotherapy.

Later she received an anti-hormonal drug, which she took until she got pregnant six years after diagnosis. Bravely, she gave birth to her daughter. When her daughter was one year old, Michal discovered metastases of the disease in her spine and ribs.

And once again she faced the ordeal of constant testing, waiting, analyzing the results, and thinking about the next move. Imaging tests and other tests revealed that she has additional metastases in the right lung.

This kind of harsh prognosis generally has predictable results. The statistics placed before the oncologists in this situation are not good predictors. It's quite similar to the medical situation I face while writing these lines.

Michal asked for chemotherapy and even proposed pneumonectomy, hoping to prolong her life and see her daughter grow up.

The conventional approach is that once the tumor metastasizes, it must be subject to systemic treatment that affects the whole body, instead of removing metastases delicately in a pinpoint procedure. Estrogen plays a major role in hormone-sensitive breast tumors, as it feeds them. Estrogen is produced in the ovaries but also in the fatty tissues of the body. Therefore, the drug Tamoxifen[15] reappeared in Michal's medicine cabinet. Since the tumors in bones plow their way more easily when the bones are brittle, Michal got infusions of Zomera to strengthen the bones.

The metastases were monitored through CT scans. As long as there is no deterioration, the drugs will not be replaced, Michal was told.

"For me it was a huge crisis," Michal wrote in an online forum. "I realized that this time there are no conventional medical means to help me get cured. It's hard to describe what I felt in those moments. I couldn't bear the thought of not being around to raise my newborn daughter.

I decided not to give up and go on a quest to heal my body. The starting point was to meet people in similar situations who achieved total recovery. I knew I could learn from the experience of others".

Following her talks with cured patients, Michael chose three courses of action. The first one was proposed by her oncologists: anti-hormonal drug and an infusion to strengthen the bone. The second option was to clear the physical body of toxins and the third was emotional cleansing.

"The rationale behind this choice stems from the perception that there is a delicate and complex relationship between body and soul, which have a strong mutual influence on each other, and that no recovery can be achieved without working in parallel on both aspects. I found two nurses who helped and guided me through the process.

The detoxification process was directed by Dr. Pnina Bar Sela, who is based in Kiryat Tivon. I also started exercising. At first I'd only go on walks and later I also started swimming in order to avoid severe pains in the bones and prevent osteoporosis. I realized that physical exercise makes the body stronger and more durable, helping the immune system cope with the cancer cells and eventually overcome them.

In addition to the physical cleansing, I started working with Vered Gliksman who treats patients with guided imagery, an ancient tool many therapists apply. Vered perfected and developed it into a new method - unique, exciting and different from anything I'd seen before. My sessions with Vered included conversation therapy, during which I realized what factors led to the development of cancer in my body.

---

[15] Synthetic estrogen-inhibiting hormone used as an anti-cancer drug for women with breast cancer and ovarian cancer.

I went through a fascinating journey, in which Vered guided me to reconsider my mindset and examine the way I perceive myself and my life. I realized that unless I change my outlook, nothing will change in my life. This observation led me to shift my thought patterns and identify when they don't serve me or cause me harm.

Following our meetings, my attitude towards life and myself changed. The emphasis was on positive thinking, viewing life from a 'glass-half-full' perspective instead of looking for the negative things; daring to dream, to want, to crave, and even to be able to see these things come to fruition in my mind. Throughout the process I had a clear image of the goals I want to achieve. It was clear that in order to achieve them, I must believe I am able to. Faith, hope, and optimism served a crucial role in the process.

Vered helped me understand that fear dictates my limitations and blocks me from achieving the goals I set for myself. I learned not to stop in the face of fear, but rather to look directly at it and dissolve it.

Happiness became a very important theme of my life. All these changes allowed the healing process to take place in my body. I learned to listen to my body and soul, and did everything possible to strengthen both of them in order to provide my body with the best conditions to heal itself.

My work with Vered was the hardest part of the healing process, since she made me aware of the way I think and my everyday choices in life.

Through guided imagery, Vered instructed me how to reduce the tumors and ultimately make them disappear.

Four months after the first CT scan that diagnosed a relapse in the disease, another CT scan was performed. During this time, my work with Vered was focused on the lungs, since the tumors in this area were a threat to my life in the short term. The CT results left us all astonished. Three out of four tumors in the lung disappeared. Of one tumor, previously 4 cm in size, only a small lesion remained. At the same time there was no change in the metastases in the spine and ribs.

The doctors told me that the bone metastases will not go away, and that I'd have to live with it like any other chronic disease. Vered and I decided that due to the welcome change in the lung, we'd focus on the spine, ribs, and the small lesion remaining in the lung. After six months, another CT scan was performed, and it showed that all the tumors in the spine and ribs were gone.

However, the same CT scan revealed two tumors in the liver. It turned out they had already been there during the previous scan, but the doctor who analyzed the results had missed it. According to the doctors, this finding probably existed already a year ago, at the time the cancer relapse was diagnosed in my body.

In light of previous successes, I was confident that the tumor in the liver can be cured. I decided to increase my sessions with Vered to twice a week. After two and a half months, the final CT scan was performed. The results showed no tumors in the liver, lung, or bones.

Today I know that it's possible to be fully cured of cancer and that my recovery is up to me. One of the major difficulties in the healing process was dealing with the doubt that it's even possible to achieve full recovery, as well as facing the fear of death and the anxieties of those dear to me who believed in the dark predictions. Vered was there for me, like a rock, constantly reassuring me that recovery is possible, and that I should persist and never lose hope.

It takes guts to dare to want to live in order to get cured, and the lust for life must be stronger than anything else. Throughout the entire process, my desire, determination, hope, and optimism regarding the prospects of full recovery were critical to the success of self-healing.

When I was diagnosed with the relapsed cancer, I looked for people who managed to be cured despite the difficult prognosis, and it wasn't easy to find any . I believe that the tools I got from Vered and Dr. Bar-Sela could serve anyone who wants to be cured, so I decided to write down the story of my healing."

This text impressed me so much that I asked Michal for Vered's contact information. It was clear that Vered is doing something special and I wanted to find out what it is.

Vered Gliksman

"Every thought, whether hidden or open, affects our body"

-*Vered Gliksman*

"People who touch creation - touch themselves," Vered told me at the beginning of our conversation when I told her I was a painter. "We yearn to touch ourselves. Painting and photography are a prism for entering the soul of man."

When Vered's son lay unconscious in intensive care after a serious traffic accident that left his cerebellum injured, the doctors feared he wouldn't wake up. And even if he would wake up, he'd be severely disabled. In the ICU room Vered learned the art of listening to herself. Not able to explain rationally what had happened to her, she began to treat her son with energy she sensed. Vered believes that creative people gain new insights in situations of survival. When she treated her son with energy, some chuckled behind her back, but when he was back on his feet two weeks later, the relatives of other patients started asking her to treat their loved ones too.

16 years have passed since then, and Vered has continued to cultivate the inexplicable gift she was bestowed. She studied Reiki, healing, kabbalah, psychodrama, and Ayurveda - incorporating all of these into her personal training studies.

"A lot of cancer patients come to see me," says Vered, "I listen to the person and try to identify when the disease broke out. Usually it happens before the symptoms appear. I encourage patients to consider the hidden and overt benefits of the disease. Many say that it revitalized them and gave them love and attention. Every disease has its perks, so I help patients see the benefits of their illness. Once identified, it's possible to change the present by giving up the benefit and moving on in life.

Recently I studied the German New Medicine, according to which, just like in kabbalah, every organ in the body is linked to a specific emotion and every conflict is linked to a specific organ in the body and specific region in the brain that controls the process at the physical level. This information is also available in kabbalah, which I teach. Every sick place in the body represents a part of the human soul that needs filling. Joy, love, stability, and self-esteem are what most people are lacking. Every organ in our body has a different meaning and the body perpetually tells the story of the soul through its various organs. If we go back and recall the recurring pains, years before the disease appeared, we can start connecting between the back pain, leg pain, and perhaps indigestion to the current illness. These signs suggest that something has gone wrong in life and project this message to the body's organs.

Every part of the body is linked to emotion or character. For example, the lungs are related to joy, the bones and liver are related to self-esteem. There is a connection between the location of the metastases and our self-perception and lifestyle. Once we understand the connection and realize that the brain controls all processes in the body, without telling reality from fiction, we can work consciously to change thoughts and habits and achieve results that are good for us. Every thought that crosses through our minds, whether hidden or open, affects our body. The instructions I give the brain shape my reality, so it matters how I talk, what I say, and what sentences are planted in my head. In the next stage, I teach the patient guided imagery and positive thinking, which are closely related. After all, everything I say is preceded by an image projecting in my head. I teach people self-healing, and impart the tools to cope with fears and anxieties and ways to communicate with themselves.

I am convinced that what the body spoils it can also repair. I witnessed total recovery in a number of people, who then resumed previous behavior patterns after a while and the cancer relapsed. This pattern repeats itself even with allergies. "

My conversation with Vered is fascinating. After all, she doesn't tell me anything new. Perhaps it's the way she says it or the tone of her voice, but the clock is not as impressed and soon I have to leave for a meeting with Rabbi Firer.

"I got a gift in this life - the ability to see into the human body," says Vered. "I can see you have an edema in the gastrointestinal tract in the colon. Healing could be good for you. I work through the energy source of the light. I learned this method through spiritual communication and I've been administering it for ten years. You can put your hand on the area that feels pain and imagine a faucet of light above your head. It fills you up and out of the palms of your hands a beam of light extends to the painful area. Try it, and you'll feel the vibration on your own."

As I speak, I place my hand, imagine the light, and wait for the feeling. I am open to accepting this proposal. So many people around me talk about energy and light and healing. I can't resist it any longer.

Although I didn't explore this area thoroughly and I don't understand this "healing", this time I will go with my gut. We are a body of energy and some of us have learned how to use the energy in the body and the energy found in the world around us. Even though I don't understand how, Gadi often manages to relieve my pain when he does healing on me. I can't argue with that. When I feel pain I call him and ask him to treat me. Usually the pain passes within a minute, thanks to the energy he sends me from afar. One can believe or be skeptical about this, but the pain passes.

All I have to do is remember to call him.

Women who change their lifestyle reduce their risk of breast cancer recurrence and improve their quality of life and life expectancy

In an article published in 2006 by researchers from the oncology departments at the Sheba and Rabin medical centers, it was determined that plumpness, little physical activity, and poor nutrition increase the risk of breast cancer recurrence. Dr. Weitzen from Sheba is quoted in Walla's health section: "This article will help physicians and breast cancer patients to lead the recommended lifestyle after the illness. Women who change their lifestyle reduce their risk of breast cancer recurrence and improve their quality of life and life expectancy." My jaw drops when I read this. They did research and reached a conclusion, but no one told me about it when I was a patient at the oncology department in Tel Hashomer Hospital.

Why do I have to read about it by chance in the paper? Why isn't it one of the main treatment protocols of the department? I feel like making a banner and hanging it in the waiting room of the breast unit. The article reminds me of an American study that examined 3,000 women and found that women who walked for 5-8 hours a week reduced their chances of getting breast cancer again by 42%.

I got sick a year after the article was published. Why wasn't I told this before in any of the annual check-ups? Whatever the doctor says has clout. I wish the doctors understood their power to help us do things outside the hospital, things that can promote our health. It's a matter of awareness and it's a lot cheaper than drugs.

CHAPTER 7

Full Self-Confidence in Recovery

It's hard to know how to talk to a cancer patient

"What about you?" asks the neighbor who lives on the street next to mine. We meet randomly about once a year. "All is well?" she continues.

"Yes, everything is fine, how are you?"

"Fine? Really?" she looks at me in disbelief, her face twitching. "Is that so?"

I don't feel like telling her what exactly is going on with me. I want to tell her that what matters is whether I live and show her what gives meaning to my life. At this moment, in this random encounter on the street – I'd rather not disclose the results of the last PET scan, or else I'd get a sad look of pity asking me: So what will you do when things get really bad? That look makes me feel like I'm in really bad condition. It saddens and weakens me. I choose to stay away from pity.

It's hard to know how to talk to a cancer patient. The chances of saying the right thing are close to zero, because there is nothing right to say. A sentence that could be relevant one day can be very annoying another day. For example, saying "everything will be fine", is really annoying. Or saying decisively "but they detected it early on, right?" is also a little annoying. Maybe just ask how you can help. And it's highly recommended to just ask and not decide for me.

Avichai Kimhi
Metastatic lung cancer spreading to the brain – conventional treatment with faith and guided imagery – 6 years after diagnosis

"I woke up in the morning fully confident that I will live. I believed I would be helped by a higher power."

- Avichai Kimhi

Studies in recent years have shown that by merely imagining physical exercise we build our muscles. Sometimes, you can go to the beach, hike, or eat a regular meal in your imagination. When Avichai Kimhi underwent intravenous chemotherapy and was only able to eat liquids, he pictured his favorite pleasures in his imagination. Looking back, his imagination guided him throughout the healing process and was probably one of the causes of his recovery.

In May 2009, a year and a half after Avichai Kimhi retired as Lieutenant Colonel following an intense military service, at age 45, he was diagnosed with metastatic lung cancer spreading to the brain. In the same year, the Israel Cancer Association announced that the cancer survival rate in Israel is among the highest in the world. I checked the percentage of men who survive lung cancer: 14.7%. Lung cancer is considered the most fatal type of cancers, killing the most people in Israel - nearly 1,700 people a year.

"The oncologist who gave me the diagnosis," says Avichai "meant to tell me that every month in life counts, but what my wife and I understood from him was that I have a month to live. This misunderstanding challenged me. At that appointment I made a deal with the doctor - I'll do my part and he'll do his. Although I am stubborn and combative, at that moment I didn't yet realize what I was committing to. I did realize I was going to work with cancer. I went along with the proposed conventional treatment, realizing that there's a good chance I won't survive. In fact, the chances of survival are nil. Meanwhile, wonderful things happened to me, which I believe made the treatment work.

As a child I believed in God even though I grew up in a secular family. After the diagnosis I reclaimed my faith. One night I dreamed I was getting a second chance. I woke up from this dream fully confident that I will live. I believed I would be helped by a higher power. After that dream I wrote to myself that I'm going to seize this opportunity the best I can. I became committed to the issue. Later I wrote a letter requesting a blessing from the Lubavitcher Rebbe, and as customary, I inserted it randomly in one of the Rebbe's letter books. Whatever's written on that page should give me the right answer to my question and request. On that random page it said: "proper health", an unusual expression for the rabbi's letters. Usually the term "good health" appears in these letters. When I saw these two words, I felt shivers and saw this as a sign. At the same time, I made a commitment to myself, as is customary when asking for something from the Rebbe, to put on tefillin every day. So I put on tefillin and prayed, and it had an unusual mystical effect on me. Putting the tefillin on my head not far from the tumor itself was a very powerful moment. This random commitment helped me substantially.

Every day I made sure to say the "Amidah prayer", which includes 18 short prayers and 18 requests, one of which is for good health. Sometimes I'd go to the Chabad House to put on tefillin. Even today, I continue to put on tefillin every morning.

Ever since I wrote the letter to the Rebbe I started documenting the disease. Almost every day I'd write about and describe my situation, holding inner conversations during the process. I believe that writing helped me reach the state I am in now. I knew from the start that I'd publish a book and speak with patients in the future. In the early years I had long conversations with patients. Usually, those who come to me were in pretty bad shape and naturally having a harder time."

The main aspects of Avichai's recovery

Relationship with Oncologist

"The oncologist who treated me, Professor Nehushtan Hovav from Hadassah Hospital, was called 'professor' by me early on when we met, even though he was only a doctor at the time. Nehushtan is first of all a human being, attentive to his patients and a first-class professional. He dedicates his full attention to his patients".

Support from Family and Friends

"Without the devoted care of my wife, I would never have survived. The love I got from my friends and associates also contributed greatly. Every cancer patient has the forsaking friends and the supportive friends. As long as I was with friends - I was completely healthy."

Avoiding sugar, listening to the body

Avichai underwent 21 rounds of chemotherapy and radiotherapy, causing him to lose his appetite. To survive, he drank Ensure formula, which he "forced" himself to love. Later he managed to eat herring. Months later his appetite gradually returned, as he remained attentive to his body and needs. This time it was steak and tomato soup, two things he rarely ate in the past. Baked fish, fries, and fresh grapefruit juice were added to the menu. "I realized that the important thing to do is eat and strengthen the immune system. Although I was tempted by sugar, as soon as I heard that cancer loves sugar I lost my desire for it", says Avichai.

Guided Imagery

"Before undergoing any kind of chemotherapy, you must check the kidneys and immune system. I constantly controlled my blood pressure by power of thought and imagination. I'm a man of imagination. It was always easy for me to imagine things, so I imagined the immune cells rising and my kidneys functioning normally, and at the same time I constantly imagined and I dreamed about my future. The near future I intend to fulfill.

For example, I promised my worried brother in the United States: 'Don't come to me', I told him, 'I'll finish my treatment and come to you, I promise'. Although this promise was detached from reality, it was binding for me and I constantly imagined that I was going to visit him.

I imagined what the cancer looks like and imagined myself sending my right hand to my chest and pulling out the cancer from my body. I imagined going to the beach, eating at a restaurant, seeing a good play. Imagination was built into my thoughts all the time."

What have I learned so far?

Zalman calls me: "There's an important gathering of 'Ta'atzumot' today. You should come, it's important to attend these events." As we talk, I get an incoming call from an unidentified caller. I call back and realize it's Shaike: "Are you coming to 'Ta'atzumot' today?" he asks, "I'll be speaking there, telling my story." I'm glad to hear that. I think Shaike has a great story. Precisely because it is not heroic, and because he didn't go to top therapists. He laboriously gathered information from books, the internet, newspapers, and an inspiring week in Alumot, and applied it to himself diligently.

I debate whether to go get an ultrasound today or go to the gathering.

I choose to go get an ultrasound at the health care clinic. The following sentences run through my head on the way there: Cancer patients can be happy people. Cancer patients should preferably realize their dreams and achieve self-fulfillment as part of the healing process.

The disk from the previous test at Tel Hashomer doesn't open at the health care clinic and the doctor can't compare the new results to the previous ones. From what she sees, the tumor I'm feeling increased by 4 mm, but that's not a final result.

Should I give up on the drug or persist?

I wait to set another appointment. The receptionist is impatient. She and the doctor are busy with a phone call from the branch in Herzliya. Someone is trying to find out if the place is available to run an ultrasound test on a patient with ALS. My ears stick out, as I wait in suspense to hear the name of the patient. Shai Rishoni. My brother... The tired and gloomy secretary comes to life and looks up at me. "Your brother? What a small world." Suddenly her energy changes. This coincidence brings her back to life. Yes, very small world indeed.

So what do I do now? The biological drug is apparently ineffective against the tumor, chemotherapy is right around the corner for me, and I can't eat. How on earth do I get rid of this cancer?

Intense guided imagery and another ultrasound at Tel Hashomer in two weeks.

I raise my level of commitment, which is already quite high due to this campaign of self-persuasion. I devote myself to finding a solution.

Every night I try to go to the bedroom by eight in order to go to sleep by nine. I prepare all my supplements for the next day. Again, I make more lists. Notes in every corner; near the spot where I do enemas; near the blender; next to the juice machine; near the stove; where the other supplements are placed. Coffee and wheatgrass enemas; walking every morning; lifting weights, exercising on the trampoline; drinking pomegranate juice, grapefruit juice, carrot juice with apple and ginger. I set a few appointments with therapists for the next two weeks. This week I'm going to begin the emotional journey with Shir's therapist. What else do I try to do every day? Eat papaya, which allows the immune system to detect tumors. Spend twenty minutes a day in the sun to absorb Vitamin D. Swallow alpha lipoic acid and pectin to cleanse the body of metals. Walk barefoot on the ground to strengthen the immune system.

I go over what I learned so far during my writing. I mostly get a strong motivation to act, and seek help from therapists instead of searching for all the solutions alone, physically and emotionally. I learned that only an insane level of commitment will enable recovery. There is no half-assed way, but it is possible.

I get out of the shower and sit on the bed to rest, trying to remember whether I finished my shower with cold water. Zalman is the only one who warms up his body as part of the healing strategy. In general, he definitely went the extra mile, doing dozens of different things to maintain his health.

I look in the mirror and see my collarbone sticking out again. In the last two weeks, I lost almost five kilograms. The biological drug weakens the immune system, exhausting the stomach. I find myself unable to eat and I vomit most of the time. I was supposed to resume the drug cycle today, but my weakness prevents me from doing it. I'm still not sure I'm doing everything possible to strengthen the body. Maybe I should sit and meditate for a few hours every day. But I can't do it. If I'm told that my life depends on it, will I be able to do it? I sigh. Who could say such a thing to me? 'How do you manage to write a book; how do you have the time?' I was asked by a woman recovering from lymphoma. At this stage she was occupied solely with her recovery. Maybe I'm wrong. Maybe there's no need to teach a class twice a week. Maybe I should only go to the beach and do meditation. Again, I wonder if it's even possible. If I want to live, everything should be possible. Do I want to live? I dry my thinning hair, which hasn't recovered since chemotherapy. The left nipple is twisted. "Yes it is because there's a tumor pulling it," said the doctor who performed the X-ray scan. That sentence comes up every time I look at it. The waist is narrow, as a result of the weight loss. I love you, I tell the figure standing in front of me. Yes. I love you, with the thinning hair and crooked nipple. You are me and that's what I got. Instead of deodorant, I grab some baking soda with two fingers and spread it under my armpit. The floor catches some of the powder. I'm curvy. I received a valuable gift, which I'm learning to appreciate. Just like I always wanted to be.

Ruth was able to arrange an appointment for me with Prof. Shoham, even though he doesn't accept new patients these days. I arrange all the paperwork and prepare to show him the list of supplements, my daily routine, my diet, and my activity. I get things in order, just the way I like it. I copy medical reports and type in the address on the Waze app. On the drive over, I find myself once again turning south to Highway 6, facing the view of the hills leading to Jerusalem. My stomach is full of air pressing from all directions. This inconvenience makes me cringe. I do not like this feeling at all. Sensing pressure in my chest, I lean over the steering wheel to let the air exit and feel relieved when it does. My notebook is placed on my lap during the drive. Holding the pen in my hand, I write down any thoughts that come up. I do it while keeping my eyes on the road. I am aware of the danger. I haven't had any sugar in five days and I'm proud of myself for that. Not that it stops the sharp pain from rushing down from my stomach to the esophagus before passing. Again I stretch towards the steering wheel to let the air out. I don't want to throw up right now in the middle of Highway 6. I find the doctor's home in the small community scattered with olive groves. A long path leads from the road to the clinic, with a wooden bridge in the middle and natural-style gardening. Just the way I like it, like the one where Pnina Bar Sela lives. I move on. I wait on the porch, the sunbeams penetrating between the bushes and generating an abstract image on the clinic wall. My stomach hurts. What insight do I want to take away from the meeting with the professor? A solution to the stomach pains. Recommendations for innovative treatments against tumors are not within his field of expertise. Whose then? As I wait for Prof. Shoham, I wonder whether my condition would have been different today had I gone to see him four years ago. I met with therapists in the past but rarely followed their prescriptions. I tend to fold the note of the doctor's recommendations, put it in my purse, and forget its main points. I already learned a hard lesson once and this may be the time to apply it. When I was 30, after two consecutive miscarriages, I went to see a therapist in the north of the country. I made a great effort to reach her. To ensure the success of the next pregnancy, she suggested that I take an aspirin pill every day. I folded the note on which I wrote her recommendation and forgot about it, until my gynecologist told me, after my sixth miscarriage, that a new study suggests a link between aspirin and prevention of miscarriages. This time I was convinced, and the pregnancy was successful. It's been seventeen years since then, and it may be time to internalize that message. Interestingly, even today I am still advised to take aspirin. A study examining women with breast cancer[16] found that those who took aspirin every day for three to five years reduced the recurrence of the disease by 60%. And they had 71% less chances of dying from breast cancer.

---

[16] www.ncbi.nlm.nih.gov/pubmed/20159825

According to another study[17] aspirin can slow the spread of lung cancer by 20% to 30%. Is it time to take a new direction? Will I leave my appointment with Prof. Shoham and make sure to apply all his recommendations or move on to the next therapist and not follow either of their suggestions? How long can I sustain the recommendations and changes before I relapse to my previous habits? The past year, during which I couldn't eat, may have mitigated some of my bad eating habits, yet I still detect a strong desire for sugar and carbohydrates when someone in my close surroundings frustrates me.

I find Professor Shoham as part of my ongoing campaign towards recovery. This is a long way with many stops and no single therapist can solve the problem. I collect bits of information from any source that comes to mind: recovering patients, therapists, medical conferences, clinical studies, and doctors. I interview people, I read, and now I'm even starting to study naturopathy. Sometimes I do the integration on my own, and sometimes in consultation with the oncologist. I'll look back at this period in a few years and try to summarize what I did, what ultimately promoted my health and what didn't. These days I'm getting the feeling that the six tumors in my body are not the end of the story. I have the power to change direction. So much so that sometimes it seems that even the sugar does not attract me. For a whole week I haven't eaten anything that's not included in the healthy menu, which is unusual for me.

The door opens. I get up from my chair, Ruth and her mother exit the room, Prof. Shoham stands behind them and waits as we hug and greet each other. "You look wonderful," Ruth complements me. "What's up? You should come inside. We'll talk, see you later".

Spacious clinic, the window overlooking an olive grove outside, a whole wall full of religious books, two other walls decorated with medical books and books about cancer. The table faces the wall, so there's no table separating me from the professor. This reminds me of the method of Dr. Bernie Siegel, who realized the table creates a wedge between him and his patients, and changed the structure of the room where he meets his patients.

I give him the documents I prepared and my daily routine. My stomach hurts and I squirm for a moment. The professor's facial features remind me of my father. His energy also reminds me of my father's determination and know-how. I'm overwhelmed by memories. It's been seventeen years since he passed away. Had I known then all that I know now, maybe I could help him. Perhaps we could have delayed the spread of the tumor in his

---

[17] www.nature.com/bjc/journal/v109/n7/full/bjc2013411a.html

stomach. At the time, I tried reading the material to a certain extent. The internet was not as developed as it is today, and I was taken aback by a sense of helplessness for not being able to find information. I read books my grandmother had left me, the same books which I practically memorized as a young women: "Life Without Disease" by Dr. R.G. Jackson, "Food, Nutrition, Diet", by Dr. Yaakov Ilani (1975).

I tried to extract from them information that might help my father.

Prof. Shoham offers me to settle for liquid oatmeal, carrot juice, Budwig porridge, squash soup with a little oatmeal, papaya smoothie with berries and cheese water. That's the menu he gives me for the coming month. In addition, he recommends a coffee enema twice a day, balanced by a source of minerals. In other words, to drink vegetable juice after the enema. The enema cleanses the intestines and helps the body remove toxins. Wheatgrass enemas are also recommended.

During the entire meeting my stomach bothers me. When I leave, I lean over a big rock at the end of the white path and throw up. Should I go back to the clinic and disturb them by going to the restroom? It's not unreasonable. You just vomited, so you are allowed to. I start walking back, but no, I'm fine. I turn back towards the car. Why not? Am I ashamed? This is no reason not to return. I turn again, but I'm just fine. I don't need to use the restroom. After a few minutes I feel better. I go back to the car and drive away.

On the way home I remember all the questions I didn't ask, even though I had a list. I left Prof. Shoham with a shopping list, and was now on my way to the store to fill my cart with natural health products. The menu I got should alleviate the digestive system and simultaneously cure it without hindering my efforts to beat cancer. The Nutren 2 formula I took until now is full of substances that negate all my efforts. It contains, among other things, corn syrup and maltodextrin, two materials that do not promote my health, to say the least. To stop my dramatic drop in weight and muscle loss, I must make sure to walk every day, lift weights, and eat proteins and other materials that strengthen the body. My lack of appetite prevents me from eating all the items on the list, and I continue to lose weight every day. Ultimately, if I fail to change this trend, I'll die of starvation, not cancer.

The next morning, I spend an hour preparing most of what I need for the day in an attempt to make life easier and make sure I eat enough.

Order of foods and drinks: camel milk with some pectin, papaya smoothie with annona, cheese water, cinnamon and some almonds. Red grapefruit juice, oatmeal drink, carrot juice with apple and ginger. Cottage cheese with flaxseed and berries based on the Budwig diet. At the end of the day - tuna and some more camel milk. That's all I'm allowed to eat, and even that's too much for me every day. Most of the items are placed in cups on a tray I installed especially in the kitchen. The rest is in the fridge, in a ready-to-use kit. And thus I am occupied with writing or painting, and whenever I remember to, I go down to the kitchen to take the next dish. I force myself to eat.

Rona
Breast Cancer - guided imagery, healing, nutrition, faith – 3 years after diagnosis

"After three years: one growth disappeared, the other remains unchanged, without any conventional treatment"

-Rona

Rona (alias) Bernie and Jim Check were ahead of their time when they said in the seventies and eighties that people can change their situation dramatically by changing their approach to life. They talked about life-changing content, and how our perspective can significantly change our lives. The theories they postulated have become mainstream long ago.

Towards the turn of the last century, I joined a friend to attend a meeting of the "Physical Immortality" group established by Bernie and Jim at Beit Hatzanchan in Ramat Gan. Dozens of people sat in the auditorium as members of the audience went on stage to share something unusual that happened them, new insights they acquired, or problems they face. Back then they were talking about all the things that would become the subject of countless articles within a few years: health, stress-free life, the body's memory of past trauma, and more. At the same time the monthly magazine "Other Life" was established, followed by the Other Life House, where workshops in the same vein were held. The ad for the meetings read as follows: The meetings are intended to prompt a physical reaction in the body, release fears and thought patterns, and promote a life without limitations. They talked about releasing fears and changing thought patterns... The content of these meetings spoke to me, and I attended several times until my friend quit the group. Then I stopped going too.

The group continued to meet until 2013. Among those regularly present in the auditorium was Rona, who thoroughly internalized the messages and lived by the principles of healthy living, both physically and mentally: eating healthy food, doing yoga religiously, going on walks and living a conscious emotional life. The small cancerous lump discovered in her breast was a big surprise to her. At first glance, it did not fit her lifestyle, but on second thought, Rona decided that it's an opportunity to learn and grow. She agreed to remove the lump surgically, but additional tests she took prior to the operation revealed that the little lump was not alone. Another tumor was emerging in a different part of the breast. This changed everything, and now the surgeon recommended complete breast removal. The other professor she went to for a second opinion concurred with the surgeon. Rona refused to take this red flag home.

"At this point I quit conventional medicine," says Rona, "and with great determination, I chose a different approach. Something inside me knew there's a better way for me. The years at 'Physical Immortality' strengthened my confidence and faith that I have inner knowledge that will allow me to heal myself. I realized this is the moment of truth for me, after years of talk about it...

Now my lesson in life is knocking on my door, and I decided I will summon my powers.

Armed with this inner knowledge, I set out to leave no stone unturned. I read many books, consulted with therapists, and stayed with two of them. For my nutrition, I'm treated by Naturopath Roi Gonik, and I receive emotional and energetic treatment from Boaz Ben Uri.

Most of my diet was based on wheat grass, green vegetables, legumes, fruits, and nuts. Roi added the cordycep mushrooms, maitake extract, and turmeric. Every once in a while, for three mornings in a row, I'd take half a teaspoon of baking soda mixed with a quarter cup of water in order to switch the body tissues to basic mode".

Rona went to Boaz Ben Uri for guided imagery treatment and healing, focusing on two issues: anger and control. "I'm a calm person, but in some cases I don't express or let out anger. Theoretically, this could be one of the causes of my breast cancer. Through guided imagery I managed to identify sensitive places. This method is faster than working with a psychologist. We touched the sources of my emotional difficulties, of anger, control, hyper emotionalism, languor, or imbalanced feelings[18]. Boaz is very knowledgeable and has tips for maintaining calm through everyday behavior. When he performs healing on me, it often feels like I'm not lying on the bed. Sometimes I actually reach down to make sure there's a bed

---

[18] Michal Boker, a holistic therapist, writes in her book "Life Choosing" that breast cancer is common among women who spend their whole lives giving but feel they do not get back in the same token and they feel emotionally exploited.

under me and I'm not hovering. Usually I lie down full of energy and get up feeling like after a week in the Bahamas. I also have visions during the healing process."

Every morning and afternoon Rona made sure to spend half an hour on meditation or guided imagery.

Rona paved the way for herself with determination and strong faith, though not without crises. After spending a year promoting her health diligently, the lump was still there and this led to fears and concerns. It happened during Passover cleaning.

Her twin daughters just started school and she wanted to see them grow. She wondered whether she's doing the right thing. The traditional meal around the Seder table was mixed with worries and thoughts about the future.

Rona managed to shake off the fears, with the support of her family and close friends, and she bravely continued on the same track, distancing herself from anyone who expresses cynicism or disbelief about the direction she chose. She was able to restore her inner faith that her actions will lead her to recovery.

"Six months ago, in the recent ultrasound test, I was happy to find out that one tumor had disappeared and a bit disappointed to find out that the other one was still there. Thankfully, it hasn't changed. The ultrasound is a good indicator of my ability to stop the development and a reminder that my work here isn't done. I must be constantly conscious at all levels, both physically and mentally. I must choose the people I associate with, my inner cycles; I must energetically determine who is right for me and who is not. I must live in great clarity – about what ought and what ought not to be."

I love reading Rona's story. Whenever I want to be stronger I go back and read it, realizing again and again that I shouldn't give up on any aspect, not on the diet, nor the guided imagery and meditation, and certainly not on the belief that it is possible.

Bracha Steinberg
Stage 3 lymphoma - conversations with the lymphatic system - 3 years after diagnosis

In 2006, the American Cancer Society documented 58,870 cases of non-Hodgkin lymphoma, and 18,840 deaths.

Bracha Steinberg - an athlete of many years, triathlonist, and aromatherapy and reflexology expert - discovered two large tumors in the groin at age 72. The tests showed another tumor in the entrances to her lungs and liver. She was diagnosed with stage-3 lymphoma. Bracha's journey includes both conventional cancer treatment and mental healing. What's special about her story is how fast the tumors disappeared.

"For my 70th birthday I received a racing bicycle as a gift. On one of my rides to Sderot and back I had a flat tire in my front wheel. The inner tube was replaced but the repair technician didn't notice the tire was damaged too. In one of the following rides the inner tube popped out through the hole in the tire and I was thrown off the bike. My left shoulder was injured. The pain was so intense, I couldn't do any physical activity or even sleep properly at night.

The pain and the physical limitations were such a drain on me, I kept telling myself, like a mantra: 'this is not how I want to live'. I believe that faith and thought can produce a chemical reaction in the body and that this statement destroyed my immune system, which started creating a weapon against itself. The lymphatic system is our defense system and I realized I had brought the disease upon myself. So I figured I could get rid of it just as I had invited it. I decided to have daily conversations with my lymphatic system in order to strengthen and rebuild it. Every day I went to meditate at the beach, even on days when I underwent chemotherapy. Since it is not recommended to be in the sun during chemotherapy, I wore only white cotton clothes to minimize the UV radiation on my body. I was my own healer. I did a lot of writing, interviewing the body's organs and the lymphatic system and discovering many insights. I took the minimum amount of drugs I could, and even during chemotherapy I continued to practice as much as I could.

In between treatments I participated in the women's triathlon in Herzliya, adapting to the fact that I mustn't catch a cold or be exposed to the sun. In addition, I did not cancel a five-week trip abroad with my grandchildren, which also took place in between treatments.

The MRI test after the first two rounds of chemotherapy (out of six) revealed that the tumors had disappeared completely. Dr. Martin Ellis, currently director of the Institute of Hematology and Blood Bank at Meir Hospital and then a senior physician at Internal Ward C, was very surprised by these results.

After the chemotherapy I embarked on a two-month-long healing journey through South America with a friend of mine. I think it gave me the final boost to recovery. "

Three years after the treatments, Bracha swims every morning and runs eight kilometers every evening. In between she works a lot in the garden, hikes through the Israel National Trail, and continues to compete in triathlons. And her body is free of tumors.

Maybe Paris?

In late October Tammy asks how she can help me with the pain. I tell her she can't. Maybe Paris? She asks. Six months ago I was looking for someone to go with me but couldn't find anyone.

Oh, thanks for reminding me of that. Just talking about it gives me joy.

We set a date and when I get home I see that Tammy already booked us a flight in November - we plan on taking off on my birthday. My brother Shai and sister-in-law Tammy give me the ticket to Paris as a birthday present. I am overcome by a thrilling pleasure.

Noa Sehayek
Brain tumor - relationship with tumor
4 years after diagnosis

"Miracles happen when you find your true self and acknowledge your feelings about what is right for you."

-Bernie Siegel

Noa Sehayik from Kibbutz Ginosar taught herself how to follow a pattern of positive thinking while talking with the tumor in her head. If the body is our subconscious, as claimed by neurologist Dr. Candace Pratt, then Noa communicated with it very intimately for a long time through writing. Her oval kitchen table became her studio. Every day, for a whole year, she sat at the table, filling it with papers and filling the papers with words. Her upstairs neighbor typed the text. At the end of the year Noa consolidated all the conversations and published them in an inspiring book called "Conversations with My Tumor." For Noa this was a fundamental process of venting emotions.

I heard about emotional processing from other recovering patients. The more of them I met the more I realized what a significant impact emotional work has on strengthening the immune system and how much it is part of the healing process.

"Can you call my landline?" she asks. I'm not surprised by this request. "I try to avoid any unnecessary radiation," she explains. Noa is not the only recovering patient who stays away from mobile phones. After dozens of studies with inconclusive results, some global health organizations catalogue radio frequency[19] as potentially carcinogenic to humans. The official recommendation is to keep phone conversations brief and try to talk with headphones while keeping the antenna away from the head. Noa and other recovering patients don't take unnecessary risks and prefer landlines over mobile phones as part of the strategy for treating the disease. I adopt this strategy and as a first step I cancel my data package to reduce radiation

---

[19] Intensive and prolonged exposure to electromagnetic fields of radio frequency may be hazardous to one's health.

from my phone and be less distracted by messages from WhatsApp, facebook, and emails.

"Four years ago I felt I was becoming physically disabled. I couldn't climb stairs, sit down, or bend over. My physical condition worsened from week to week. The medical tests discovered a brain tumor - hemangioblastoma - composed of multiple capillaries and unorganized cell clusters. It turned out it was impossible treat it surgically. Any strain, the doctor told me, would cause the tumor full of blood vessels to explode. I'm sorry, but there's no way I can help you.

The doctor sent me home to count my days. Before the tumor was detected, I was in charge of the dining hall. Now, as the tumor doubled in size in each test, I sat at home for three months and I bemoaned my fate. I lamented the life I was missing".

Eventually the panic made way for Noa's natural curiosity.

"I viewed the tumor as something very interesting I stumbled upon, not as something that's going to kill me. According to all the studies on the specific tumor I had, I was supposed to die at the age of 50 and I was already 54. This figure gave me hope. Doctors had no cure for me. They only gave me painkillers. I realized that I was done looking for solutions in conventional medicine. However, I felt very alone and I was startled by the responsibility I carried. I asked myself: Can I heal myself?"

War in the South

War in the south, Operation Protective Edge. We feel it well, everyone I know is in a gloomy mood. The sirens are heard even in the rear, in the southern and central cities. Every morning and evening my family members enter the shelter as rockets are fired at us. Sometimes the siren catches me while driving. I look at the other motorists, but most of them continue to drive fast. On the radio they announce where sirens are sounded. I am undoubtedly within range of the rocket fire. I press the gas pedal to reach a safe place to pull over. I have a minute and a half to take cover. I quickly get out of the car, taking my phone and keys with me. I jump over the metal railing and rush down to the woods next to the road. I stand with my back against the direction of the shooting. Others stand on the side of the road, ducking behind the cars. I start blubbering insistently. Our reality bursts out even in my tears. I park the car near the home of Ilan, a film director, and send him a message informing him that I am outside. Ilan joins me on a visit to Noa at kibbutz Ginosar. On the radio they announce that the funeral of a soldier from kibbutz Ginosar killed in Operation

Protective Edge will commence at five in the afternoon. We get on the highway in silence and drive away from the rocket range. When we arrive at the kibbutz we see groups of youngsters on the lawns, some in uniform. Sorrow and heartbreak fill the air.

"I spent all day painting this mandala" – Noa explains the colorful painting on the table on her porch. "I knew that the funeral would be difficult. This difficulty releases in the brain very different substances from those released when I meditate or paint. So I was preparing my body". Noa is not familiar with Pert's theory - but she knows that stress weakens the immune system and that this system must be protected. Always, certainly at such a time. After all, *this* is our war. Our war does not involve being glued to the TV in suspense. It is here anyway."

Noa's house is surrounded by a heavenly garden of papaya trees, Moringa trees, muscat grape vines climbing on ropes prepared in advance, a small waterfall rippling persistently. There's a reason the waterfall is there. Noa explains:

"It was built following a meeting with a brain tumor specialist who told me that my tumor is clogging the cerebral circulation. If it grows more it will block the circulation and put my life in danger.

I realized I needed a waterfall in front of me to constantly see the free flow of water and imagine that my brain is enjoying steady and continuous flow."

Benny, Noa's partner, gets up and picks a jasmine flower stalk and puts it on the center of the table. The smell of jasmine envelops us.

"My tumor is so friendly. Though it sits on the brainstem, it doesn't cause any harm. It's fine by me, we have an extraordinary relationship."

Noa is happy to share with me all the things she does for her health. And she does a lot. I came to experience her rigorous daily routine. I observe all the details, plants, and colors, searching for clues to what cured her. I can't help but compare between what she does and what I do. The similarities between us amaze me. Noa tells me how she began her recovery process:

"I said to myself: I will find a cure, I'm going to discover one now. I really believed it. I didn't think I was going to die, even though I had no idea how to avoid it.

It happened after three months of endless weeping over my looming death. As if all the waterworks inside me were drained, my tears dried. One day I turned on the computer and suddenly saw a video of an Osho meditation course in an ashram in the desert. 24 hours later I was there. I found the course very intense, interesting, and healing. The meditation opened my life. For ten days I studied breathing exercises, meditation, and guided imagery.

I came back from the course reinvigorated. I knew now that meditation will lead me to inner healing. I practiced breathing meditations all the time, and started walking, writing, and recording what happens to me every day. I felt a strong urge to write. Every day when I woke up from meditation I'd write down on a notebook whatever was on my mind and heart. I love talking to people, asking questions and investigating. I realized I had a chance to talk with my own tumor. Just to talk to it, nothing more. I started writing, and it answered me. In each meditation I asked the tumor questions and each answer became a chapter in the book.

In fact, I achieved emotional cleansing by writing continuously every day for eight to ten hours, for a whole year. When I started writing I was practically disabled. I had trouble with all basic functions of the body. Throughout this year, from day to day, week to week, my physical and emotional condition gradually improved.

Writing helped me identify my habitual behavioral patterns. I also understood why the tumor came to me. Now I could check whether I wanted it to leave me. I felt like I became the tumor's student and it became my friend. We nurtured a relationship of mutual understanding and respect, separating between the tumor's menacing nature and its educational nature. Once I started regarding the tumor as a close friend who came to support and help me, instead of seeing it as a threatening factor, it stopped growing.

A year later I had a book, which was written entirely through a meditative process. I had so much to say and let out. Today I believe that writing can cure people. It allows things that speech does not allow. Writing alone in silence is your own private experience. You can write personal and intimate things. In the meantime, I decided to defy my physical weakness and started walking every day. I'm limited, but I'll do it anyway. I called these excursions 'my walks of happiness'. In such walks I cannot cry. In such walks I seek happiness, look for birds, pick fruit, trim leaves from my organic vegetable garden, and enjoy the flowers, the shades of green and tones of happiness along the way. Suddenly I realized I can be happy even though I have a brain tumor. Happier than anyone else – let them be jealous.

Following the publication of the book, many people approach me and ask to talk, create groups, and spend time together – as we share a common fate. People say that I wrote exactly what they think. I also studied personal coaching and I combine my experience and knowledge to help new patients suffering from the same panic I still remember facing myself. I invite those seeking guidance to my long morning or evening walks. I talk to them and instruct them while walking. My life is now more pleasant and meaningful. I'm really grateful that the tumor appeared. Before that my life was shallower. The brain tumor changed everything, so it's not so bad that I got it. The happiness I have now is different from before. I understand life differently and there is meaning to everything I do.

I went to countless festivals and spiritual workshops, just to meditate and meet people. I was thirsty for a spiritual life. The body was sick and I wanted to absorb spirituality to distract myself from the physical hardship. 'Body and soul' is not just a cliché. I saw it work on me. I felt the workshops were really contributing to my physical health. I attended a workshop called 'Love Yourself'. There I decided I wanted the tumor to be outside the skull so that I could talk to it more easily. I performed an imaginary act of energetically removing the tumor from the brain. My friend gave me a stone shaped like a tumor, which my husband placed in a niche he carved in the top of a eucalyptus tree, and that is where the tumor's menacing nature is placed. The tree grew around the stone as if it swallowed it. As far as I'm concerned, nature is a full partner to this process - a sublime act on its part.

I kept the tumor's educational aspect, which I believe in strongly. Through imagination I brought it to my inner truth. Therefore, the tumor can make me live a better life, and I can feel more joy, love, and pleasure in my life. I devoured the entire shelf of spiritual books at the Steimatzky bookstore. I read all the time, and then moved on to medical school textbooks. I found out that no one in the world with my condition has ever passed the age of fifty. Today I'm fifty-eight. When I discovered that statistic, I started to believe I have a chance. Since then my life has become beautiful and fascinating. Now I constantly think of delightful experiences to organize, and ask myself what I want to do but haven't yet done. I set up a group of friends aimed at:

Having fun. Every two weeks we meet for our activity. There is only one rule – you're not allowed to talk about the problems of the kibbutz. I go on trips to pick plants and flowers in the mountains. In other words, I have a blast."

What's your secret? I ask her.

"You need a fiery passion for self-healing. 95% of what I do during the day is devoted to my health. I make sure to spend an hour every day discussing philosophy: In order to recover, I have to occupy my mind with contemplation on a daily basis. It reinforces my healthy lifestyle. As part of this hour, I listen to Adiel Tal's youtube lectures on healthy nutrition or Arieh Avneri's talks on 'The Milk Fools' ", explaining how dairy products are bad for us. Sometimes I play these videos while working at home. My brain gets the message and it fuels me. Without this fire, I don't know how I would heal. This is my eternal flame, my life vest in the middle of the sea. Instructing others also keeps me on my toes.

I'm proud of myself. The tumor came to the right address, and thanks to it I became a writer. My gain from the disease is emotional cleansing. I fell in love with the disease. I investigated my need to be sick through writing and the discovery also became one of the steps in my healing process."

Before we leave Noa I open the book lying on the coffee table: "Miracles arise from finding your true self and acknowledging your feelings about what's right for you," Bernie Siegel writes in his book "Love, Medicine and Miracles".

The last MRI showed with certainty that Noa's tumor stopped growing. Her treating Prof. at Ichilov Hospital said: "I don't understand what you're doing, but keep doing it."

Noa's Daily Routine

Noa wakes up at six.

After drinking a glass of water, she sits down for a breathing meditation on the porch in front of a small waterfall (to release the pain).

In the garden she picks leaves for tea, which she drinks after her walk: lemongrass, vervain, ginger, sage, white-leaved savory and cinnamon.

In boiling water she soaks cumin seeds, coriander, green tea, fennel, cloves and stevia for sweetening. After going on a walk, she will drink it as a medicine.

Before her morning walk, Noa drinks wheatgrass.

On her morning walk she is usually accompanied by someone who needs advice or assistance regarding their health.

As she walks she picks and eats natural foods.

When she returns home, she sits down near the waterfall again for some guided imagery and then writes 150 thanks to God for all the good things she has in life.

Then she writes down what she wants to devote her energy to today.

At the end of this part of the day, Noa has time to work as editor of the kibbutz newspaper, which she does until lunchtime.

For lunch she prepares vegan food based on a list of anti-cancerous plants .

As she prepares the food, Noa listens to youtube videos.

She spends the hours after lunch with friends, strolling in the fresh air. In the afternoon she has another meal, followed by some reading and writing.

She goes to bed at 11:00

She drives to Alumot occasionally and often reads Bernie Siegel's book, "Love, Medicine and Miracles "(a book which many recovering patients and therapists mention).

"I have a great life," says Noa.

"And what do you dream about? "

"Painting".

"So come to Akko with me next month to paint."

"I will."

She is indeed coming.

I returned from Noa full of energy to start the changes. My encounter with her encouraged me to sit down and practice breathing meditation, regular meditation, and talk to the tumor. I have a feeling that it halted in recent days. I put my hand on the spot, and it is not warm. I know that the spot is warmer when there is activity. So I have short conversations with it. I explain to it that now I am the one growing, and that it can rest assure, for it can retain its size if it so wishes or diminish. It's fine by me. But only a few days later I find myself lying in bed, once again reaching for the breast tumor, and this time it feels like it actually grew significantly in recent days. Below it, another bulge appears on the rib. This discourages me. "Damn it, it grew", I say, turning my head to Gadi. He looks at me in silence. He knows it's better this way. There's nothing he could tell me right now that would soothe me. I get up and go to my study. I should have gone to sleep long ago. I am overcome by sadness and exhaustion. The first image that appears on facebook is of my brother, sitting in a wheelchair, connected to a respirator, holding hands with his wife. They are at the beach, in a photo in the back. Their son is lying on the couch in front of them. My brother writes 'LG', meaning 'Life Is Good' - his motto in general and particularly in the last three years. He received 180 likes.

Inspired by Noa I continue to talk to the tumor in automatic writing

Tumor: You're hanging me out to dry

Me: I will write and create instead of you. It's no big deal if you dry up a bit

Tumor: I have no space. I am suffocated

Me: Diminish yourself and I'll take your place

Tumor: I am tired and exhausted

Me: I will treat you gently, I have power. You rest. You require discipline and sensitivity. Discipline through action and sensitivity through love, acceptance, compassion, and venting. I know you halted because I am softening, since I have more love in me. I'm not afraid of you anymore. You are in your place. You want to talk to me. Do you have something to say to me?

Tumor: I love you and don't want to leave

Me: Then don't leave. Stay, but don't bother me. You can talk, I'm listening. I can grow in essence and in action and you can stay in your size. You don't have to grow in order for me to listen to you. Yes, it's true you've grown. I noticed that and now I'm listening. I have all the time you need. You're so small, cute, and sweet. You will gradually shrink, because I am growing and you've done your part. Your task was to get me to pause and pay attention and examine my life. I am doing that. The remedy is delaying and giving us time. I'm free, I have plenty of time, all the time I need in order to stop. Here it's working. At home there are too many things I want to do and repair. Perhaps I can do it even at home. Every morning until 11:00 is plenty of time to sit down and observe, to think, to write, to walk, to brush, to take a shower, to love my body, my life, my growth. I work on the book with love. A lot of love for those around me. It's my job. Your job is to be quiet.

Chapter 8

My Emotions, My Body, and Me

Suzanna Marcus

Breast cancer - changing diet, lifestyle, and emotional work - 16 years after diagnosis

I'm standing near the kitchen sink peeling carrots to make juice. The kitchen door is open to the yard and the summer heat rushes in and mixes with the chill inside the home. It's clear to me that mental and emotional change strengthens the body. It's the hardest thing to do. It's easier for me to prepare food and juice every half an hour. To that I can devote myself. But I can't force myself to rejoice, dance, or paint... How to make it come naturally from within, that is the great mystery. I have no choice but to continue to look for my personal answer. For now, I still don't know how.

Suzanna Marcus has been working as a healer, psychotherapist, and spiritual teacher for over twenty years now.

When she discovered she had breast cancer, it had already spread to the glands and was identified as stage 3. During the weeks prior to the diagnosis she had trouble sleeping continuously and woke up every night covered in sweat. In retrospect, she learned that the cold sweat at night was a symptom of the cancer.

After the surgery (lump removal and lymph node sampling to see how far the tumor had spread) she was offered to undergo chemotherapy followed by radiotherapy and a bone marrow transplant. Suzanna asked for time to think about it. She remembers facing great pressure from her doctors.

"After I got the diagnosis, I had to be very honest with myself," Suzanna recalls. "I asked myself whether I want to live or die. I realized that the very thought, even for a moment, of wanting to die might actually hasten my death. I pitied myself for the hard times I was enduring. Now I had to honestly choose again. I knew I wanted to live and do the best I can. I asked myself what it is I need to do to muster the strength to live. Eventually the panic subsided and a new awareness emerged. Introspecting through meditation and guided imagery, I tried to find calm and pacify all the systems. I decided to strengthen my immune system and reduce toxins in my body and mind. I didn't fight cancer, I decided to make peace with it and with my past. I chose the path of recovery and committed myself to it completely. I was like an arrow locked in on a target. I created my path to mental, physical, and spiritual recovery. I respect those who choose to undergo chemotherapy, which may be right for them, but I knew it's not right for me. I chose a holistic approach to healing, trusting the body's internal capacity while clearing it of toxins and strengthening the immune system. The doctors and my friends had a hard time accepting this decision. They thought I was being reckless."

Suzanna closed her successful clinic in Tel Aviv. "I realized that I must focus on my recovery only. In any case," she said to herself, "if I fail, I won't need the money anyway."

Suzanna looked back at the years preceding the disease and saw repressed pain, guilt and fear. As far as she was concerned, all those created fertile ground for the development of the disease.

"I realized how important it is to release all the pain and anger. Even if the anger is justified, you should let go of it. Your life depends on it. When I treat patients I see how their reaction to trauma weakens their immune system. No matter what treatment we choose, it's important to concurrently work on letting go of traumas to support the healing process, because what happens in the mind affects the body.

For many years I was a prisoner in my own story. I invested a lot of energy in the dramatic events that I believe led to my illness. Once I learned how to work with my emotions and memories, I could regard the cancer as a gift, because it pushed me to let go of past traumas and appreciate the present. I didn't die, but my old ways did. I call them 'my old song'. I'm often wonder how I summoned the courage and strength to face my extraordinary journey. I'm not religious in the conventional sense of the word, but I can say that my faith in the grand scheme of things served me well and helped me overcome the challenges I faced. In my view, a crisis is an opportunity to change old patterns."

In order to recover, Suzanna listened to her soul, maintained awareness of everything that was happening, and tried to be very honest with herself about her feelings for her family, her friends, and the food she eats.

At that time, she was desperately searching for other recovering patient who she could identify with and be inspired by. She wanted to hear their stories and see if they experienced any trauma in their lives before the disease was detected, and if so, what they did about it. Did they take responsibility? Did they change old patterns? What was the healing process? Which healing methods did they choose?

But she couldn't find anyone to tell her such an inspiring story, so she promised herself that when she gets well she will write a book about her journey, hoping to encourage those facing tough challenges to find their inner strength and determination.

Eight months prior to the diagnosis of the disease she had already moved to Zichron Yaakov. Suzanna preferred the colony's different, slower pace than Tel Aviv's bustling streets. Now that she was in the process of recovering, she grew her food in the garden and squeezed wheatgrass juice at a time when very few people in the country were familiar with that drink. Later she grew her own grass and started following the "Ann Wigmore" diet. In addition, she took dietary supplements, and drank essiac tea, known for its anti-cancerous properties, which she ordered from England. Later she replaced essiac with Chinese herbs.

She drank leaf and green vegetable juice four times a day and avoided eating fruits and sugar. Six months after she started the recovery program, she could see that the values in her blood tests were starting to drop back to normal.

She followed the diet religiously for one year and the 'raw food' protocol for a total of five years, gradually adding 20% cooked food.

She did meditation and guided imagery for a year to let go of past traumas.

Since then it's been sixteen years.

Ten years after the diagnosis, she published a book called "Six Months to Live Ten Years Later."

Today Suzanna treats people who want to grow and stay healthy, as well as cancer patients. The aim is to teach them how to regain their inner healing powers while continuing to grow.

"My treatment is intended for those willing to take responsibility for their healing rather than pass it on to someone else. It is necessary to work on the body and soul alike. I help people deal with the challenges they face and ask:

- What is the source of my problem?
- Where am I stuck?
- What do I need to change in my life at all levels to resolve the problem I face?
- How can I achieve the change I need to live a full life of happiness and health?

"As far as I'm concerned, it's vital that the patients be full partners in the recovery process, believe in the path they chose, and have faith that they can indeed recover. Whether they chose conventional or complementary treatment, in my opinion their positive attitude and faith are the most crucial factors.

Together with the patients, we search for traumas, thoughts, and events that poisoned their souls and weakened the immune system, allowing the cancer to take over the system. I teach them how to remove internal and external toxins, how to relieve stress, past traumas, pain, and anger. Once they let go of all those, they have a better chance at healing. Even if the disease is terminal, it's worth it to perform this cleansing process and leave the world in greater peace."

What did Suzanna do?

6:00	-	Drinking wheatgrass juice
6:30	-	Walking for an hour in the open air – walking meditation and physical exercises
7:30	-	Wheatgrass enemas
8:30	-	Green juice
9:00	-	Breathing exercises while sitting down
9:30	-	Meditation with breath counting and guided imagery – for letting go of old patterns
12:30	-	Lunch: fresh vegetable food that removes toxins
1:30	-	Outdoor activity, walking, gardening
3:00	-	Green juice

4:00	-	Wheatgrass juice
4:30	-	Wheatgrass enemas
5:30	-	Green juice
6:30	-	Dinner: fresh vegetables, sprouts, dried crackers
7:00	-	Meditation

Evening – time for music or reading - things that bring enjoyment

Going to bed before midnight.

This daily schedule doesn't seem simple at all. But Suzanna says the hard part is making the decision. Once she decided she really wants to live, it wasn't hard for her to follow this protocol at all. Today she eats regular food (except for junk food), protects herself emotionally, occasionally fasts, and sometimes goes back to drinking juices and wheatgrass. She balances

Suzanna's website: www.suzannamarcushealing.com

Back when he was an advertising executive, busy and stressed out all day long, he began to feel severe pain in the stomach. After a week of suffering, he went to get tested, and it turned out he has a tumor in the colon that already metastasized. Ten years have passed since then. Today Boaz does things more slowly, does healing and guided imagery, illustrates, surfs every morning, sometimes sails at sea in the afternoon, reads, and spends a lot of time with himself.

There are two things he is certain of: First - that cancer is the main cause of the dramatic change in his life. Second – that this new activity affects all those around him. "Our home has undergone a real transformation," he says.

"The great transformation in my life began with one sentence I heard in a random meeting with Nader Butto, a senior cardiologist who treats patients outside the hospital with 'energy wash-outs'. After his lecture, as a large crowd tried to greet him, I managed to get a hold of him for a moment. With dozens of people standing behind me, wanting to talk to him, I was able to tell him briefly about my illness and ask for suggestions. "So you want me to tell you how to get cured from cancer?" he asked me. "I'll tell you: 'be happy,'" then he turned and walked away. I realized that I was stuck in old patterns that lead to incorrect behavior, which were outside my correct frequency.

I thought it was a job for life and realized that in order to be happy, I need to get rid of everything that creates negative feelings. And that's exactly what I did. I examined every single thing that gives me satisfaction in life (relationship, work, kids) and said goodbye to the things that bothered me.

The path to Boaz's extraordinary recovery from colon cancer began when he asked to postpone the surgery by two months so he could strengthen his immune system. Then he stopped chemotherapy on his own volition. His friends, family, and doctors, (basically everyone around him) were angry with him. They screamed at him and expressed their discontent.

The patient's loved ones usually feel helpless and deeply afraid. The doctor is often the only authority and unless we do what he says, who knows what will happen? Boaz claims our ability make decisions is skewed by the white coats and the statistics the doctors present to us.

I remember my father lying at Hadassah hospital with abdominal sarcoma. We wanted to help him so badly, but didn't know how. We waited, not knowing why. The doctor called me to his room, opened a binder, and showed me graphs and figures indicating that if my father undergoes a particular kind of chemotherapy there is a 40% chance the tumor will diminish. Otherwise, there's a 100% chance the tumor will soon block the main blood vessel in his stomach and kill him. I felt as if heavy clamps were gripping my lungs. I don't remember him mentioning the possibility that the chemotherapy itself would harm the bodily systems. My father wanted to undergo the chemotherapy because he felt it was his only chance. Reluctantly, I was convinced by the graphs. But my father's body could not withstand the treatment, and shortly afterwards we parted from him. I often think that if it had happened to him today we'd have much more tools to help him.

49-year-old Boaz was not impressed by the reactions of others, who were convinced he wouldn't survive without chemotherapy. This retired major (having dived in the Kishon river during his military service) who received a citation in Lebanon, mustered the strength and courage to let go of conventional thinking and chose his own way of treatment. Understanding what's right for him and dissatisfied with the doctors' answers, he decided to stop the chemotherapy and imaging tests and told himself he'll do whatever it takes to avoid conventional medicine.

"I was looking for another way to overcome the disease," Boaz says. "A friend told me about a new medical method by Dr. Hamer, according to which our emotional experience directly affects the physical body. And in the meantime, I started studying guided imagery. My situation began improving and I became totally committed. Then I learned Dr. Eric Pearl's reconnection method."

---※●※---

New Medicine" is a medical approach discovered and developed by Dr. Ryke Geerd Hamer. It enables us to thoroughly understand the causes of various cancer diseases and other serious illnesses, the logic behind the development of the disease, and the physiological processes that occur during the disease.

Dr. Hamer, who treated cancer patients, began his research after being diagnosed with testicular cancer. He couldn't find any logical reason for his illness apart from the trauma involving the tragic death of his eldest son two months earlier.

As a first step in his research, he questioned all cancer patients in his department and discovered that in 100% of the cases there had been some kind trauma in the background.

---※●※---

---※●※---

Based on the assumption that all bodily activity is controlled by the brain, Dr. Hamer started running head CT scans on all of his cancer patients. This resulted in another important discovery: in the brain of every subjects there was a spot with concentric circles around it, like a drawing of a grouping on a shooting range target or ripples created when a rock is thrown at still water.

Among all subjects, he found this shape located in the center of the brain or the part that controls the organ or bodily system afflicted by the disease.

After interviewing a large number of cancer patients and running CT scans on their brains, Dr. Hamer identified a pattern and found a direct link between the type of trauma experienced by the patient, the location of the circles in the brain, the type of disease and its location in the body.

Until then, no studies had examined the brain in search of the source of diseases or the brain's role as a mediator between the mind and the sick organ.

Dr. Hamer argues that all diseases are caused by shock, conflict, or trauma that catch us by surprise, totally unprepared. Once the conflict takes place, the shock affects a specific area in the brain (which changes depending on the type of trauma), causing harm that can be seen in the

CT scan. Until then, radiologists thought the circles appearing in brain scans are irrelevant side effects caused by malfunctions or disturbances in the CT devices. Siemens, which manufactured the CT scanners Dr. Hamer worked with, examined the issue and confirmed that the circles appearing in the images are genuine findings.

Dr. Hamer named the phenomenon of shock or unexpected conflict 'Dirk Hamer Syndrome' or in short - DHS, in honor of his son Dirk who died in a gun accident. He found that DHS assaults 3 systems simultaneously: the person's mental/emotional system, the brain, and one of the body parts or tissues. The circles that appear in the brain as a result of DHS became known as 'Hamer Focus' or HH.

The brain cells affected by DHS send biochemical signals to the cells of the organ that match the type of damage. These signals prompt physiological processes that manifest as a disease in the same organ. These physiological processes can be of three types: 1. Tumor. 2. Dissolution of cells or tissues. 3. Dysfunction. What determines which physiological process occurs in the relevant organ is: which area in the brain received the shock and which layer that area of the brain belongs to. Apparently, every part of the brain is programmed to prompt a different kind of physiological response in the event of shock. This is related to the evolutionary process, which programmed every area of the brain to respond in the most effective way for survival. Dr. Hamer found that all physiological responses, which manifest as cancer or some other inexplicable disease and often appear like a glitch of nature, are essentially special and important biological programs, each with a clear biological purpose. Over the years, Dr. Hamer has come to understand the profound biological significance of each of these programs.

For more information on New Medicine, courtesy of Idan Saar, Healthy Choice: www.healthychoice21.com

---≪•≫---

Boaz is convinced that the main thing that kept him alive was the emotional preoccupation. "After all, it touches every aspect of life - my relationship with myself and with others, my children, my job, the whole universe. To maintain this, I check my level of joy every day.

Whatever triggers my emotions I process immediately – so that it doesn't stay with me for more than a few minutes. I compare this emotional navigation to the app Waze. When I'm off course, I tell myself just like the app says: "Recalculating route".

I work on my free will and constantly reselect the things I do and the way I like doing them.

We need to shatter all our taboos that consume our energy. We need a new set of tools to live life differently. I didn't fight anything, I speak with the cancer. True freedom is to allow myself to choose how to respond and behave. Today, as a therapist, my greatest difficulty with patients is reducing their levels of fear.

I'm also mindful of nutrition. It's an important issue but not absolute. There are many methods, not one single winning approach. I eat effectively, using the minimum amount of energy to digest the most nourishing foods. Lots of vegetables without meat, sugar and flour. I don't find unhealthy foods tasty anymore.

I am convinced that the medicine of the future will revolve around frequencies. Food, music, and colors are all frequencies and therefore I do sound washing every morning. When I meditate every morning, I lie on the exam bed in my office, play my favorite music, and let it wash me. If I like this music, it means it contains frequencies that I need. The frequencies restore my balance every time. In Tibet they treat people with sounds of Tibetan bowls. I encourage you to spend half an hour every day listening to music. "

Shir
Metastatic Breast Cancer - nutrition, sports and psychological treatment– 2 years after diagnosis

"In alternative clinics I saw less toxic treatments and better results."

-Shlomo Guberman

In April 2013, I discovered that I had a metastatic tumor in the liver. In addition to all the tests and appointments with oncologists, I turned to Shlomo Guberman (Gubi), who wrote the book "Cancer Can Be Beaten." Gubi lost his sister and mother to cancer and decided to dedicate his life to finding articles and studies that confirm the effectiveness of anti-cancerous supplements. He explains that "since the early '70s very little progress has been made in oncology. Compared to the developments in modern medicine, chemotherapy remained almost completely stagnant. Some life-extending biological drugs were invented and radiotherapy was improved, but no revolution has occurred. Conversely, in alternative clinics I saw less toxic treatments and better results.

The integrative clinics administer chemotherapy in lower doses and at timings that correspond with the body's biological clock.

In his view, the most important elements in the anti-cancerous diet are:

1. No sugar. Empty carbs cause the proliferation of cells. In PET-CT scans they use sugar to detect concentrations of cancer cells.

2. No trans fats. Minimal consumption of omega-6-rich fats and oils that are not cold pressed. Use of healthy oils such as: black cumin, hemp, avocado, flaxseed, grape seed, olive, and coconut.

3. Have a general preference for organic food.

4. Eat very little any animal source foods, especially dairy products (goat milk is ok).

5. Add superfoods - especially algae, chlorella, spirulina, and combo sea weed, which contain iodine and anti-cancerous substances.

6. Soybeans contain unhealthy substances, but fermented beans are free of toxins. Tempeh, soy sauce, and miso are healthy. The rarity of breast and prostate cancer in Japan and the Far East is attributed to the consumption of soy. However Guberman does not recommend drinking large amounts of soymilk.

7. Eat a lot of fruits and vegetables without fear of fructose, which doesn't cause much secretion of insulin or boost blood sugar levels.

8. Organic dried fruit can be eaten. Non-organic fruits contain sulfur.

9. Atlantic sea salt dries naturally in the sun, not through chemical processes, and is therefore good.

In addition to nutrition, he tries to cheer up his patients, who often come to him in low spirits after their days have been numbered. "Statements relating to fixed periods of times have a psychological impact on people, but on the other hand, I have no doubt that optimism affects the healing process. I bring up the subject and refer patients to mind-body therapy, healing, meditation, and qigong".

I left my meeting with Gubi with two large papers containing a list of supplements and precise instructions for when and how much to take. In addition, I ordered all the supplements from a website abroad and hoped for the best[20]. But I could not see well. I noticed the tumor was doubling in size in each test. I remembered Gubi saying how unpleasant it is when the tumor in the liver is very large. I panicked. I asked him for the names of people who successfully used his services.

Gubi sent me to Shir, a young woman who was a mother of a four-month-old girl and two-and-a-half-year-old boy when diagnosed with hormone-sensitive breast cancer. Shir underwent all the conventional treatments, including chemotherapy, surgery and radiotherapy. Then she got a prescription for an anti-hormonal drug and hoped for the best. Despite all the treatments, only one year had passed before she discovered large metastases in the liver and the area of the left shoulder. Her oncologist suggested chemotherapy. "This time," says Shir, "my husband and I decided to radically change our attitude towards my recovery. I stopped working immediately, realizing that I needed to be active and deeply involved in the healing process. We started collecting information on complementary medicine. I went to consult with Gubi regarding dietary supplements, with

---

[20] Recommended site for ordering dietary supplements: http://www.iherb.com?rcode=ZAR168

Edna Mintz regarding nutrition, and went to Meirav Yehoshua to practice the Journey Method (see box) with her. In addition, I started doing sports, qigong, guided imagery, acupuncture, and shiatsu.

The Journey method was conceived by Brandon Bays, who teaches awareness and holistic healing. A student of Deepak Chopra, she wrote a book about the process by which she naturally eliminated a tumor from her womb.

The "Journey" Method entails an emotional quest, in which the inner essence and personal potential are revealed, and deep emotional obstacles are removed.

The 'emotional journey' is followed by a process called the 'physical journey', which exposes old memories and limiting patterns. In this process, these memories are cleaned, allowing the healing process to begin. Both journeys are a process of guided imagery. The first is related to emotional aspects and the second treats physical organs in the body with guided imagery.

"I started working very hard on the healing process, and within a month I could boast a significant drop in the markers in the blood test. These welcome declines motivated me to continue in full force, while maintaining strict discipline. Mentally speaking, it was very hard to face all the things I love to eat.

In every visit the oncologist would bring up the issue of chemotherapy, but I kept stalling. After six months, the PET-CT results were amazing. There was an 80% reduction in the sizes of the tumors, and on the bottom of the page it was written: excellent reaction to treatment. Perhaps those who analyzed the results thought I was undergoing chemotherapy.

I believe it saved my life, even though the oncologist never showed signs of joy, maybe because, clinically speaking, I still have a metastatic disease and it's just a matter of time before the cancer comes back."

Despite the oncologist's pessimism, Shir's disease remains dormant, and I envy her. Especially her ability to do everything she did. When we spoke a year ago, I told Shir that I kept myself healthy for two years with proper nutrition and dietary supplements and when I stopped, the disease came back with greater intensity. When I visited her recently for another interview, she told me that my statement is constantly on her mind. She remembers it well and it is, in part, what gives her the strength to continue.

Shir says she doesn't sleep well at night either. The fear that the cancer will relapse is always in the air. But for now, Shir's cancer has been dormant for two and a half years.

I tell her I ordered medical cannabis oil, which I take by drops at night because that's the only way I can I fall asleep and sleep through the night. Shir also started taking cannabis now.

"I know that as long as I maintain this lifestyle the disease will remain dormant," says Shir, "but I gave myself some dietary exemptions." Minor exemptions, like eating some whole grain bread, or cooked soups. I take less supplements but make sure to drink citrus pectin every day as well as the Ban Zhi Lian formula Gubi suggested that I try. I continue to drink wheatgrass every morning, as well as smoothies and juices. I exercise, and even go out and have fun. I look at my children and remember how I used to dream of my son's first day of elementary school – which I actually lived to see. I continue to set landmarks that I aspire to reach in life. As long as I saw the markers drop, my motivation was sky-high. Now the difficulty is greater. I'm much more afraid that the disease will relapse, and I've noticed that when I talk with patients about what I did - the fear comes back. "

I offered Shir to send written material on her recovery to those interested in her story and ask them to read it before speaking with her, so that she can filter out some of the calls. Most people who reach out to her can't sustain the natural healing protocol. I learned this from myself and other recovering patients I interviewed. I used to send callers to my blog - "Suddenly Cancer", where I presented many of my thoughts. I asked them to call me after they read the blog post and its featured links. Most people I referred to my blog didn't call me back.

Inspired by Shir - I go on the "Journey"

I want to do what Shir does. I want to stop the tumors. The natural endeavor is harder than chemotherapy. It requires great discipline and changing your habits, in addition to coping with resistance from your close circles, be it doctors or family members. I decide to go on the "journey" with Meirav Yehoshua. On the way to Meirav I pull over at the side of the road, feeling shivers, nausea, pain in the side, and sweating heavily. I try to catch my breath. With cars passing by quickly, I moan in pain, my stomach swelling, and I consider vomiting intentionally. I shove a finger, and feel the gag that brings the food up to the mouth. Only after I'm able to throw up do the pain and shivers pass. I manage to arrive at Meirav's clinic on time as scheduled. Her treatment room has two armchairs from IKEA. These chairs are popular among therapists, I note to myself. I've seen them in several clinics. I quickly devote myself to the process. After a few words of introduction and background, I close my eyes and Meirav instructs me to identify feelings in the body, to link emotions to feelings and life situations to emotions... At one point I even sat around a campfire in my mind and invited my parents, myself as a child, and an external counselor. Meirav asks me to look at a specific situation involving my father that caused me anger, frustration, and despair. Slowly, like embroidery work, Meirav guides me to the point where I can see my father and myself as a being of light and love. It's not easy to change emotions. It took me two and a half hours. Was I able to let go of the emotions of that event? Maybe. I leave the journey with a list of very comforting phrases: "I am an essence of light, serenity, and joy. People are essentially light and love, with good intentions in in their heart, and the ability and desire to heal. Life is pleasant and it is possible to live happily. I'm full of white light, I am open to what life gives me. I'm a loving and compassionate being. I have inner confidence. My personal guide in the imagination process asked to convey several messages to me: "Preserve what you understood today. Maintain the light and try to see those around you as entities operating with good intentions." I read these sentences again and again. I recorded them on my phone so I can listen while driving. These sentences convince me, softening a hidden place inside me.

The Ho'oponopono Method

The phrases I wrote down after the journey are similar to the message that arises from the Ho'oponopono method. Meirav Zamora teaches Ho'oponopono – an ancient tribal Hawaiian healing art. Ho'oponopono means "correcting the mistake" and restoring the divine order. Dr. Pnina Bar Sela, who treats with the Ann Wigmore method, recommended this method to me. Meirav emphasizes the healing power of forgiveness and the significance of forgiveness in Judaism, to ourselves and to others. "Forgiveness and self-love can lead to correction and healing. Without forgiveness we cannot heal," says Meirav." We feel there is much more in the world than what we experience and see and we look for something beyond our reach. With the Ho'oponopono method, we clear fears, anxieties, and beliefs. We clean what's unnecessary and fill up with the healthy faith that there is someone or something protecting us."

To implement the method, Meirav makes sure to be constantly mindful of everything that goes on around her, the energies between the members of her household, the inner sadness that might be afflicting her, and her relationships. She is constantly aware of what she's experiencing, without judging whether it's good or bad. Where she identifies problems, worries, and skepticism, Meirav utilizes the mental work of Ho'oponopono through four sentences aimed at the little girl inside her. That is, her subconscious. These are the sentences:

1. I love you
2. I'm sorry that what's inside me makes me experience the difficulty I want to clean
3. Please forgive me, I'm sorry. Please forgive me for what's inside of me
4. Thank you

"This is a labor of forgiveness, love, and compassion for one's inner child," says Meirav. "We are fulfilling what our subconscious is programmed to do. When I tell my subconscious: Thank you for helping me let go – the subconscious lets go and we are visited by an energy of healing, love and correction. That's the basis of the method. And that's what I work with all the time.

Sometimes the inner child feels anxious, afraid, tense, and insecure. Whenever I feel any of those things I immediately recite the four sentences. I understand that my relationship with my inner child is the key to everything. When I feel love and compassion and goodness, I create change.

Cancer patients need peace and quiet to enable the healing process. Ho'oponopono allows this quiet, as well as balance, letting go of pain and sorrow, and bringing joy."

Once again I hear about letting go of fears and beliefs. Vered Gliksman also talks about letting go of fears, perhaps Boaz does too. It seems that some things are recurring in the various treatment methods.

Michel Bubta
Bile Duct (Cholangiocarcinoma) Cancer - conventional treatment with change in outlook on life, change in diet, meditation –
8 years after diagnosis

"My lifestyle is mostly meditative. For example, when I eat I only notice the food"

-*Michel Bubta*

I contacted Dr. Danny Keret, a naturopathic physician, to hear about his approach and his patients who were cured of metastatic cancer. Danny told me something that startled me: "Most patients with metastatic cancer eventually die." I followed up on that point, asking him if he think it's nevertheless possible to recover, even from metastatic cancer. "Of course it's possible. It has been proven by quite a few people, but it's difficult to achieve," he answered. "I suggest you talk with Michel Bubta".

Michel, a resident of Ganei Tikva, married with two children and grandfather of three grandkids, an educated man, is a chemist by profession and an avid trekker in his spare time. Eight years ago, at age 56, after a very long series of tests, he found out he has cholangiocarcinoma - bile duct cancer.

"The tumor was not sensitive to chemotherapy or radiotherapy," Michel recounts. "I'm good with statistics, and after looking up information online I realized I was in big trouble. I discovered that my chances of making it to the New Year's celebrations are very slim. What could I do? I searched for a surgeon who would agree to operate on a tumor in the liver 7.5-cm in size."

Prof. Ahmed Eid from Hadassah Hospital in Jerusalem, a senior surgeon specializing in organ transplants, agreed to perform the complex surgery to remove part of the liver. Following the operation, it was decided to try an experimental drug that wasn't yet released to the market. This drug had a side effect of frequent delusions. While watching TV, reading, or listening to music, Michel started imagining that he was seeing transfusion tubes all around him.

Michel, who kept away from psychologists his entire life, set his first appointment with a psychologist. Coincidentally or not, Michel found a psychologist who works with guided imagery.

"In my sessions with her I addressed severe emotional baggage from my childhood and felt I was starting a new life. My outlook on life changed completely. I became happier and more content with life.

After recovering from the surgery, I went hiking for a month in northeastern India, submerged in a meditative atmosphere and surrounded by stunning views of the Himalayan Mountains, with snow-capped peaks, glaciers, lakes, fertile valleys, lush green forests, and rivers. "

From then on - every ten months a new metastasis appeared: twice in the lungs and twice in the liver. Each time a new one appeared I underwent surgery to remove it. Again I tried the experimental drug and again reacted badly to it. I gave up and stopped taking it. With a 2% chance of surviving for over five years, the statistics were still not on my side. From the outset, I decided to open a parallel avenue of complementary medicine, although I had no idea what it entailed. I reached Dr. Danny Keret, Graduate of the Technion's Medical School with a Ph.D. in Naturopathy from Bastyr University in the United States.

Following the meeting with Dr. Keret, I changed my whole way of life. I underwent a radical transformation, altering my diet to natural unprocessed foods without industrial additives, food coloring or preservatives, and increased the amount of fruits and vegetables I ate. I completely stopped consuming dairy products and added dietary supplements to my menu. Besides the gradual change in diet, I entered a routine of meditation. After maintaining this lifestyle religiously for four years, all the unpleasant symptoms in my body disappeared, and the tumors haven't returned ever since. My treating oncologist, Dr. Ayala Hubert, director of the department of gastrointestinal tumors at Hadassah hospital, said she never encountered such a case and that no such phenomenon appears in the medical literature. Since then I've been regularly monitored, and I view life very differently: I enjoy every moment and everything in my life and when I face a problem I fix it with the least possible negative emotions. I returned to my psychologist, who is also a spiritual mentor to me, and who drastically affected my outlook on life. I live in the present only, and I've managed to let go of a lot of baggage from my distant past.

When we feel spiritually strong, our body feels well physically. Being a part of nature, we humans have a body structure intended for specific foods. When we eat the right food – it's easier for us to maintain our health. I made this my philosophy of life." Michel says.

As mentioned, it's been eight years since Michel got sick. His story too gives me a lot of hope. It allows me to change the image of my future. Suddenly there's a chance that the metastasis in my body, as well as the stage I'm in, are alterable. I am inspired and reinvigorated to continue and seek my own path.

what did Michel do?

Diet

Natural diet without any processed or industrialized foods. A lot of fruits, vegetables, and legumes in accordance with the recommendations of naturopath Dr. Danny Keret. No food coloring or preservatives. Not necessarily organic food.

Meditation

At first I practiced meditation to stop the flow of thoughts. Today my lifestyle itself is mostly meditative. For example, when I eat I only notice the food. I devote my attention solely to whatever specific activity I'm doing. I focus on the moment, not the past nor the future. I do the opposite of multitasking now. To me, single-tasking is like meditation.

Emotional cleansing

Working with psychologist on emotions from the past.

Physical Exercise

I gradually got back in shape to my level of fitness before undergoing the surgery and I continue to maintain it. In the mornings and evenings I walk 8 km and exercise.

Dietary Supplements

Omega-3 - 2 grams per day

Vitamin B12

Vitamin D

Naturopath Dr. Danny Keret's therapeutic approach to cancer patients

"In principle, I try to stress that in complex situations of cancer, conventional therapy is not enough and must be actively supplemented with other things. I instill content into the patient's activity. The content that comes up in the sessions revolves around what the patient can do to reduce the chances of relapse or stop the cancer from spreading.

The simpler activities are physical, relating to nutrition, movement, supplements, and herbs. Then I move to content that's beyond the body and I ask the patient: Do you feel hope or despair? If they feel hopeful, there is no need to tackle that aspect. If the patient feels desperation, I suggest a cognitive exercise I learned from Dr. O. Carl Simonton: identifying unhealthy beliefs and replacing them with healthy thoughts.

For each belief one must ask himself: Is the thought based on fact and does it make you feel the way you want to? Does it help you protect your life and your health? Does it help you solve significant problems in life?

Does it help you achieve your short and long term goals?

If the answer is no, then it's not a healthy thought, and therefore we will create a healthy thought to counter it.

For example, a potential recurring thought could be: the cancer will relapse in the coming months and I will die in agony. The healthy thought instead would be: I might die, and perhaps not. Those most hopeful patient will say: I might die in the coming year, but probably not. And then add optimistically: and what I do significantly affects and improves my chances. It's very important to realize that I have the ability to influence the results; that I am doing things actively, creating change, meeting with friends and doctors, asking for help; and that I'm not a victim.

I help the patient identify negative thoughts surrounding the brain uncontrollably, and then create alternatives. These alternatives are very effective in dealing with fear and terror, which are prevalent emotions in any experience of cancer.

Cancer is associated with a frightening cultural suggestion. We keep hearing about people who die of cancer – the best medicine out there can't even help wealthy and successful people like Steve Jobs. Fear reduces the ability to cope and the person must have the tools to cope. Some deny that they have cancer and as a result have an easier time. They don't come to me anyway. But the majority is afraid, especially when there are metastases. The overwhelming and paralyzing thoughts affect the quality of life. I want to help the person with his existential suffering, and not just solve the problem of cancer. Inspired by the book "Cancer as a Turning Point" by Lawrence Le Shan, I help people find whatever it is that will give them enthusiasm and meaning in life.

I talk a lot about the issue of assistance, advising patients to give clear instructions to friends and family regarding what help they need. The ability to accept help is a gift to everyone. People want to help but don't know how.

There is a personality component among people prone to getting sick. Often these people fail to strike a balance between their concern for the world and their concern for themselves. I talk with patients about ways to care more about themselves, and ask them to create a list of actions that reflect self-interest.

In the case of heart disease, prevention through sports and a fat-free diet is quite obvious. In the case of cancer, the confusion is pervasive. Patients are exposed to dozens of diet methods, but there isn't one single method that's good for everyone. Each patient must devise the right program for himself. This is a process of examination, among other things, to find out who's the best oncologist or alternative therapist for me and what diet I should choose.

I talk with patients about potential diets and research-based dietary supplements. I encourage them to ask and examine whether it's the right diet for one's own body, to be attentive to their body and avoid fanatical approaches or directions that aren't right for them.

I highly encourage them to search for information online, join forums of patients from all around the world to draw ideas from, and mainly to be very active, trust their intuition and do unusual things."

Cancer as a Turning Point

Psychologist Dr. Lawrence Le Shan believes that a mental change combined with medical treatment can mobilize the immune system for the sake of healing. According to Le Shan, living a full and satisfying life optimizes the immune system. Half of his patients whose prognosis was very bad achieved long remissions in the disease and the lives of others were extended well beyond expected. "Miracles... were not caused by witchcraft, but by dedication and hard work that made cancer a turning point in the life of a person, instead of a precursor to their demise," Le Shan writes in the introduction to his book.

Noa Sehayek, who discovered a tumor in her head, summoned her mental powers and realized her dream of writing a book... Her immune system may have responded in return by keeping her healthy.

Wonderful news!!!

Another ultrasound test at Tel Hashomer. The doctor asks why I do ultrasound every two months and not mammography. I look at her but don't answer. "What?" she says, "because of the radiation? Come on, you already have cancer..." She doesn't realize I am going to get better, or just isn't taking it into account... In any case, she performs the ultrasound test.

The result: "No change in the size of the metastases."

Yay!!!!

This confirms that I can keep doing what I'm doing.

Eitan Ben Ami the oncologist writes to me in response to the news: "Wonderful news!!!"

In two days I submit the manuscript. Next week I celebrate my 51st birthday in Paris. Perfect timing.

Cancer is definitely a turning point in my life. The opportunity to write this book is a dream come true for me, just like it is for Noa Sehayek. Another dream. The journey has reached the point where I present the book to a publisher. But this is not the end of the exploration. The stories of recovering patients continue to reach me and I continue to collect them. At the same time, I remain vigilant about methods of treatment for my body, about the food I eat, and how I conduct myself in all areas.

Along the way I met many people. They all had an impact on my way of thinking and my conduct. The most uplifting statement I heard, and still hear in my mind today, was said to me by the oncologist: "Survivors have certain qualities that help them, and I have no doubt you have them too."

The current writing labor is part of my recovery journey. It's fascinating and difficult, including moments of crisis where I think the tumors are growing and don't have an answer, as well as moments of spiritual elevation. Facing my fears, during the writing of the book I came across patients who didn't give up even when a year or four years had passed and the tumors still did not diminish. Shaike waited two years before seeing any results. Others have been living with cancer for over 25 years. Gradually, as I met and heard more and more recovering patients, I realized it is possible to eradicate cancer. What I didn't expect to find, and yet was presented to me again and again was the combination of conventional and complementary medicine. Many of the recovering patients received partial conventional treatment because they decided to take responsibility over themselves or because a family member took the helm, as in the case of Zvika. I have no doubt that changing lifestyles, lowering toxins, ensuring good nutrition, proper sleep and emotional work strengthen the body, allowing it to better cope with cancer and with chemotherapy or other drugs. I learned that it's not necessary to choose between conventional and complementary treatment, because they are not contradictory but rather complement each other in many cases. Just as modern medicine has many different disciplines and we have to see specialists in various fields, the same goes for complementary medicine. The hard part is finding a therapist who knows exactly what we need. So we often find ourselves running from therapist to therapist, getting bits of medical treatment from each one, or as some cured patients do, conduct online research independently and read books.

The common trait among all the people featured in the book is that they took responsibility and had a strong desire to live. The responsibility for the treatment methods did not remain in the hands of the doctor, but rather was assumed by the cured patients without any hesitation. This initiative led them all to find their own way. It led Nir Malchi to the clinic in the United States to get a special chemotherapy cocktail; it led Zalman to the most renowned therapists in the country; Dr. Henin investigated mushrooms and Shuka conducted an in-depth mathematical study on the causes of the disease. The second important thing I learned is the power of mental strength and conviction, which got Rachel Bornstein out of bed forty years ago, and me this year. I was surprised at how significant emotional work is. Those who've lived for the most years after diagnosis are precisely those who made a dramatic change in their outlook on life, like Avner Shilo and Boaz Ben Uri.

I think the research I've done here can serve as a starting point for recovering cancer patients. The stories I heard are inspirational, providing practical advice and instilling hope. Throughout the book I repeatedly urge the readers not to take supplements based on rumors or bits of information. It is not recommended to attempt the various healing methods alone. Today there are many excellent books in Hebrew on various methods and new approaches to combination cancer therapy. I highly recommend to study, read, and seek consultation.

I completed the craft of writing, but the physical and emotional journey continues, as I work hard to maintain the progress I already made. Today the tumor is small and quiet. I give it love, compassion, tenderness, and we live in peace. I wish every person who reads this book faith and patience to embark on their own journey, without leaving any stone unturned.

EPILOGUE

Collecting the stories of "my heroes" was an inspiring experience for me. I embarked on this journey in great confusion, wondering what I should do to get cured. In my mind, I envisioned a dire future. As I progressed with the craft of writing, I realized how significant my thoughts are to the healing process, and how much the mantras in my head and the images I can see influence the process. Before writing the book, I focused mostly on diet and physical exercise as the key factors for strengthening the body. But suddenly, I was opened up to a whole new world that I was aware of, but never delved into: the power of our subconscious, or the power of the mind, the power of faith and prayer. The strong desire to live and actively search for a way to survive was very prominent in these stories. Every conversation with a cured patient made me think of my own direction, things I want to add, or therapists I want to meet. I was amazed at how they each decided to cope with their illness and inspired by the determination that led them to where they are.

Following my conversations with cured patients, I met new and good therapists. I learned many new things, including the importance of breathing for raising oxygen levels in the body, creating movement in the abdomen, and alleviating pain. I learned about determination and perseverance even when the solution is not in sight. I learned about dietary supplements, rehabilitating mushrooms, and most of all - the high value of emotional work and finding joy in life. I find myself reading the interviews again and again, seeking to be inspired by them.

I continue my physical and emotional journey to recovery, making sure that I enjoy myself along the way.

APPENDIX 1

What I'm doing today following my private research

After all the conversations, books, conferences, and sources of information I was exposed to in recent years:

- **I go to bed at nine o'clock.** Following my talk with Sara Hamo I started going to bed early in order to strengthen the immune system.
- **I apply aromatic oil to alleviate stomach pains.** I started studying naturopathy, and learned that aromatic oil significantly relieves abdominal pain - so I apply it every morning and evening on the gallbladder area.
- **I apply anti-cancerous aromatic oil on the tumor area.** I learned that citrus peels contain a substance called limonene, which chemically kills breast cancer cells. I asked Eti Bracha, a therapist who treats with aromatherapy, to give me an oil containing limonene to rub on my skin near one of the metastases. Guberman suggested that I rub cannabis oil on the area near the tumor.
- **I take a high dose of the agaricus mushroom**, on the recommendation of Shlomo Guberman, to strengthen the immune system.
- **I take a biological drug by special approval of the Ministry of Health.** I managed to get the biological drug, which Estelle found for me through articles that she read online. I receive it as a compassion drug.
- I drink camel's milk every morning and evening, inspired by Zalman.
- **I eat a lot of papaya and annona.** Before bedtime I take 8 drops of cannabis, vitamin D and calcium.

- **I avoid sugar entirely.** As Guberman suggested, I take a pill of Glucomin in the evening to lower my blood sugar levels.
- I take an aspirin pill every day, inspired by Shuka and various studies.
- Every day I drink soup with astragalus, seaweed, ginger, three types of chopped vegetables, and cooked artichoke water. Each ingredient in the soup has a different role.
- I prepare a mixture of flax, black cumin, milk thistle, seaweed, ground moringa and scatter it on the food.
- I do a coffee enema twice a week.
- **I walk, brush, jump on a trampoline**, and take hot and cold showers, alternately.
- **I continue to read** material on cancer treatments - physical and emotional.
- I study naturopathy.
- **I make time for emotional and physical therapy.** Following my interviews with the cured patients, I realized the significance of the emotional aspect in the healing process, and I continue to meet with Vered Gliksman for imagination exercises and healing through light; with Yona Luria for guided imagery; with Meirav Yehoshua for the "Journey" method to let go of more old pains; with Motke Eilon for shiatsu and acupuncture to relieve the digestive system; and with Tal Rishoni for Japanese acupuncture.
- **I began treatment in a hyperbaric chamber** to repair the damage caused to the digestive system by radiation.
- **I fill my world with love and joy**, mostly observing my familial and social ties, examining what is right for me, and filling my relationships with love and positivity.

Besides all that, I can still picture a future.

Thanks

I'd like to take the opportunity to thank all those who participated in one way or another in the compilation of the material for this book and in the journey I've undergone during these years. A journey that led to the writing of this book.

First, to all the inspiring 'strangely cured' patients, who shared with me their journeys, their fears, and their joys. I drew strength and encouragement from all of you and I hope the same will happen to those who read this book. We all took part in bringing forth this helpful information and knowledge, which we all collected.

Thank you for sharing your stories.

To Lilach Galil, who I met on a hiking trip. She reminded me that I love and dream of writing and encouraged me to realize this dream. Thank you, Lilach. To Ruth Roi Weinstein, who referred me to the first people I spoke with and kindly gave me the names and phone numbers of therapists and cured patients. To all the wonderful people who agreed to share their experience with me. To Dr. Shaul Tal, CEO of Focus Publishing who called me immediately after receiving an email suggesting that he should publish the book; who supported, advised, accompanied, and encouraged me very wisely and warmly. Thank you very much, Shaul.

I'd like to say thanks to my therapists: to Guberman (Gubi) for his care, assistance, and knowledge. To my sister Tal, Motke, Sharon Bar-Gil, Eitan the oncologist who was willing to examine the strange ideas I presented to him; to Luria, Vered Gliksman, Meirav Yehoshua, Dr. Shlomo Segev, and Dr. Efrat Broida.

Thanks to Dr. Danny Keret for referring me to his "special" patients and helping me expand the book's body of knowledge.

To my sister-in-law Tammy Rishoni who reviewed the text again and again, providing her comments and insights, and encouraging me to go on a sweet vacation with her in Paris during the writing of this book. To my partner Gadi, who read and helped and advised and provided guidance - you are my best friend.

To my mother Rachel, the woman of iron and silk who plows through the events of our lives with great courage and generosity. Thank you, mother. Thanks to Yael, Anat, Hani, Hilat, Galit, Efrat, Ronit, Debbie, and Yifat, my best friends who remained by my side during the painful and frightening year of severe abdominal pain; to my sister who constantly reminded me that it's possible and preferable to treat abdominal pain; to my brothers, Tal and Shai, and my two dear sons, Amit and Nadav, who are simply present in my life and fill me with love.

I am sincerely grateful for all the love that I have.

APPENDIX 2

Recommended therapists and complementary treatments

During my personal journey to recovery, I met many therapists. The list includes therapists I met personally, with the exception of Dr. Winkler and Dr. Shai Pasternak, whom I only interviewed over the phone after getting warm recommendations from their patients.

The therapists I met charge fees ranging from 200-1,000 shekels. The complementary medical centers at the hospitals employ top therapists – and although appointments with them are brief, the prices are much lower. Something to think about. Before choosing therapists and dietary supplements, it's a good idea to give it some thought. There's no need to take every dietary supplement you hear of. A qualified naturopath or supplements consultant can determine the exact dosage you should take. Sometimes it's possible to make a blend containing several dietary supplements and thereby save considerable sums of money. Some therapists offer bi-weekly appointments, rather than weekly, so as not to burden the patient's schedule and pocket. Meditation, guided imagery, walks, and outdoor hikes with loved ones are highly recommended, and do not cost any money.

I recorded my talks with therapists so I could hear them again and again and figure out whatever I didn't get during the appointment. Every time I heard one again it was like being at another appointment, and I realized that the things I was hearing, although important, were starting to repeat themselves.

Dr. Meir Winkler - strengthening the body with plants

Dr. Meir Winkler has specialized in internal medicine for 30 years. He also specializes in herbal medicine, treating a variety of diseases. When it comes to cancer, the primary use of herbs is for strengthening the body and eliminating side effects. "Chemotherapy damages both the cancer cells and healthy cells in the body. When treatment suppresses bone marrow activity, we see a drop in red and white blood cells. As a result, the immune system is weakened, sometimes to the point where effective oncological treatment must be paused. Other body parts are also damaged by the medication: liver, kidneys, digestive system. Medicinal herbs can be used to strengthen the body, so much so that it's possible to resume the treatments.

Some herbs treat against the strong fatigue caused by treatment. Some herbs treat anemia and others increase the number of white blood cells and boost the body's defenses. Some herbs alleviate painful mouth sores (Aphthous stomatitis) and treat against gastrointestinal disorders. Note that Apte also appears among healthy people suffering from a digestive disorder, and the herbs can be useful in their case too.

I decide what to prescribe the patient based on the blood tests and the medication they are receiving, their general feeling, and the side effects. Depending on all those factors, I concoct a mixture of herbs, usually in the form of tea.

A dose for three weeks costs around 100 NIS. Usually one session is sufficient and after that patients stay in touch with me via telephone."
Website: www.medicenter.co.il

Sara Hamo - Kingston Clinic method

Sara Hamo recovered from cancer through the Kingston Clinic method. Today she advises people how to change their eating habits and lifestyle to allow their body to cope with the disease.

Sara asks patients to read her book, "Golden Path to Natural Healing", which describes her journey to recovery. Before going to see her, patients should know what it's all about and see if they're ready for change. "Recovering patients must realize that health is not just about food. Things like hours of sleep, exercise, and sometimes even major mental changes are highly important too. Once you get used to it," she claims, "it gets easier."
Website: www.naturalway.co.il
You can send questions to Sara via email: sarahamo@netvision.net.il

Edna Mintz - Raw food based on the Ann Wigmore method

Edna Mintz is one of the founders of Kibbutz Alumot and currently works as an independent nutritionist. I first met Edna Mintz on my visit to Alumot. She's a petite, slim woman who learned the secrets of herbal nutrition at the Hippocrates Institute in the United States, and together with her ex-husband Jerry Mintz founded the Alumot health farm for recovery through diet and healthy lifestyle education. A year and a half ago, when I came to consult with Edna at her apartment in Tzahala, she was already divorced from her husband Jerry and worked independently as a respected nutritionist. At the "Ta'atzumot" gathering held at the Bnei Dan Hostel in Tel Aviv, Edna talked about summoning the healing powers of cancer patients and the effect of one's mood on the acidity of their body. A state of stress activates hormones that produce a layer of acidity in the body. I am already very familiar with the theory of raw food, but I enjoy listening to Edna speak again: "Chlorophyll is a key player," Edna assures us, "it purifies the blood, removes toxins, and is rich in magnesium. Make sure that 50% of your diet is comprised of vegetables and leafy greens. Even for healthy people I recommend drinking vegetable juice and eating a large amount of vegetables every day." Edna mentions a patient whose tumors disappeared from her body after six months of proper nutrition. As for dietary supplements, she recommends 4-6 grams of curcumin a day, 600-4,000 international units (IUs) of vitamin D per day, melatonin, astragalus for strengthening the immune system, omega-3, flaxseed oil, B12, thistle, and lion tooth for protecting the liver.

Edna's website: www.ednamintz.co.il

Edna accepts patients at her clinic in Tzahala.

Dr. Shai Pasternak - Ayurveda

Dr. Shai Pasternak is a western MD, director of the Northern region for Maccabi Tivi health services. He also treats patients with Ayurveda and Bach flower remedies

at the Clalit Health Care clinic for Complementary Medicine. Shai views his therapy as complementary, helping to reduce side effects and recover from surgery. "When the side effects are diminished, the body is able to receive more chemotherapy and suffer less damage." Shai explains. "Conventional medicine doesn't kill the cancer, it only reduces it. The complementary treatment balances the body, cleanses it of toxins, and improves the chances of success of the treatment. The complementary treatment is not a substitute to surgery. In Ayurveda, we use a formula called Maharishi Amrit Kalash, which significantly reduces the side effects of chemotherapy, strengthens the immune system, and supports and enhances the success of the treatment.

Some of my patients have recovered and some have not. I presume that the treatment with Ayurveda and Bach flower remedies raises the rate of recovery".

Chinese and Japanese Acupuncture

Today almost every hospital in Israel has a department of complementary medicine that offers acupuncture treatment. This treatment involves the insertion of thin needles into specific points in the body for about 20-15 minutes. Acupuncture is used for treating symptoms associated with cancer and cancer treatment.

Tal Rishoni - Japanese Acupuncture

"I believe that cancer is the result of a disruption in the body's delicate control mechanisms. To fix the disruption, the body needs sufficient available energy. Therefore, there needs to be as little distraction and energy disruptions (like toxins or stress) as possible. We need a strong immune system.

Acupuncture is personally tailored to patients based on their condition and stage of treatment. Japanese acupuncture originates from Chinese acupuncture. It's a variation that includes the release of reflex points. During treatment I get immediate feedback indicating that I chose the right spot in the body to affect.

Japanese terminology is more modern and goal-oriented than Chinese terminology. This is a practical and effective method. I often see quick results with Japanese acupuncture".

Tal treats patients in Tzahala. Tel. 054-5505009

Motke Eilon - Chinese medicine: acupuncture, medical herbs, and shiatsu

Acupuncture and shiatsu do not directly treat cancer but help to strengthen the patient and reduce the side effects of "Western" medicine in order to advance the fight against the disease itself.

Medicinal herbs can have a positive effect on benign and cancerous tumors, and some herbs even reduce the chances of relapse. In China, most cancer patients receive medicinal herbs, sometimes even years after the disease disappears. Motke recommends periodic 'maintenance' treatments even after the conventional treatment is completed. The treatment itself varies depending on the patient's condition and circumstance: chemotherapy, radiotherapy, biological therapy, intervals between treatment rounds, or post-treatment; pain following surgery or as a result of the disease itself; treatment of scars and physical disorders that remain after surgery.

Motke approaches each stage as needed, applying the therapeutic tools of Chinese medicine. If necessary, he advises patients to adjust their lifestyle to the new situation and refers them to nutritionists, yoga, meditation, and qigong.

Motke treats patients in Moshav Herut. Tel. 097962275

Gadi Lahat – Meditation, Guided Imagery and Healing

My beloved partner, who has supported me since the first day of diagnosis and constantly reminds me of the important work I have to do. He does energy therapy when I am in pain. He helps me realize my dreams and make time for the important things: meditation, mental work, guided imagery, and nutrition. Following the disease, Gadi studied patient support and he now treats with guided imagery, healing, and conversation.

Gadi treats patients in Ra'anana. Tel. 054-4458428

Prof. Yaakov Shoham - Dietary supplements, guided imagery, meditation

Prof. Shoham is an internal medicine specialist and researcher in the field of life sciences and medicine. He's trained in oncology, nutritional medicine, Chinese and Western herbal medicine, and other non-toxic treatments. He has also studied psycho-oncology, medical hypnosis, and guided imagery.

He developed a unique medical approach, from a systemic perspective.

Most patients who turn to Prof. Shoham have cancer. His therapy includes the alleviation of side effects, acceleration of healing processes, rehabilitation of systems in the body damaged during surgery, radiotherapy, or chemotherapy (to the extent that they are relevant to the specific case); prevention of relapse after conventional treatment, and – direct treatment of the disease if there are no other options for conventional treatment.

Prof. Shoham: "Cancer can be prevented by leading a healthy lifestyle that includes a healthy and balanced diet that provides the body with antioxidants, exercise, positivity, and equanimity. The combination of conventional and herbal medicine will lead to better results when treating and curing existing cancer."

Prof. Shoham accepts patients at Moshav Gimzo. Tel. 08-9285043

Yona Luria - Hypnosis and guided imagery

Medical psychology specialist. Graduate of Hebrew University in Jerusalem, majoring in Psychology and Jewish History, with an M.A. in Clinical Psychology from the Academic College of Tel Aviv-Jaffa.

Clinical psychologist, specializing in cardiology, neurology, bone marrow transplantation, somatic disorders, and pain. Also works in education and instruction of people with learning disabilities and ADHD.

Psychologist of the Department of Bone Marrow Transplantation at Hadassah Ein Kerem Hospital.

Psychologist of the Diabetes Clinic of Meuhedet Health Care Services - Jerusalem region.

Treats patients in private clinics in Modi'in, Jerusalem, and Kibbutz Rosh Tzurim. Covered by Meuhedet Health Care. Tel. 050-5172868

Dr. Eitan Ben Ami, oncologist

The most humane doctor I encountered, after spending eight years meeting dozens of doctors. I met Eitan back during his residency, and together we marched to recovery. Eitan was available by email and telephone, he responded to articles and studies that I sent to him, and when I found a drug that wasn't available in the country he helped me obtain it. Eitan didn't rush to send me to the ground floor where they administer chemotherapy. In her study from 1991, Prof. Sandra Levy found that the second most important predictor of the survival of women with breast cancer is happiness. She also claims that the woman's relationship with her doctor has an effect on the recovery. Eitan definitely played a big role in my journey.

Dr. Sharon Bar-Gil - Naturopathic oncologist

Dr. of Nutrition, specializing in diet, herbs, and dietary supplements, mainly for cancer patients at all stages of the disease.

"Proper nutrition and medical herbs can assist in coping with various side effects, and slow down the disease." Sharon says.

She treats patients at the Davidoff Center of Beilinson Hospital in Ramat Hasharon. Tel. 054-8187275

Ayelet Bar-Levav - Teaches the Yemima Method

Around the same time I started writing the book, I began to study at the Ma'ane Center. Is it run by Ayala, the niece of the great Yemima. There I learned to connect with myself, to my good essence, which I always wished to have at the forefront of my personality. To let go of my mental-emotional burden and act out of love. There I learned the notion that only great love can stop the tumor.

Classes are held in Kfar Saba. Tel. 054-2473247

Meirav Yehoshua - Certified therapist, Brandon Bays's "Journey" method

Meirav uses the "Journey" method to cure depression and anxiety. Her personal experience gave her the faith and ability to perform emotional, mental, and physical self-healing.

"I realized the power of healing lies within us if we are willing to dive into our inner world and learn to let go of what's blocking us. Our life energy will flow freely and allow us to rejuvenate and grow in all aspects of our lives.

After all the journeys I underwent in life, both as a patient and therapist, it became clear to me that we are the ones responsible for our lives. We are free to pursue a full and healthy life and have the power to realize it. If something is stuck in our lives or we become ill, it means that a part of us that knows who we truly are, in essence, is signaling to us to wake up. It is inviting us inside for self-discovery, cleansing, forgiveness, liberation; to replace beliefs that don't serve us with new beliefs and make internal, cognitive, and sometimes even physical changes as well as changes in lifestyle.

Every person has a powerful energy of life, so when I meet someone who is sick, as far as I'm concerned I'm meeting a healthy individual (with a disease). The disease is the body's clever way to lead us back to ourselves, to listen to our inner world, to search and explore: what is truth and what is at the root of the disease."

Meirav treats patients in Rosh HaAyin. Tel: 054-3042322

Vered Gliksman - Working with light, guided imagery, kabbalah

Conversations including guided imagery. Vered is a master of Reiki, healing, kabbalah, psychodrama, and Ayurveda, all of which she integrates with coaching.

"A lot of cancer patients come to see me. I listen to the patient and try to determine when the disease started. Usually the disease appears before it is detected. I encourage patients to seek the hidden and apparent benefits of the disease. Many say the disease gave them a boost of energy, love, and attention. Every illness has its perks. I help patients see where it's coming from, and once we identify it, they can change the present by giving up the perks and moving on in life."

Vered treats patients in Rishon Lezion. Tel: 052-8688299

Rafi Mintz - Macrobiotics

Quote from Rafi's website: "'Complementary medicine' means bringing the person back to the conditions best suited for his personality. For this reason, whenever a new customer comes in for consultation, I meet with them, and even with their life partners or business associates, primarily to diagnose their personality. After these meetings Rafi matches foods based on the macrobiotic diet. Rafi provides a list of recommendations tailored to the particular situation of the individual patient". Rafi lives and treats patients in Givat Ada.

Website: www.rafim.com/cosmology.htm

Eti Bracha- Aromatherapist

Aromatic oils. Eti concocted one kind of oil for my inflamed gallbladder and another kind to apply externally on the areas of the metastases. Eti makes products: mixtures of oils, creams, ointments, sprays for cosmetic and medical use... She studied reflexology, Swedish massage, practical and clinical aromatherapy, Bach flower remedies, Reiki 1 & 2, and she also treats patients with Hopi ear candles and cupping.

Website: www.xcore.co.il/maga/index.php

Tel. 052-4648880

Shlomo Guberman (Gubi) – Dietary supplements consultant

Guberman has vast experience and extensive knowledge in dietary supplements tailored for the various types of cancer. Guberman also talks about nutrition.

Gubi treats patients in Ra'anana. Tel. 09-7403031

APPENDIX 3

Lists to prepare for yourself while and after reading the book

My beliefs:

A sentence that comes to mind about my health – my faith	Is that a fact?	Does it help me achieve my goals?	Alternative constructive thought
Example: The cancer will certainly relapse	No	No	What I am doing is perhaps helpful or perhaps not. It is possible that I will recover.

Daily Routine for Recovery

I recommend preparing several such lists and hanging them in the kitchen, on the fridge, in the bathtub, next to the bed. These lists help us remember all the actions we've decided to undertake.

Time	Activity	Specifics
	Wake up	
	Exercise	
	Trampoline/brushing/hot-cold shower	
	Breakfast	Recommended food
		1
		2
		3
		4
	Morning supplements	1
		2
		3
		4
		5
	Coffee enemas/wheatgrass	
	Meditation/breathing/guided imagery	
	Lunch	Recommended foods. Food and drink
		1
		2
		3
		4
	Dietary supplements	1
		2
		3
		4

		5
	Snack	
	Meditation	
	Fun activity	List of options to choose from:
6:00 pm – 7:00 pm	Dinner	
	Preparing food for tomorrow	
	Dietary supplements	
	Going to bed not later than 10pm	

Questions for myself to explore

Question	Potential answers	What can I do
What should I change in my life?		
What can I do to be happy?		
What do I want to achieve?		
What perks do I have in life?		
What am I thankful for in life?		

List of supplements and intake schedule

I recommend keeping it in the same place with the supplements. Also, based on my experience, I recommend setting the dates for ordering the supplements in advance, to avoid being out of stock.

Name of supplement	Dosage	Time of intake	When to order more

About the author

Dorit Rishoni-Mandil was born in Israel. She grew up in the Tel Nof Air Force Base until the age of six, when her family moved to Ramat Hasharon, where she lived most of her life. As a daughter of an El Al pilot, she traveled a lot around the world and was influenced by the many cultures she was exposed to. Dorit debated between studying biology and art, eventually choosing photography, painting, and writing. She worked as a journalist for the Schocken Publishing House and other newspapers, and later pursued an independent career as a painter, lecturer on creative thinking, and art teacher. Her paintings are displayed in various galleries and private collections.

Dorit was diagnosed with cancer in April 2007. From that moment on she began to explore the stories of cancer survivors from around the world and apply what she had learned to her own situation. Dorit gives lectures and holds workshops for recovering patients and people who want to maintain their health.

Dorit currently lives in Ra'anana with her two sons and her partner. She is studying naturopathy and plans to do research in the field.

Dorit invites people who've experienced any dramatic remission of cancerous tumors to send their story to dorit.rishoni@gmail.com

Also, visit her website www.heal4cancer.com for additional information.

Printed in Great Britain
by Amazon